WITTGENSTEIN

Robert J. Fogelin

Professor of Philosophy
Dartmouth College, Hanover, New Hampshire

Second Edition

Routledge & Kegan Paul
London and New York

First published in 1976
Second edition published in 1987 by
Routledge & Kegan Paul Ltd
11 New Fetter Lane, London EC4P 4EE

Published in the USA by
Routledge & Kegan Paul Inc.
in association with Methuen Inc.
29 West 35th Street, New York, NY 10001

Set in Garamond 10 on 12pt
by Input Typesetting
and printed in Great Britain
by T J Press (Padstow) Ltd,
Padstow, Cornwall

Library of Congress Cataloging in Publication Data

Fogelin, Robert J.
Wittgenstein.
(The Arguments of the philosophers)
Bibliography: p.
Includes index.
1. Wittgenstein, Ludwig, 1889–1951.
I. Title.   II. Series.
B3376.W564F63   1987   192   86–17851

British Library CIP Data also available
ISBN 0–7102–0975–4

For F C F

Contents

Preface to the First Edition   page xi
Preface to the Second Edition   xiii
Abbreviations   xv

Part One   WITTGENSTEIN'S *TRACTATUS*   1

   I   The Atomistic Ontology of the *Tractatus*   3
        1 *Introduction*   3
        2 *Facts in logical space*   3
        3 *Wittgenstein's version of ontological atomism*   5
        4 *States of affairs and the world*   11
        5 *Wittgenstein's defense of his ontological atomism*   14

  II   Picturing the World   18
        1 *Introduction*   18
        2 *The pictorial relationship*   19
        3 *Pictorial form*   20
        4 *Thoughts*   25

 III   Propositions   27
        1 *Propositions and propositional signs*   27
        2 *Simple signs*   29
        3 *Names in the context of a proposition*   31
        4 *Elementary propositions*   34
        5 *The primacy of elementary propositions*   36

  IV   The Logic of Propositions   39
        1 *Negation*   39
        2 *Logical "connectives"*   41
        3 *Logical truths*   45
        4 *The general form of the proposition*   47

vii

　　　　5 *Logical inference* 　　　　　　　　　　　50
　　　　6 *Probability* 　　　　　　　　　　　　　　51

　　V Generality 　　　　　　　　　　　　　　　54
　　　　1 *The problem of general propositions* 　　54
　　　　2 *Functions and expressions* 　　　　　　55
　　　　3 *Functions and type theory* 　　　　　　57
　　　　4 *Generality and the operation N* 　　　　60
　　　　5 *Fully general propositions* 　　　　　　66
　　　　6 *Identity* 　　　　　　　　　　　　　　71
　　　　7 *Propositional attitudes* 　　　　　　　74

　　VI The Naive Constructivism of the *Tractatus* 　78
　　　　1 *A fundamental error in the logic of the* Tractatus 　78
　　　　2 *Proposition 5 and proposition 6* 　　　83
　　　　3 *Numbers and equations* 　　　　　　　83

　　VII Necessity 　　　　　　　　　　　　　　　86
　　　　1 *Necessity and the doctrine of showing* 　86
　　　　2 *Are there non-tautological necessary propositions?* 　88

　VIII My World, Its Value, and Silence 　　　　　93
　　　　1 *Solipsism* 　　　　　　　　　　　　　93
　　　　2 *Values* 　　　　　　　　　　　　　　96
　　　　3 *The insignificance of the sayable* 　　　97
　　　　4 *A critique of showing* 　　　　　　　100

Part Two WITTGENSTEIN'S LATER PHILOSOPHY 　105

　　IX The Critique of the *Tractatus* 　　　　　107
　　　　1 *The problem of interpretation* 　　　　107
　　　　2 *The motley of language* 　　　　　　110
　　　　3 *The critique of ostensive definition* 　　115
　　　　4 *Inner acts of ostention* 　　　　　　118
　　　　5 *A remark on meaning and use* 　　　　121
　　　　6 *Simples* 　　　　　　　　　　　　　122
　　　　7 *Transcendental illusions surrounding the idea of* 　127
　　　　　simples
　　　　8 *The attack on analysis* 　　　　　　　130
　　　　9 *Family resemblance* 　　　　　　　　133
　　　　10 *Comments on family resemblance* 　　136
　　　　11 *Wittgenstein's treatment of proper names* 　138
　　　　12 *Some remarks on philosophy* 　　　　140

　　X Understanding 　　　　　　　　　　　　144
　　　　1 *Introduction* 　　　　　　　　　　　144

2 *"Now I can go on!"* 145
3 *Deriving* 147
4 *Experiencing the because* 149

XI   Sceptical Doubts and a Sceptical Solution to These 155
     Doubts
1 *The same again* 155
2 *The machine as symbol for itself* 156
3 *A "paradox" and its solution* 159

XII The Private Language Argument 166
1 *Its occurrence in the text* 166
2 *Privacy and certainty* 169
3 *The idle ceremony* 172
4 *The training argument* 175
5 *The public-check argument* 179
6 *The subject concluded* 183

XIII Topics in Philosophical Psychology 186
1 *Introduction* 186
2 *Plan for the treatment of psychological concepts* 187
3 *Expression* 188
4 *Linguistic expression* 191
5 *Seeing as* 201
6 *Wittgenstein's know-nothing approach* 205

XIV Topics in the Philosophy of Mathematics 211
1 *Introduction* 211
2 *Anti-Platonism without conventionalism* 211
3 *Invention and discovery* 217
4 *Infinity* 218
5 *Wittgenstein's anti-foundationalism* 223

XV   Wittgenstein and the History of Philosophy 226

Notes 235
Selected Bibliography 249
Index 252

Preface to the First Edition

Except for the two closing chapters, this book is a careful examination of Wittgenstein's chief works: Part One considers the *Tractatus Logico-Philosophicus;* Part Two considers the *Philosophical Investigations.* For the most part I have referred to other materials only when it helps to illuminate these texts. The exceptions to this are Chapters XIV and XV of Part Two. Chapter XIV, which considers topics in philosophical psychology, draws heavily on *Zettel.* Chapter XV, which considers topics in the philosophy of mathematics, is largely concerned with the *Remarks on the Foundations of Mathematics.*

Following the charge of the editor of this series, I have tried to offer a critical evaluation of the arguments presented in these works, but I confess that there may be too much exegesis and not enough critical evaluation of arguments in this book. I beg as a partial excuse for this that Wittgenstein's writing is often obscure and the text is surprisingly lacking in explicit arguments for one to evaluate. In general I have resisted the temptation of reconstructing the text into an argument—especially when this is done as a prelude to showing that the argument is no good.

Concerning the *Tractatus,* I am chiefly indebted to F. P. Ramsey and Bertrand Russell for the general form of my approach. Although Russell's introduction to the *Tractatus* contains some mistakes, I do not hold it in the low regard that others seem to. Discussions of the *Philosophical Investigations* have been so much a part of the philosophical climate for the last twenty years that it is impossible for me to decide which writers have influenced me most. This general acknowledgment implies no general responsibility. Throughout this book I have avoided, again for the most part, criticisms of competing interpretations of the text. An infinite regress is best stopped at the start.

I owe a personal debt to my colleague Robert Jaeger who read the first part of this work with care and made invaluable suggestions for its improvement. I also wish to thank Russell Abrams and Douglas MacLean who helped with suggestions on the manuscript and Betsy McCaulley who heroically converted my drafts into finished copy.

Preface to the Second Edition

Since the publication of the first edition of this work, I have had second thoughts concerning my interpretation and evaluation of Wittgenstein's philosophy. I do not think that I simply got Wittgenstein wrong—others may—but I am still not sure that the emphasis is always correct. Perhaps I have the words right, but not the music.

This new edition differs from the original in a number of ways. I have made changes throughout the text in the direction of simplicity, and I have cut back on digressions. There are a number of substantial changes in the discussion of the *Tractatus*. I have rewritten Chapter VI to state more clearly my argument that the logic of the *Tractatus* is fundamentally flawed. I have also responded in detail to criticisms of this claim that have been made by Peter Geach and Scott Soames. I have expanded Chapter VIII in order to make clear what I had in mind in saying that "the task of the *Tractatus* is to reveal the foundations of the Tower of Babel; its point is to show the insignificance of that structure." This claim was central to my original interpretation of the *Tractatus*, but was not expressed forcefully enough.

The most important revision in the second part of the book concerns the private language argument and the discussion of following a rule that precedes it. (These are now Chapters XII and XI respectively.) There is no substantial change in the content of these two chapters, but they are now presented in a simpler format that makes clear, I think, just which aspects of Wittgenstein's argument I accept and which aspects I reject. I have also added a long footnote, amounting to a brief appendix, comparing the interpretation that I presented in the first edition of this work with a very similar interpretation recently published by Saul Kripke. Finally I have added a closing chapter examining the place of Wittgenstein's later philosophy in the history of philosophy. I argue that his closest antecedents are the Pyrrhonian sceptics.

These revisions present a more critical view of Wittgenstein's philosophy. This is certainly true of the section entitled "Wittgenstein's know-nothing approach," which has been expanded and relocated as Section 6 of Chapter XIII. But even if I am more critical of Wittgenstein's philosophy, my general assessment of his later philosophy remains unchanged: I think that the *Philosophical Investigations* is the most important work in philosophy published in this century.

Lynne McFall read most of the revised material and made thoughtful and incisive comments on it. Florence Fogelin and Teri Albright contributed their editorial skills to help bring this revision to completion under very tight time constraints. The cost of preparing the manuscript was underwritten by the Dartmouth College Faculty Research Fund.

Abbreviations

In this work I have used the following standard abbreviations:

NB   *Notebooks 1914–16*, Basil Blackwell, 1961
PT   *Prototractatus*, Routledge & Kegan Paul, 1971
TLP   *Tractatus Logico-Philosophicus*, Routledge & Kegan Paul, 1961
      (Pears and McGuinness translation)
PG   *Philosophische Grammatik*, Basil Blackwell, 1969
PB   *Philosophische Bemerkungen*, Basil Blackwell, 1965
BB   *The Blue and Brown Books*, Basil Blackwell, 1958
PI   *Philosophical Investigations*, Basil Blackwell, 1953
RFM   *Remarks on the Foundations of Mathematics*, Basil Blackwell,
      1956
Z   *Zettel*, Basil Blackwell, 1967
OC   *On Certainty*, Basil Blackwell, 1969

When a man is proud because he can understand and explain the writings of Chrysippus, say to yourself, if Chrysippus had not written obscurely, this man would have had nothing to be proud of.

Epictetus

PART ONE

WITTGENSTEIN'S
TRACTATUS

I

The Atomistic Ontology of the *Tractatus*

1
Introduction

The central concern of the *Tractatus* is the status of propositions,[1] yet the work begins with a discussion of the character of the world. To many commentators this seems backwards, since it is often maintained that Wittgenstein derives his basic ontology from commitments concerning the nature of language. Certainly a case can be made for this reading, but at the start, at least, I think that we will do better to avoid heavy reconstruction of the text. In any case, Wittgenstein's order of exposition is natural in one way: it begins with the claim that the world is all that is the case (the totality of facts) and then proceeds to consider a centrally important subset of this totality; i.e., those facts that are used to represent other facts. Wittgenstein calls such facts "pictures." Thus in whatever direction the argument may move, the *exposition* of the picture theory presupposes the *exposition* of the theory of facts. I shall therefore begin at the beginning.

2
Facts in logical space

The opening propositions of the *Tractatus* introduce themes or motifs that echo throughout the text. Though lacking detail, they introduce ideas that give the *Tractatus* much of its "characteristic physiognomy." At the start we are told that the world is all that is the case: a totality of facts, not merely a totality of things (1 and 1.1). The world cannot be identified with a totality of things, since the totality of things can constitute a variety of possible worlds depending upon their arrangement. At this point, however, we cannot say with confidence what Wittgenstein means by saying that the world *is* the totality of facts, for we have yet to be told what facts are.[2]

These opening passages also contain a principle of *closure* or limitation:

1.11 The world is determined by the facts, and by their being all the facts.

This is systematically important because it allows Wittgenstein to argue—as he does on a number of occasions—that something cannot lie *within* the world just because it is not a matter of fact or a feature of a matter of fact. Of course, what this closure principle comes to can be seen only after the central idea of a fact is itself explained, but right from the start we see the kind of system with which we are dealing. It is not a descriptive theory, open-ended and subject to further developments perhaps of a wholly unexpected kind. It is a closed system that, at various points, invokes this feature of closure for argumentative purposes.

The opening propositions introduce a further notion that has persistent influence in the text:

1.13 The facts in logical space are the world.

Here the central idea of a *logical space* is introduced without explanation. Even so, the idea of *space* is rich in analogical suggestions and these are exploited throughout the *Tractatus*. To begin with, space, i.e., physical space, presents us with a set of locations, positions or places. Space is a manifold. At the same time, this set of locations forms a *single* space where each location or place stands in a wholly determinate relationship to every other. At this stage we cannot say what *logical* space is, but the analogy indicates this much: facts do not compose the world as a heap; they are somehow embedded in a manifold of systematically related "places."

This broad sketch of the world is completed by a principle of atomism:

1.2 The world divides into facts.

and as an elucidation of this:

1.21 Each can be the case or not the case while everything else remains the same.

Now this idea that the *world* divides into facts seems to go against the earlier idea that facts are embedded in an internally related manifold, but a closer comparison with the character of physical space overcomes this difficulty. The set of places in physical space forms an internally related manifold, but this manifold is wholly indifferent to the way things are disposed in its various places. This interplay between a structure of necessary connections (logical space) and a purely contingent set of items embedded in it (the totality of facts) is fundamental to the Tractarian world view.

3
Wittgenstein's version of ontological atomism

Although Wittgenstein begins by talking about *facts*, it becomes clear that the idea of a *state of affairs* is more fundamental:

2 What is the case—a fact—is the existence of states of affairs.

At this point it is not clear what kind of reduction is implied by this proposition, so I shall proceed naively (but quite literally) by identifying each fact F_i with the *obtaining* of a set of states of affairs $(S_i, \ldots S_n)$. In the limiting case the set contains a single state of affairs and thus every state of affairs is a fact, but not conversely.[3] States of affairs in turn are explained through the notion of objects (or things):

2.01 A state of affairs (a state of things) is a combination of objects (things).

It is this relationship between objects and states of affairs rather than the relationship between states of affairs and facts that will be the subject of the present section.

Wittgenstein's elucidation of the role of objects in states of affairs is *atomistic* in a traditional sense of this word. *Classical* atomism is more or less adequately characterized by the following fundamental theses:

1   Change (in a wide sense) is a matter of the combination and separation of constituent entities.
2   Not everything is subject to change, for there must be an unchanging basis for change. Atoms, entities that are not the result of combination nor subject to division, constitute this unchanging basis.
3   Combination and separation are possible because atoms exist in a void (in a space) that provides a field of possible combinations.

Wittgenstein's version of this "perennial philosophy" is purified in at least two ways: it is not restricted in its formulation to physical entities (bits of matter), and it is not supported by empirical considerations. But granting these differences, the similarity between the Tractarian system and ancient atomism remains striking. The possibility of change, in the wide sense in which it was used by the ancients, approximates the more modern notion of *contingency*, and the text of the *Tractatus* will make it clear that Wittgenstein accepted the following variation on the first thesis of atomism:

5

1w Contingency is always a matter of the combination and separation of objects and (conversely) the combination and separation of objects is always a matter of contingency.

Although the reasoning that lies behind it is extremely complicated (and perhaps unsatisfactory), it is also evident that the *Tractatus* is characterized by a commitment to the second thesis of atomism given above. Unlike the believer in *infinite divisibility*, Wittgenstein holds that not everything can be the result of the combination and separation of constituent entities. In general terms, he accepts the following thesis:

2w There is a set of entities upon which all contingencies are non-contingently based.

I shall say something about Wittgenstein's version of the atomist's third thesis (concerning space as the field of possible change) after we have a better hold upon the notion of a *logical* space.

In the sections that follow, I shall look at Wittgenstein's atomism in two ways. I shall first show how Wittgenstein *elaborates* or *unfolds* his atomistic theory. This is largely a matter of examining his way of thinking through the commitments I have labeled theses 1w and 2w. I do not think that this side of his philosophy has received the attention it deserves. Later I shall examine Wittgenstein's *defense* of his atomistic ontology. This reasoning involves (or, at least, seems to involve) a transcendental deduction from the structure of language to the structure of the world. This side of Wittgenstein's philosophy has received considerable attention, but for the moment I shall set it aside.

In explaining how objects constitute states of affairs, Wittgenstein is unsurpassed in grasping the fundamental consequences of an atomistic ontology. Consider, for example, the following claim:

2.011 It is essential to things that they should be possible constituents of states of affairs.

Suppose for a moment that it is not an essential feature of objects that they are possible constituents of states of affairs. This would mean (given 2w) that for it to be possible for an object A to be a constituent in states of affairs, some further contingency, i.e., some further combination of objects, would have to obtain. Then, however, A would not count as an object (i.e., something essentially basic) in the sense demanded by atomistic theory. Somewhat more surprisingly, we are given the following claim:

2.0121 It would seem to be a sort of accident, if it turned out that a situation would fit a thing that could already exist entirely on its own.

This goes against a natural way of viewing an atomistic theory. We tend to think of atoms moving about freely, combining and separating again. In between they are uncombined. Here Wittgenstein flatly denies the possibility of an object having a potential for both a combined and an uncombined status. There are no eligible bachelors in the Tractarian world.[4] Wittgenstein seems to be reasoning in the following way: if a thing could exist entirely on its own, then it would be an accidental (contingent or inessential) feature of such an object that it could also exist in combination with other objects. But if this feature were accidental, then it must concern the combination and separation of objects and, once more, the envisaged object fails to meet the standards of objecthood.[5] Objects, then, that do enter into combinations forming states of affairs are said to be unable to enjoy a status outside of states of affairs.

Wittgenstein might have developed a *purely combinatory* theory, i.e., he might have held that all objects are alike in being fit to enter into combination with any other objects. The *logical space* of this world would be all the possible ways in which its objects can combine. Although I do not think he talks about the matter directly, Wittgenstein's language suggests that he is not presenting a theory of this kind, but rather one where objects are sorted into different *categories* and combine accordingly.

> 2.0123 If I know an object I also know all its possible occurrences in states of affairs.
> (Every one of these possibilities must be part of the nature of the object.)
> 2.01231 If I am to know an object, though I need not know its external properties, I must know all its internal properties.

All this would be strangely out of focus if the world did not contain different kinds of objects, for if any object could combine with any other, then all objects would have the same internal properties. It is thus a *general* feature of objects that they are fit to enter into states of affairs. It is in virtue of this that they *are* objects. It pertains to the nature of various *kinds* of objects that they can enter into a certain limited range of combinations. It is in this way that objects can be different in their internal properties or, alternatively, different in their *form*.[6] Furthermore, an actual combination is always one combination out of a range of possible combinations, a notion that Wittgenstein points to with his concept of a *space:*

> 2.013 Each thing is, as it were, in a space of possible states of affairs.

I think that what this says is that every object—to be an object—must be involved in some state of affairs out of a range of possible states of affairs.

We can summarize this discussion of the *combinatory* relationships between objects in states of affairs in the following four theses:

C_1 If something is a possible constituent in states of affairs, then it is necessarily a possible constituent in states of affairs. (from 2.011)

C_2 If something is a possible constituent in states of affairs, then necessarily it is a constituent of *some* state of affairs. (from 2.0121)

C_3 If something is a possible constituent of a certain *kind* of state of affairs, then it is necessarily a possible constituent of that kind of state of affairs. (from 2.0123)

C_4 If something is a possible constituent of a certain kind of state of affairs, then necessarily it is a constituent of *some* state of affairs of that kind. (from 2.0131)

Here I think that it will be helpful to construct a simple world that satisfies the main features of the Tractarian system so far examined. This model will also provide the basis for a more careful discussion of the notion of a *logical space*. The world we postulate contains indefinitely large sets of two different kinds of things. Things of the first sort will be symbolized by upper-case letters; things of the second sort by lower-case letters. The combination rule for this world is that a state of affairs can contain only two objects, one drawn from each basic category. I shall stipulate that every object must be combined with at least one object of its range but that the combination of one object with another in its range does not exclude it from combining with another in its range. We thus get the simple representation shown in figure I.1 of what Wittgenstein calls a logical space (Figure I.1).

Here the shaded areas represent actual combinations of objects: the unshaded areas represent possible combinations of objects that do not, in fact, obtain. The diagram as a whole represents a region of the logical

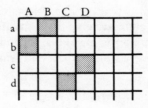

Figure I.1

space of possible states of affairs generated by the two kinds of postulated objects.

The thrust of theses C_2 and C_4 can now be expressed in the following way: C_2 says that each object must exist at some location in logical space. Thesis C_4 goes beyond thesis C_2 in introducing *limited* ranges of logical space that are open to objects. But still the object must occur somewhere in this range. That there is a range of places open to an object constitutes its *independence:* that it must occur in at least one of these places is an aspect of its dependence. This is what Wittgenstein is getting at in the following difficult passage:

> 2.0122 Things are independent insofar as they can occur in all possible situations, but this form of independence is a form of connexion with states of affairs, a form of dependence. (It is impossible for words to appear in two different roles: by themselves, and in propositions.)[7]

But if objects are dependent upon the logical space they inhabit, Wittgenstein also makes clear that a strong dependence runs in the opposite direction as well. Objects, in virtue of their form, determine the structure of the logical space of possible states of affairs:

> 2.0124 If all objects are given, then at the same time all *possible* states of affairs are also given.

Since logical space is just the system of all possible states of affairs, we now see that the dependence relationships among objects and states of affairs are in equilibrium. This idea that a "space" will depend for its structure upon the objects that inhabit it constitutes an important difference between Wittgenstein's atomism and classical atomism. For the classical atomists, space is an independent and neutral medium through which things move. Atoms demand space, but not conversely. By establishing a systematic parity between the two fundamental principles of atomism (matter and the void or being and non-being), Wittgenstein gives this position its most coherent articulation.

There is, however, a passage that may suggest that this praise, however well intentioned, is misplaced.

> 2.013 Each thing is, as it were, in a space of possible states of affairs. *This space I can imagine empty, but I cannot imagine the thing without the space.* (my italics)

The italicized sentence suggests that logical space is wholly independent of the objects it contains, since it could exist entirely without objects. There are two things to say in response to this: (i) if the passage is given the suggested reading, then we encounter sharp inconsistencies with other things said in the text and, anyway: (ii) there is no need to give the passage this troublesome reading.

(i) As will emerge later in our discussion of propositions, the only thing that can be thought or even imagined is that objects are or are not disposed to each other in given ways.[8] From this it follows at once that we can neither think of a world nor imagine a world that contains no objects whatsoever. (ii) Furthermore, there is a natural reading of text that avoids these difficulties. Wittgenstein is not talking about space as an individual totality. He is drawing the following contrast: we cannot conceive of a particular object except as located in space,[9] but any portion of space (however large) may be thought of as empty of objects.

Thus the relationship between space and its objects can be expressed as follows: an object must exist somewhere in logical space, but nothing about space determines a definite location. In reverse fashion, without objects there would be no space, but nothing about the form of those objects determines what portions of space are filled.

So far we have concentrated upon the combinatory characteristics of objects. We can now turn to the signal trait of atomism, i.e., that its basic entities are atoms. An atom is an object that is neither the result of combining constituent entities nor the potential victim of dissolution through the separation of constituent entities.

2.02 Objects are simple.
2.021 Objects make up the substance of the world. This is why they cannot be composite.
2.027 Objects, the unalterable, and the subsistent are one and the same.
2.0271 Objects are what is unalterable and subsistent; their configuration is what is changing and unstable.

It should go without saying that substance is not used in the sense of that in which properties *inhere*. Properties do not inhere in objects, but rather the material or contingent properties of things are *constituted by* the configuration of objects. A change in material properties is a change in the configuration of objects. Substance is that which remains unchanged through all changes. It is in this Kantian sense that "objects make up the substance of the world."

This reasoning is of a piece with the idea that objects, via their form, determine all possible states of affairs. Reality has a determinate form because the objects that determine its form are unalterable. Now we might think that objects themselves might change their form and with this the form of reality would change as well. However, from the atomistic point of view this entails that objects, if they change, must have their nature determined by the combination and separation of other objects. We now lose the basic image of the Tractarian world view, for, instead of having a contrast between a set of contingencies forming a mosaic within a necessary structure of possibilities, we find that possibilities are themselves only contingent. The contingency would go all the way down.

4
States of affairs and the world

2.04 The totality of existing states of affairs is the world.

Given the totality of states of affairs, the totality of facts is also given and that totality, we already know (from 1.1), equals the world. So states of affairs now occupy the privileged position initially held by facts and, as we might expect, the original claims about facts are rewritten as claims about states of affairs. We have already seen that it is the totality of existing states of affairs (in place of the totality of facts) that is the world (2.04 for 1.1 and 1.11). And just as "the totality of facts determines what is the case, and also whatever is not the case" (1.12), Wittgenstein now says that "the totality of existing states of affairs also determines which states of affairs do not exist" (2.05). And the ontology is closed (i.e., it has a *that's all* clause) under the category of states of affairs:

2.06 The existence and non-existence of states of affairs is reality.

Reality contains nothing that cannot be elucidated via the notion of states of affairs.

Finally, the atomistic thesis is enunciated with respect to states of affairs:

2.061 States of affairs are independent of each other.
2.062 From the existence or non-existence of one state of affairs it is impossible to infer the existence or non-existence of another.

This is a reformulation of 1.2 and 1.21, but, given the discussion of the way objects determine the form but not the actual disposition of logical space, we have a better idea what this independence comes to. Indeed, we here avoid a puzzle concerning the independence of *facts*. If a given fact is composed of the states of affairs S_1 and S_2, then there are at least two facts for which this independence breaks down. In particular, the states of affairs S_1 and S_2 are facts whose existence or non-existence is not independent of the existence or non-existence of the fact they compose. Presumably what Wittgenstein had in mind at 1.21 was that a given fact is independent of all those *other* facts that lie outside it. Without the analysis of facts via states of affairs, this remains an empty metaphor, for we would not know what it means for one fact to lie outside another.

Having come to the doctrine of the independence of states of affairs,

I can now explain the restrictions placed upon the world model given in section 3. These restrictions were introduced to provide just the right sort of independence. I first stipulated that the two sets of objects must have endlessly many members. Without this restriction, the following breakdown occurs. Suppose object A enters into combination with objects only in a class K. K contains only a finite number of objects n and we know that it is not combined with some $(n-1)$ of these objects. From this it follows that A *is* combined with the remaining object. Thus with a world containing only finitely many objects of a given kind, the required independence of states of affairs is lost.[10] I further stipulated that although an object must occur in *at least* one state of affairs, we cannot further insist that each object must occur in *at most* one place in logical space. Less figuratively, for states of affairs to be genuinely independent, an object's role in one state of affairs can have no bearing upon the existence of further combinations of objects including its own further combinations. Thus, if an object is involved in two or more states of affairs, this does not result in fusing these various states of affairs into a single larger state of affairs. More formally, if A is combined with B and is also combined with C, we may not infer from this alone that B and C are combined.

These purely formal considerations touch upon a feature of the Tractarian system that eventually played an important role in Wittgenstein's decision to abandon it. In elucidating the notion of the form of an object, Wittgenstein relied upon the comparison of a determinate under a determinable:

> 2.0131b A speck in the visual field, though it need not be red, must have some colour: it is, so to speak, surrounded by colour-space.

This nicely captures the idea that objects occur only *within* the range of their possible combinations with other objects; however, it also carries the unwanted implication that an object will only occur *once* within its range of possible combinations. Thus if an object is entirely blue, then it cannot be entirely red, entirely pink, etc. Wittgenstein notices examples of this kind, but holding to his high *a priori* road, passes them by with a hastily written promissory note.[11]

We can go into the details of this particular issue later on;[12] here it is more important to see why the *Tractatus* absolutely demands a strong sense of independence that does not allow even the incompatibility of two determinates under a single determinable as unanalyzable. Objects give both the form to the world and supply its content (2.025). But if the combination with one object excludes an object from combining with another in its range of combination, then the world has more form than is given by the set of objects alone. The world, we might say, contains *dimensions* of combination out of which only a single combination can hold at a time. Now, however sensible a movement in this direction may seem in its own right, it actually subverts the basic principles of atomism. If we employ the notion of dimensions of combination, then we can no longer say that the form of the world is given *wholly* by the possible combinations of its basic contents. These combinations now take place within a system of higher structures that are not themselves atomistically based: possibilities will wax and wane in accordance with what other possibilities are actually realized.

Before closing this discussion, let me consider one of the more difficult problems in interpreting Wittgenstein's ontology. It has been noticed by a number of commentators that Wittgenstein's terminology seems inconsistent. The following propositions seem incompatible:

2.04 The totality of existing states of affairs is the world.
2.06 The existence and non-existence of states of affairs is reality.
2.063 The sum-total of reality is the world.

The problem is transparent. 2.04 identifies the *world* with the existing states of affairs. In contrast, 2.06 identifies *reality* with both the existence and non-existence of states of affairs. Finally, 2.063 at least seems to identify the *world* with *reality*. Thus the set of existing states of affairs seems to be identified with the set of existing *and* non-existing states of affairs.

I do not think that there is any way to restore perfect terminological consistency to the text, but I think that it is possible to show that this slip is quite natural and, in the end, innocent of deep systematic importance. We may first note that 2.04 and 2.06 are connected by the following proposition:

2.05 The totality of existing states of affairs also determines which states of affairs do not exist.

This claim follows from principles already laid down. Given that every object must occur in some state of affairs or other (2.0121), we know that given all states of affairs, all objects are given as well. But we have already seen that given the totality of objects, all *possible* states of affairs are given (2.0124). In other words, given all *existing* states of affairs, we can construct, through the objects they contain, all *possible* states of affairs—both those that exist and those that do not exist. It is in this way that the structure of reality is implicated in the structure of the world. For quite trivial reasons, the structure of the world is implicated in the structure of reality. Of course, it still remains a mistake to *identify* the world with reality, but, in the end, this is something that can be set right without undermining the basic principles of the Tractarian ontology.

5
Wittgenstein's defense of his ontological atomism

So far we have been concerned with the way Wittgenstein thinks through and articulates the basic tenets of an ontological atomism. We can now examine his *grounds* for adopting this particular standpoint. This will prove a difficult task because Wittgenstein says little on this score; most of what he says is obscure; and all of it anticipates matters that occur later in the text.

In the portion of the *Tractatus* that we have examined, the arguments in behalf of the atomism are subsumed under the claim that objects are simple.

> 2.0201 Every statement about complexes can be resolved into a statement about their constituents and into the propositions that describe the complexes completely.
> 2.021 Objects make up the substance of the world. That is why they cannot be composite.
> 2.0211 If the world had no substance, then whether a proposition had sense would depend on whether another proposition was true.
> 2.0212 In that case we could not sketch out any picture of the world (true or false).

First let me sketch what I take to be the general form of Wittgenstein's argument. I think that we must see 2.0201 as laying down a condition that every statement must meet in order to express a *sense:* every statement concerning complexes can be resolved into a set of statements in which all reference to complexes is eliminated. Furthermore, this analysis is made in a way that the original complexes will be completely described. The conclusion is now reached along the following lines. If analysis always generates names that are in their turn names of complexes, then the criterion of sense laid down in 2.0201 would forever remain unsatisfied. Thus without simples there could be no propositions with a sense and we could not sketch out any picture of the world (true or false). Since we obviously can sketch pictures of the world, we cannot deny the existence of simples.

I confess that there are some difficulties with this reading of the text. They turn upon proposition 2.0211 where Wittgenstein remarks that without substance "whether a proposition had sense would depend on whether another proposition was true." Suppose we have a proposition that attributes a feature to the complex of *a* combined with *b:*

(a combined with b) is *p*

What proposition must be true in order for this proposition to have a sense? The naive answer is this: it must be true that *a* is combined with

14

b. However tempting this interpretation may be, it apparently runs contrary to the stated text:

3.24 . . . A proposition that mentions a complex will not be nonsensical, if the complex does not exist, but simply false.

It thus seems that if there are no simples, then the *truth*—not the *meaning*—of one proposition will always depend upon the truth of another. This, perhaps, is a bad enough result, but it is not the result Wittgenstein speaks about at 2.0211. In sum, I do not know how to make the argument in the 2.02s square with the statement at 3.24.

In any case, it is the thesis given at 2.0201—the thesis of analysis—that should command our attention, for, given that thesis, we might be able to arrive at the doctrine of simples, pursuing a line of reasoning verbally different from that presented in the text. Now I think that the first thing that strikes us about 2.0201 is that it seems obviously false. My desk should count as a complex, yet it seems completely implausible that some statement about it (e.g., "My desk is cluttered") can be analyzed in such a way that the names contained in the analyzed form of the statement would refer only to *objects* in the sense in which Wittgenstein uses this notion. Certainly I cannot perform this reduction; nor could Wittgenstein. Wittgenstein's reflections on this are revealing. Consider this passage from his *Notebooks:*

It does not go against our feeling, that *we* cannot analyse
PROPOSITIONS so far as to mention the elements by name; no, we
feel that the WORLD must consist of elements. And it appears as if
that were identical with the proposition that the world must be
what it is, it must be definite. Or in other words, what vacillates is
our determinations, not the world. It looks as if to deny things
were as much as to say that the world can, as it were, be indefinite
in some such sense as that in which our knowledge is uncertain and
indefinite. The world has a fixed structure. (NB, p. 62)

This passage is remarkable on a number of counts. First, it suggests that we believe that the world contains elements *despite* the fact that our thought seems uncertain and indefinite. Here, at least, the primary atomistic instinct concerns the *world* rather than thought and those propositions that formulate it.

But the passage shows something more significant: a brute commitment to the *determinacy* of the world together with the assumption that determinacy can only be founded on a system of determinate *entities* (things, objects). There is no reason to suppose that the commitment to either of these doctrines is forced. Proceeding in reverse order, it seems that things may be wholly determinate without being composed of elementary irreducible parts. There seems to be no incompatibility

15

between *determinacy* and *infinite divisibility*, as the number line illustrates.

I think that Wittgenstein was, in a way, aware that there was no good argument available in behalf of the doctrine of simples. This comes out in another passage in the *Notebooks:*

> And nothing seems to speak against infinite divisibility. *And it keeps on* forcing itself upon us that there is some simple indivisible, an element of being, in brief, a thing. (NB, p. 62)

I think that the phrasing here is just right: the doctrine of simples was something that Wittgenstein found himself forced to adopt. I do not think that Wittgenstein's genius lies in replacing this inclination with a reasoned argument; instead, it consists in his ability to think through this commitment once made.

Just as there seems to be no compelling reason for identifying the doctrine of determinacy with a doctrine of simples, there seems to be no compelling reason for adopting the doctrine of determinacy at all. Without scouting the regions of modern particle theory, there are any number of things that exist without being determinate, e.g., rumors and clouds.

Looking ahead to the treatment of language, we again find this commitment to determinacy via simples:

> 3.23 The requirement that simple signs be possible is the requirement that sense be determinate.

Once more we have a double movement: the insistence upon determinacy and the equation of determinacy with the demand for simples. Now there really does not seem to be any obvious reason why determinacy of *sense* can only be grounded in a system of simples. Furthermore, the notion that a sense—to be a sense at all—must be determinate seems to go *against* our intuitive inclinations. It is a commonplace that many of the propositions that we formulate about the world are vague or in other ways indeterminate. Wittgenstein, of course, was aware of this commonplace, but held in the face of it that "in fact, all the propositions of our everyday language are in perfect logical order just as they stand" (5.5563).

But again, why should we believe that senses must be determinate, and what, more pointedly, does this mean? The idea that something can be determinate or exact in some wholly unrelativized way is precisely an illusion that Wittgenstein attacks in his later writings, and this constitutes one of the deep criticisms he has of the Tractarian system. Beyond this, why should we hold that determinacy can be made good only by way of a theory of simples? When determinacy is used in a perfectly natural way, there seems to be no difficulty in thinking of instances of determinacy where a system of irreducible entities is missing. When determinacy is used in some extended and sublime way, then it is difficult to know what to think at all.

In sum, I think that we shall search the *Tractatus* in vain for arguments supporting Wittgenstein's atomistic commitments. Admittedly, there is some argumentative prose in passages cited at the beginning of this section that seems intended to support ontological atomism. But when we follow these leads to Wittgenstein's discussion of language, we find passages like 3.23 cited above, i.e., bald statements of the atomistic position. I do not, then, think that the importance of Wittgenstein's work lies in the manner in which he gives atomism a new linguistic base. It lies in the way in which he develops the atomistic program co-ordinately both for language and the world.

II

Picturing the World

1
Introduction

Wittgenstein begins his exposition of the picture theory with the following claims:

2.1 We picture facts to ourselves.
2.11 A picture presents a situation in logical space, the existence and non-existence of states of affairs.[1]

The natural reading of this passage is that a situation (*Sachlage*) is a distribution of states of affairs in a region of logical space. A picture presents the region in a logical space as disposed in a given way: out of a limited range of possible combinations, some obtain, others do not.

An interesting feature of this portion of the text is that it repeats a pattern of development used earlier. In expounding his ontology, Wittgenstein begins with a discussion of *facts* and then goes on to elucidate *facts* through the notions of *states of affairs* and *objects*. Here Wittgenstein begins with a general account of picturing, then moves on to consider propositions (or word pictures), and finally gives his deepest analysis using the notions of *elementary propositions* and *names*. It is only after we reach this deepest level of analysis that we see clearly how Wittgenstein's theory of symbolism matches his ontology. There, however, the fit is perfect.

To return to the idea of picturing, Wittgenstein uses this notion in a very wide sense. We can say that a picture is anything that is "a model of reality" (2.12). Of course, for something to be a *model of reality*, it must (i) be *of* reality and (ii) *model* it. Pictures pertain to reality (are of it) because objects in the world "have the elements of the picture corresponding to them" (2.13). Eventually this object-in-the-world element-in-a-picture correlation is spelled out as a kind of name relation.

18

But a picture is plainly more than a mere set of elements correlated with items in the world. Although I may use a list as a picture (e.g., of the order in which the bands will march by), most lists are not pictures.

2.14 What constitutes a picture is that its elements are co-ordinated with one another in a determinate way.

It is via this determinate structure that the second condition is satisfied, i.e., that pictures are *models* of reality.

2.15 That the elements of a picture are related to one another in a determinate way represents that the things are related to one another in the same way.

This is all very general, but at least we can see that the picture theory demands development on two sides. First, we need an explanation of the elements of a picture showing how they are related to the objects in the world they represent. Here Wittgenstein speaks of the *pictorial relationship (abbildende Bezeihung)*.

2.1514 The pictorial relationship consists of the correlations of the picture's elements with things.

Second, we also need an account of the way a picture represents *how* things are related to one another. Here Wittgenstein speaks of *pictorial form:*

2.151 Pictorial form is the possibility that things are related to one another in the same way as the elements of the picture.

I shall consider these ideas one at a time.

2
The pictorial relationship

The details of the pictorial relationship are spelled out only later using the notions of simple signs as they occur in elementary propositions. Here, in a context largely concerned with pictorial form, Wittgenstein does, however, make some general remarks of importance.

A persistent feature of the *Tractatus* is Wittgenstein's alertness to the dangers of third man arguments. His task is to work out certain fundamental relationships, and he will fail in this if the fundamental notions simply generate the very sort of problem that they are intended to solve. This concern already comes up for the structure of states-of-affairs: "in a state of affairs objects fit into each other like links in a chain" (2.03). We saw that, unless the possibility of combination pertained to the very nature of objects, then, given the atomistic framework, we would have to posit some deeper set of objects to account for this contingency. Thus the combination relationship among objects is an immediate relationship depending upon nothing else. In the same way, and for the same reasons, Wittgenstein insists upon the immediate character of the correlation between the elements in a picture and the objects they represent:

> 2.1511 *That* is how a picture is attached to reality: it reaches right out to it.

If a picture did not "reach right out to reality" then the question of a picture's correctness would always wait upon settling a further contingency, i.e., whether things were so arranged that the needed correlation obtains. Wittgenstein captures this doctrine of immediacy in a striking image:

> 2.1512 (A picture) is laid against reality like a ruler.
> 2.15121 Only the end-points of the graduating lines actually *touch* the object to be measured.

Another matter concerning *pictures* and the *pictorial relationship* may seem only terminological, but since it can cause confusion later on, some care at this point will not be wasted. In painting a picture of a barn, I may have some *particular* barn in mind which I am trying to paint. Then again, in painting a picture of a barn, I may *not* have any particular barn in mind, for I am only trying to represent how barns look. We could reserve the word "depictions" for pictures of the first sort, i.e., for pictures where a definite pictorial relationship has been established. In the present context, then, Wittgenstein is clearly speaking about depictions:

> 2.1513 So a picture, conceived in this way, also includes the pictorial relationship, which makes it into a picture.

In other contexts, Wittgenstein will make use of the notion of a picture in the second way mentioned above, i.e., without reference to an established pictorial relationship. For example, when he says that a picture is a *fact*, I do not think he can mean that a depiction is a fact. This, in turn, is related to Wittgenstein's willingness to call a propositional *sign* a fact, but not a *proposition* a fact.[2]

3
Pictorial form

Of the two notions, *pictorial relationship* and *pictorial form*, the second is the more important and, in the end, the harder to understand. The notion of a *form* is important to Wittgenstein and its use recurs throughout the text. It is connected with possibility in one way and with necessity in another. With respect to *objects*, form is the possibility of their occurring within a determinate range of states of affairs, but this range of possibilities is itself unalterable, hence, necessary. Although we did not touch upon this earlier, Wittgenstein also speaks of *form* relative to states of affairs:

2.032 The determinate way in which objects are connected in a state of affairs is the structure of the state of affairs.
2.033 Form is the possibility of structure.

Of course, 2.033 is connected with the remark that precedes it, but it holds quite generally: wherever we have the possibility of structure we have form.

So far, the notion of a form should strike us as rather empty, but when it is applied to pictures, yielding the notion of a pictorial form, it begins to do heavy work. The idea of a pictorial form will serve at least two main purposes: (i) It allows Wittgenstein to generalize the notion of a picture beyond its primitive base. It allows him to get from pictures (as ordinarily understood) to language (as ordinarily understood). (ii) The form-structure distinction allows Wittgenstein to separate the conditions of *meaning* from the conditions of *truth* and thereby provide a solution to the ancient puzzle of the possibility of false judgments.

(i) As a set of elements co-ordinated with each other in a determinate way, a picture is a fact (2.141). In correct picturing, *two* facts are correlated with one another through their elements. But "if a fact is to be a picture, it must have something in common with what it depicts" (2.16). The two facts do not share elements and thus, following Wittgenstein's nomenclature, they do not share a *structure*. What they share instead is the same possibility for a structure, i.e., a *form:*

2.17 What a picture must have in common with reality, in order to be able to depict it—correctly or incorrectly—in the way it does, is its pictorial form.

We can make some sense out of this claim even at the level of common sense. I can represent the color and shape of a barn using pigment on canvas just because a picture so constructed is itself part of the world exemplifying the world's color and spatial features. Needless to say, the details of representation (perspective, etc.) are complicated, but the basic idea is simple enough:

2.171 A picture can depict any reality whose form it has.
A spatial picture can depict anything spatial, a coloured one anything coloured, etc.

We might even have a convention that allows us to assert that Harold's barn is red by writing "Harold's Barn" in red ink. Setting aside worries about an appropriate supply of colored inks, it is clear in advance that all color predications could be made in this way and thus we could get along without our color adjectives, at least for all those contexts that readily come to mind. Here we might say that the picture and the thing depicted share certain *material* features of the world, and in this way the picture has the same capacity to represent diversity as the pictured object has to exemplify it. Being made of the same thing, they are made for each other.

Suitably impressed that we *could* employ a symbolism that uses the very features of the world that it is intended to represent, we can next reflect upon the fact that most of our symbolism does *not* work this way. Although I could assert that Harold's barn is red by writing "Harold's Barn" in red ink, I do not do this. Mostly I just say "Harold's barn is red" and nothing could seem more different than the phrase, "is red," that I utter and the color of Harold's barn. What is needed, then, is a generalization of the idea of pictorial form that no longer ties it to the material features of particular modes of picturing. This is given in the following set of difficult passages:

2.18 What any picture, of whatever form, must have in common with reality, in order to be able to depict it—correctly or incorrectly—in any way at all, is *logical form*, i.e., the form of reality.
2.181 A picture whose pictorial form is logical form is called a logical picture.
2.182 Every picture is *at the same time* a logical one. (On the other hand, not every picture is, for example, a spatial one.)

Before examining these passages in detail, let me give an informal sketch of what I take to be the driving force behind them. Commentators often repeat the story of Wittgenstein's fascination with the use, in a courtroom procedure, of toys to represent a traffic accident. It was this experience, so the story goes, that provided the original insight that eventually developed into the picture theory of meaning. Setting aside questions of biographical accuracy, we can imagine how a person might generalize from this case. To begin with, he notices that the arrangement of toys can represent the accident because both are spatial. Placing the toys in a certain spatial arrangement shows how the cars were (or supposedly were) spatially arranged. Furthermore, if the cars are placed in some particular arrangement, this shows that the cars at least *could have been* so arranged. Here we have the primitive base for the thesis that "what is thinkable is possible too" (3.02).

Now if this particular case is to serve as the model for a *general* theory of representation, everything inessential about it must be expunged. Upon reflection we come to the surprising conclusion that the very spatial character of the representation, which so impressed us to begin with, is itself inessential. We are, after all, familiar with methods of representation that do not exploit spatial relations representationally, and that is enough to show that a reference to space will be out of place in a general theory. One by one all the special features of our methods of representation will be eliminated in this way. It now seems that if we wish to hold on to the original idea that representation takes place in virtue of shared forms, we are forced to posit a conception of form that exploits no empirical characteristics essentially. This, I suggest, is the task assumed by *logical* forms.

If the above remarks indicate the motive for the introduction of the notion of a shared *logical* form, they still leave this basic idea unexplained. Here we must take seriously the initial identification of *logical form* with the *form of reality*. I think what Wittgenstein is getting at is this: Every picture, of whatever kind, is a fact—a part of reality (2.141). Now just as any region of physical space can be used to represent any other, any region of *logical space* can similarly be used to represent any other. The ontology of facts was presented in the opening parts of the *Tractatus* and one important consequence of that theory was that every fact is related in *form* to every other *possible* fact. This is the underlying reason why facts have the capacity to represent other facts of an utterly diverse material quality. I think that Wittgenstein's identification of logical form with the form of reality amounts to saying that a picture has a representational capacity simply in virtue of the form it has as a part of reality. Indeed, he seems to make even the stronger claim that, in the last analysis, all representation takes place in virtue of logical form. I take this to be the point of the following assertion:

2.182 Every picture is *at the same time* a logical one. (On the other hand, not every picture is, for example, a spatial one.) (Wittgenstein's italics)

If the general thrust of this interpretation is correct, then we can hardly emphasize enough the importance of the claim that pictures are *facts*.[3]

If we turn now to criticism, there is little to say that is not obvious. The identification of logical form with the form of reality builds the ontology of the *Tractatus* into the picture theory itself. This speaks for the unity of the *Tractatus*, but has the disadvantage of infecting the picture theory with whatever reservations we have about the Tractarian ontology. But the concept of a logical form raises difficulties that are independent of its ultimate identification with the form of reality. Earlier I remarked that at a certain point we seem forced to introduce the notion of a logical form. Of course, we are forced in this way only if we hold fast to certain antecedent commitments. Chief among these is the belief that there must be a *single* mechanism underlying a picture's capacity to picture the world or, more generally, a model's capacity to model the world. This tendency to posit a *logical* form is reinforced when we attempt to extend the picture theory to regions where representation takes place without recourse to *any* shared material properties, e.g., with musical scores and most propositions used in everyday life.

To summarize: given the following three theses:

(1) There is such a thing as a perfectly general theory of representation;

(2) Representation always involves the notion of a form shared by the representation and the thing represented;

and

(3) There is no single material feature that is exploited by all forms of representation;

the doctrine of a logical form (= a form of reality) seems inevitable. Of the three theses, only the third seems obviously true.

(ii) A second way that the notion of *form* plays an important role in the *Tractatus* turns upon the ancient problem of false judgments. This emerges as a problem whenever the criteria of meaning and the criteria of truth are so formulated that anything satisfying the first criteria must automatically satisfy the second. To give a crude example, if we maintain that the meaning of a proposition is the fact to which it refers and at the same time hold that a proposition is true just in case this selfsame fact obtains, then it is impossible for a proposition to be both meaningful and false. In this crude form, it may seem impossible for a thoughtful person to find this perplexing, but there are, in fact, genuine pressures in the direction of absorbing the criteria of truth within the criteria of meaning. After all, there must be some very close connection between meaning and truth.

In the fashion of the *Tractatus*, the central ideas concerning meaning and truth are first sketched in a general way with details added only later. 2.2 summarizes and brings into prominence what it is that a picture must have in common with what it depicts:

2.2 A picture has logico-pictorial form in common with what it depicts.

But there is more to picturing than a mere *sharing* of logical form. There is more in common between two successively minted coins than we expect of a picture and what it depicts, yet for that reason alone we do not say that each coin depicts the other. For depiction, the form of a fact must be projected on the logical space of states of affairs picturing the way a set of represented objects are supposed to stand to one another.

2.201 A picture depicts reality by representing a possibility of existence and non-existence of states of affairs.

2.202 A picture represents a possible situation in logical space.

Returning to Figure I.1, we can notice that "aB" is meaningful and true. It is meaningful because it corresponds to a place in logical space; it is true because objects are combined in that place. "aA" is meaningful and false. "BC," on the other hand, is meaningless since there is no place in logical space corresponding to it—either empty or filled. So Wittgenstein has a right to say:

2.22 What a picture represents it represents independently of its truth or falsity, by means of its pictorial form.

The *Tractatus*, then, has the right sort of structure to avoid the ancient problem concerning the meaningfulness of false judgments.

I believe that it is also important to notice that the *Tractatus*, although it keeps truth and meaning separate, does not simply set them adrift. There is an important systematic connection between meaning and truth which can be stated roughly in the following way: to know the meaning of a proposition is to know just those conditions that must obtain in order for it to be true.

4
Thoughts

The complete generalization of the notion of picturing is highlighted by the introduction of a new terminology:

3 A logical picture of facts is a thought.[4]

Using this new terminology, Wittgenstein can go on to say:

3.01 The totality of true thoughts is a picture of the world.

This parallels, in an obvious way, the earlier claim that the world itself is "the totality of facts" (1.1). ·

The reference to *thoughts* introduces one of the more puzzling aspects of the *Tractatus*. It has been a traditional view that whatever is thinkable (conceivable, imaginable, etc.) is also possible. Wittgenstein affirms this doctrine:

3.02 A thought contains the possibility of the situation of which it is the thought. What is thinkable is possible too.

On the most natural reading, this remark seems entirely empty. This follows definitionally since a thought is a logical picture of the world, and any picture of the world, just to be a picture, "represents a possible situation in logical space" (2.202). So what is the point of all this? The answer seems to come out in the following passage:

3.031 It used to be said that God could create anything except what would be contrary to the laws of logic.—The reason being that we could not *say* what an "illogical" world would be like.

The second sentence, of course, gives Wittgenstein's account of this supposed limitation on God. The point is that there is no way of specifying such a limitation. To picture the impossible, the picture itself must exemplify in its structure the impossibility it is supposed to picture. It must be an impossible picture, i.e., not a picture at all.[5]

Using similar reasons, Wittgenstein rejects the idea that a thought could be true *a priori:*

> 2.223 In order to tell whether a picture is true or false we must compare it with reality.
> 2.224 It is impossible to tell from the picture alone whether it is true or false.

Now elevated to a higher level of prominence in Wittgenstein's numbering system, we find these remarks about *thoughts:*

> 3.04 If a thought were correct *a priori*, it would be a thought whose possibility ensured its truth.
> 3.05 *A priori* knowledge that a thought was true would be possible only if its truth were recognizable from the thought itself (without anything to compare it with).

I take it that 3.05 is a conscious reference to 2.223 and 2.224.

Here a cautionary note is needed. The notion of *a priori* truth is important in philosophy, and the above remarks may suggest that Wittgenstein is committed in advance to saying that there are no *propositions* that are true *a priori*. This, however, is a mistake. Wittgenstein does extend the picture theory to encompass propositions, but in a complex way that allows for the possibility of propositions that are true *a priori*. Such propositions (e.g., tautologies) picture nothing—express no thoughts—but they gain their propositional status through standing in systematic connection with propositions that do picture reality or express thoughts. To use traditional terminology, Wittgenstein attempts to accommodate *analytic a priori* propositions within his system. This subject will be canvassed in close detail later on.[6]

Incidentally, we can now see why there can be no single-object states of affairs. The thoughts representing them just in being meaningful, would be true—i.e., *a priori* true. This eliminates inveterate bachelors along with eligible bachelors.

III

Propositions

1
Propositions and propositional signs

Finally at 3.1 Wittgenstein turns to the central concern of the *Tractatus*, propositions:

> 3.1 In a proposition a thought finds an expression that can be perceived by the senses.

This remark is descriptive, not definitional, for there are many different ways in which a thought can find expression perceivable by the senses. The distinguishing thing about a proposition is that here the perceptible elements are words forming sentences. For Wittgenstein, *propositions are word pictures*.

> 3.12 I call the sign with which we express a thought a propositional sign.—And a proposition is a propositional sign in its projective relation to the world.

Thus a proposition is not an entity distinct from a propositional sign, for example, it is not the *meaning* of the propositional sign; it is just the propositional sign taken together with its *pictorial relation* to the world.
Turning now to *pictorial form*, we may recall that Wittgenstein made the following general claim about pictures:

> 2.14 What constitutes a picture is that its elements are co-ordinated with one another in a determinate way.

Now in parallel with this he tells us:

> 3.14 What constitutes a propositional sign is that in it its elements (the words) are co-ordinated with one another in a determinate way.

But if a propositional sign has its elements co-ordinated with one another

27

in a determinate way, then, on Tractarian principles, a propositional sign
is a *fact* (3.14).

We might pause for a moment over the claim that it is a propositional
sign rather than a proposition that is called a fact. If any determinate
and co-ordinated structure of elements is called a fact, then a propositional sign merits the title. What about a proposition (i.e., a propositional sign in its projective relation to the world): is it also a fact?
Wittgenstein never calls a proposition a fact, for the pictorial relationship
is wholly immediate and is not itself an object that can be a constituent
of a fact.

We have already seen why it is important for Wittgenstein to treat
pictures (now including propositional signs) as facts: facts, as part of
reality, are capable of representing other facts. Here Wittgenstein makes
the same point from a different perspective:

3.142 Only facts can express a sense, a set of names cannot.

The assertion that a set of names cannot express a sense is the counterpart
of the earlier claim that the world is the totality of facts, not of things.
The world is constituted by things standing in determinate relationships
to one another, and a proposition expresses a sense by indicating that
things stand to one another in determinate relationships. The latter
cannot be achieved by a set of words that merely tabulate things.

In this context, Wittgenstein speaks for the first time about the *sense*
of a proposition. Some of his remarks about this crucial notion are not
altogether easy to follow.

3.11 We use the perceptible sign of a proposition (spoken or written)
as a projection of a possible situation.
The method of projection is to think the sense of the proposition.
3.13 A proposition includes all that the projection includes, but not
what is projected.
Therefore, though what is projected is not itself included, its
possibility is.
A proposition, therefore, does not actually contain its sense, but
does contain the possibility of expressing it.
("The content of a proposition" means the content of a proposition
that has sense.)[1]
A proposition contains the form, but not the content, of its sense.

If we read these passages carefully, it should be clear that the *projection*
is identified with the propositional sign, and that which is projected into
the sign, i.e., the *sense* of the proposition, is a possible situation. From
this we can see that a proposition includes all that the projection includes,
since the projection is a propositional *sign*, and a proposition just is the
propositional sign in its projective relationship with reality. Furthermore,

if the *sense* of a proposition is the possible situation projected, then the proposition does not contain its sense. Finally, in order for one thing to depict another, the two must have something in common, i.e., a form. It then follows that even though a proposition does not contain its sense, it must exemplify in its structure the form of its sense.

2
Simple signs

3.2 In a proposition a thought can be expressed in such a way that the elements of the propositional sign correspond to the objects of thought.

The proper elements of a proposition Wittgenstein calls "simple signs" or "names" (3.201 and 3.202). This dual nomenclature brings out the two sides of their employment. As *simple* signs, they are signs that admit of no further analysis via other signs. They are rock-bottom on the side of language. As *names*, they represent things. Furthermore, this rock-bottom level of language locks into the rock-bottom level of the world:

3.203 A name means an object. The object is its meaning.

Thus the *pictorial relationship*, which we first examined with respect to pictures in general, is now established through an immediate correlation between the simple signs of the language (names) and the simple entities of the world (objects).
Pictorial form is expressed by the way simple signs are put together:

3.21 The configuration of objects in a situation corresponds to the configuration of simple signs in the propositional sign.

By correlating simple signs with simple things and arranging the simple signs in a definite way, I am able to say of simple things that they are arranged in this same way.
Given this general account of propositions, the only thing that a proposition (employing a configuration of signs) can picture is some situation (i.e., a combination of objects). Objects themselves cannot be pictured:

3.221 Objects can only be *names*. Signs are their representatives. I can only speak *about* them: I cannot *put them into words*.
Propositions can only say *how* things are, not what they are.

Earlier Wittgenstein remarked that, in a manner of speaking, "objects are colourless" (2.0232). Objects can have features in virtue of entering into combination with other objects, but in themselves, although they have a determinate form, they have no structure capable of description.

Since there is nothing about them to be *described* (put into words), they can only be *named*. In a similar way, we might also speak of names (simple signs) as being colorless, for again, they express no structure capable of articulation:

3.26 A name cannot be dissected any further by means of a definition: it is a primitive sign.

Once more, then, we are dealing with the standard atomist's exploitation of the notions of complexity and simplicity. If we now ask why the theory demands a system of simple *signs*, we get the following answer:

3.23 The requirement that simple signs be possible is the requirement that sense be determinate.

This, of course, raises the two questions asked earlier: (i) why should we require that a sense be determinate, and (ii) why should we assume that it is only through a doctrine of simples that this demand can be met? On the first point, a glance at the actual workings of language does not suggest that this requirement is met; indeed, it suggests just the opposite. Wittgenstein was, at the time of writing the *Tractatus*, fully aware of this disparity between the claims of his theory and the actual appearance of language, but his demand for determinacy (his "scholastic instincts") was given precedence over the contrary manifest evidence. The disorderly character of our actual language was not a "discovery" of Wittgenstein's later period.[2] What changed was Wittgenstein's attitude toward this disorderliness: in the Tractarian period he held that it *hid* the determinate structure of thought, whereas in the later period he held that it revealed that thought itself could be indeterminate.

The second question points to the great missing argument of the *Tractatus:* the reasoning that takes us from the demand for determinacy to the need for simples. When we canvassed this issue earlier, we were sent forward to the discussion of simple signs we have now reached, but here no argument presents itself showing that determinacy of *sense* can only be achieved through a system of simple *signs*. Now unless we can find some background argument taking us from the demand for determinacy to the need for simples, little systematic importance attaches to the question whether Wittgenstein reasoned from the structure of language to the structure of the world or conversely. Wittgenstein had a commitment to determinacy that he cashed in through a doctrine of simples, and this reasoning emerges—in a co-ordinated way—for both language and the world. I do not think that there is much more to say on this subject and I shall not return to it again.

3
Names in the context of a proposition

3.3 Only propositions have sense; only in the nexus of a proposition does a name have a meaning.

I wish to pause over this proposition because it introduces ideas that are important not only for the *Tractatus*, but for the whole development of Wittgenstein's thought. The proposition is an echo of—and surely a conscious reference to—the thought of Frege. The allusion has two sides, each difficult in its own right: (i) the passage invokes the contrast, exploited in a technical way by Frege, between the sense and reference (*Sinn und Bedeutung*) of an expression;[3] (ii) the second half of the proposition repeats, in a somewhat altered form, a principle enunciated by Frege in his *Foundations of Arithmetic*:

[N]ever . . . ask for the meaning of a word in isolation, but only in the context of a proposition.[4]

I shall first say something about Wittgenstein's use of the contrast between sense and reference and then go on to examine the claim that a name has meaning only within the context of a proposition.

(i) It seems reasonable to suppose that Wittgenstein's account of meaning is consciously presented as an alternative to Frege's. Frege held the sensible view that expressions like "the largest river in New York State" can have both a sense and a reference. The sense of this expression is what is normally understood as its meaning or significance. The reference of an expression (if there is one) is just that thing which uniquely satisfies the sense of the expression, in this case, the Hudson River.

Frege extended this reasoning in two problematic ways: he held (a) that *proper* names also have a *sense* as well as a reference and, more surprisingly, (b) that propositions can have a *reference* as well as a sense. Now holding to Frege's technical employment of these notions of sense and reference, we can characterize Wittgenstein's position in the following way:

I   Names (genuine names) have only a reference, but no sense (from 3.203).
II Propositions, in contrast, have a sense, but no reference (from 3.3 and 3.143).

Though we can describe Wittgenstein's position using Frege's technical distinction, this leaves open an entirely different question: does Wittgenstein take over the terms *Sinn* and *Bedeutung* and use them in Frege's manner? I am not asking whether Wittgenstein adopts Frege's sense-reference *theory*, for we have just seen that he does not. I wish, instead, to ask whether we must, in order to capture the thrust of Wittgenstein's

31

position, always render *Sinn* and *Bedeutung* as *sense* and *reference* respectively. The answer to this question, I'm sure, is no!

In particular, if we attend to Wittgenstein's employment of the term *Bedeutung*, we see that it is not restricted to a technical use meaning "reference." For example, Wittgenstein speaks about the *Bedeutung* of a logical constant at 5.451:

> . . . once negation has been introduced, we must understand it both in propositions of the form '~p' and in propositions like ~(p v q)', '(x).~fx' etc. We must not introduce it first for the one class of cases and then for the other, since it would then be left in doubt whether its meaning [*Bedeutung!!*] were the same in both cases.

This is the crucial passage on this matter, for it is a central theme of the *Tractatus* that logical constants are not *representatives*, i.e., that they do not stand for things or have a reference (4.0312). Yet here Wittgenstein speaks, without apology, of the *Bedeutung* of a logical constant. He also speaks of the *Bedeutung* of a logical schema (at 5.13), and in general he uses the verb *bedeuten* freely throughout the *Tractatus* without giving the slightest indication that he is following Frege's technical conventions governing this term. Again:

> 5.6 *The limits of my language* mean [*bedeuten*] the limits of my world.

I have made a fuss over this point since it runs counter to a suggestion made by Elizabeth Anscombe on the proper translation of *Sinn* and *Bedeutung*. She is speaking about the *Notebooks*, but her remark *seems* to encompass the proper reading of the *Tractatus* as well:

> I render "Bedeutung", here and elsewhere, by "reference" in order to bring it especially to the reader's attention (a) that Wittgenstein was under the influence of Frege in his use of "Sinn" ("sense") and "Bedeutung" ("reference" or "meaning" in the sense of "what a word or sentence *stands for*") and (b) that there is a great contrast between his ideas at this stage of the *Notebooks* and those of the *Tractatus*, where he denies that logical constants or sentences have "Bedeutung".[5]

(ii) With this terminological point behind us, we can look at the more important claim that occurs in the second half of 3.3:

> [O]nly in the nexus of a proposition does a name have meaning.

Now a name has a meaning in virtue of representing an object. Why does it have to be in the nexus of a proposition to do this? "George Washington" seems to name George Washington both inside and outside of propositions. Part of the reasoning behind this doctrine involves a deep commitment regarding the relationship between a proposition and its constituents. This commitment is alluded to—without accompanying explanation—in a parenthetical remark that occurs early in the *Tractatus:*

2.0122 (It is impossible for words to appear in two different roles: by themselves, and in propositions.)

In the *Prototractatus* this parenthetical remark is part of a much larger independent entry all written as commentary on what eventually becomes the first sentence of the *Tractatus*, 2.0122:

PT, 2.0122 What this comes to is that if it were the case that names had meaning both when combined *in* propositions and outside of them, it would, so to speak, be impossible to guarantee that in both cases they really had the same sense of the word.

It seems to be impossible for words to appear in two different roles: by themselves and in propositions.

Using this suppressed passage as commentary, we see that the parenthetical remark in 2.0122 exactly parallels an important claim about the role of objects in situations:

2.0121 It would seem to be a sort of accident, if it turned out that a situation would fit a thing that could already exist entirely on its own.

In sum, Wittgenstein holds that if names occur in propositions, it must be essential to their nature to occur in propositions. If it were not essential to their nature, then it would be a sort of accident—a contingency—that a combination of signs constitutes a proposition. For reasons (good or bad) that we have already examined, Wittgenstein would consider an outbreak of contingency at this fundamental level an altogether impossible result. At the most abstract level, then, we can say that *any* question we raise about names must be posed relative to their role within propositions, since a propositional role is essential to names.

Descending to a lower plateau where we can breathe some richer air, it may help to begin again by simply asking what names are like. I think that we are first struck by the fact that names are typically correlated with actual objects. "Harold Lloyd" is the name of Harold Lloyd. Yet we rightly feel that there must be more to the name relation than this bare *correlation* for, among other things, the relation is directed. Where "A" is the name of A, it is usually not the case that A is the name of "A."[6] What, then, turns a correlated mark into a name—what gives such a mark its life? The answer concerns the way this mark is employed:

3.22 In a proposition a name represents an object.
3.221 Objects can only be *named*. Signs represent them.

Here the German verb is *vertreten*, a word that could be translated "to act as a substitute for." Now if we seriously maintain that names *represent* objects or *act as substitutes for them*, we must mean that names somehow behave as their proxied objects behave. What objects do is stand to one another in determinate relationships, and names must do the same thing in representing them. This is not something that a name can do in isolation! So for names to represent objects they must be correlated with objects (the pictorial relationship), and the way the names are put together is intended to show how the proxied objects stand to one another (pictorial form). This is just to say "only in the nexus of a proposition does a name have meaning."

Although the position has been subjected to powerful criticism, later on by Wittgenstein himself, it should not be treated with contempt. In particular, it cannot be dismissed out of hand through considerations of the following kind: the word "brie" is a sorry substitute for the cheese and, for that matter, where the word is needed, the cheese will make a mess. This, however, is not serious criticism, but parody. The philosopher who holds that names *take the place* of things (or act as their substitutes) is not suggesting that the word takes over the thing's role in the world. The name is not a *material* substitute for the thing: "Brie" is not ersatz brie. The general idea is that the words play a structural role in a proposition that represents the way things stand to each other in the world. Whether this is a good or a bad theory will depend upon whether it can generate an adequate account of language. The *Tractatus* is one attempt, perhaps the most sustained attempt, to think this idea through and give it substance.

4
Elementary propositions

From what has come before, it should not be surprising that the truth conditions of a proposition are established via a relationship with *states of affairs* whose existence and non-existence constitute reality. Furthermore, the sense of a proposition is just that set of possibly existing and non-existing states of affairs that are projected into the propositional sign.

4.1 Propositions represent the existence and non-existence of states of affairs.
4.2 The sense of a proposition is its agreement and disagreement with the possibilities of existence and non-existence of states of affairs.

But if the truth-conditions of propositions (quite generally) are established by a relationship to states of affairs, then there must be some mechanism in our language that establishes this relationship. Wittgenstein introduces elementary propositions precisely to perform this task. Just as the theory of simple signs completes the account of the *pictorial relationship*, the theory of elementary propositions completes the account of *pictorial form*.

Concerning elementary propositions, Wittgenstein makes the following important claims:

> 4.21 The simplest kind of proposition, an elementary proposition, asserts the existence of a state of affairs.

As a state of affairs consists solely of objects concatenated in a determinate way, so too, an elementary proposition is nothing more than a determinate combination of names.

> 4.22 An elementary proposition consists of names. It is a nexus, a concatenation of names.

The way in which the names are concatenated in an elementary proposition is intended to represent, by a rule of projection, the way in which objects hang together in a state of affairs. It is at this fundamental level that the picture theory is extended to propositions. Furthermore, it is at this level, and really at no higher level, that names perform their representative function:

> 4.23 It is only in the nexus of an elementary proposition that a name occurs in a proposition.

Just as states of affairs are independent of one another (2.061 and 2.062), elementary propositions are logically independent.

> 4.211 It is a sign of a proposition's being elementary that there can be no elementary propositions contradicting it.

Finally, since the world just is the totality of existing states of affairs, a complete description of the world is given by the set of true elementary propositions.

> 2.04. The totality of existing states of affairs is the world.
> 4.26 If all the true elementary propositions are given, the result is a complete description of the world.

This, then, is how matters stand. On the side of the world, states of affairs are the fundamental *picturable* items. They are wholly constituted by a set of objects being combined in a determinate way. On the side of language, elementary propositions are the fundamental *picturing* items. They are composed solely of simple signs combined in a determinate way that is intended to represent, by a rule of projection, the way in which the objects they proxy are combined. It is thus in their deep

35

structures that language and the world meet in a way that is immediate and perfectly congruent.

5
The primacy of elementary propositions

The claim that the totality of true elementary propositions gives a complete description of the world has important consequences. It assures us that whatever can be said by other kinds of propositions can at least be *encompassed* by a set of elementary propositions. The total set of elementary propositions, after all, says everything that there is to say. But the *Tractatus* contains a stronger claim: every individual proposition can be *analyzed* using elementary propositions. Specifically, at proposition 5, Wittgenstein says that every proposition is a truth-function of elementary propositions. That is, any non-elementary proposition P, can always be analyzed using a set of elementary propositions P_1 through P_n.

To see the source of this doctrine, we can return to a proposition touched upon earlier:

4.1 Propositions represent the existence and non-existence of states of affairs.

Using alternative terminology, propositions "present a situation [*Sachlage*] in logical space, the existence and non-existence of states of affairs" (2.11). Previously, I have depicted a situation in logical space as a region within a larger grid. Since we are not here interested in the way in which objects generate logical space, reference to objects has been dropped. The letters A, B, C, etc., are abbreviations for the elementary propositions that picture particular states of affairs in logical space. They are not names of these states of affairs.

We can now consider the non-elementary proposition P that represents the situation shown in Figure III.1:

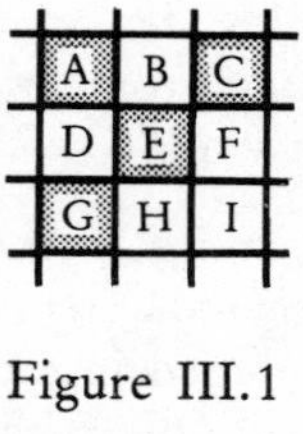

Figure III.1

We see in the first place that this situation is a mixture of existing and non-existing states of affairs. Somehow, then, P must indicate that certain states of affairs obtain, whereas others do not. Of course, the content of P is already given in the complete list of true elementary propositions. The list will show that the elementary propositions A, C, E, and G are true just because they appear on the list. But it will also establish that there are such elementary propositions as B, D, F, H, and I, and that they are false. From the list of true elementary propositions it is possible to construct the list of all possible elementary propositions. That B, D, F, G, and I appear on the list of elementary propositions, but not on the list of true elementary propositions, shows that they are false. This, of course, is just another version of the argument that the character of the *world* determines the character of *reality*.[7] In any case, the complete list of elementary truths—the Whole Truth—encompasses all lesser truths.

These reflections, though important, do not settle the present problem of finding a way to picture some *particular* region in logical space. We want to find a way of saying something short of saying everything. Given the short list of elementary propositions A, C, E and G, the structure of the situation is not determinately specified, for the string of propositions is simply silent about the remaining regions in the situation. In asserting P we do not intend to say that *no* other states of affairs obtain. It thus seems that we cannot express the structure of most situations simply by giving a partial list of elementary propositions.

It should be clear, then, that some further device is needed to tailor our propositions to the structure of a particular situation. Without worrying for a moment what this notion brings with it, a *negation* sign will do the job. Using this notion in a natural way, we can represent *any* situation in logical space by means of two lists: the one is a set of elementary propositions indicating that certain states of affairs obtain; the other is a set of negated elementary propositions indicating that certain states of affairs do not obtain. (In principle, either list can be empty.) We then get a representation of P that looks like this:

$$
P = \quad
\begin{array}{ll}
A & \sim B \\
C & \sim D \\
E & \sim F \\
G & \sim H \\
  & \sim I
\end{array}
$$

But there is something wrong with setting P equal to a *set* of propositions. In order to achieve the unity missing in a mere list of propositions, we can make use of another familiar notion in logic: *logical product*. We shall express the logical product of a set of *n* propositions by means of the following notation:

37

$$\pi \, (P_1 \ldots \ldots \ldots, P_n)$$

A proposition formed this way is true just in case all of its constituent propositions are true and false otherwise. Finally, then, we can express P this way:

$$\pi \, (A, \, C, \, E, \, G, \, {\sim}B, \, {\sim}D, \, {\sim}F, \, {\sim}H, \, {\sim}I)$$

It should be clear at once that any situation (the existence and non-existence of states of affairs) can be represented by a schema of this kind. Furthermore, since propositions "represent the existence and non-existence of states of affairs," it also follows that whatever can be said by a proposition can be exactly matched by such a schema. We thus see, in advance of the explicit statement in the text, that every proposition is a *truth function* of elementary propositions. This brings us to an important feature of the Tractarian system: Wittgenstein's distinctive treatment of the truth-functions of logic.

IV

The Logic of Propositions

4.0312 The possibility of propositions is based on the principle that objects have signs as their representatives.

My fundamental idea is that the "Logical constants" are not representatives; that there can be no representatives of the *logic* of facts.

1
Negation

We can begin our examination of the role of logical terms in propositions with *negation*, for of the logical constants, negation seems to raise the most philosophical difficulties. In some way negation allows us to construct new propositions out of old, for given any proposition we can generate another by denying it. What seems baffling about negation is the way in which it enters into the structure of a proposition. The problem arises within Wittgenstein's picture theory in a particularly sharp form. If a proposition pictures a situation in logical space, what exactly does its denial picture? The same thing?—Then how can the one picture be correct and the other incorrect? Something different?—Then why does the one picture actually *exclude* the other? Furthermore, if negation is part of a picture, how can the negation of a negation take us right back to where we started? How can an item disappear in this way?

Wittgenstein answers these questions through exploiting the *ideal* features of elementary propositions. We can introduce this topic informally by comparing elementary propositions with ordinary pictures (e.g., paintings). There are two ways in which we might use a painting to "say" that something is not the case: (i) We rule something out by exemplifying things not standing in that relationship and saying that this is how things are, (ii) We rule something out by exemplifying it in a

39

picture and saying that this is not how things are. In the first case the exclusion is exemplified *in* the picture itself, in the second case it is not.

A striking feature of an elementary proposition is that it can be used as the basis for ruling something out only in the second of these ways. An elementary proposition represents a combination of objects purely through a combination of signs; it exploits no shared material properties with the objects it depicts. Thus, if the names in an elementary proposition could speak, they would say (in chorus):

I The objects we proxy stand to each other as we stand to each other.

They could also say—now producing the denial of an elementary proposition:

II The objects we proxy do not stand to each other as we stand to each other.

However, they could make neither of the following declarations:

III The objects we proxy are uncombined just as we are uncombined.
IV The objects we proxy are not uncombined as we are uncombined.

There is no way that an elementary proposition can *exemplify* the non-combination of objects without becoming a set of uncombined names, i.e., *not a proposition at all*. Regular pictures can, of course, exhibit a non-combination of objects and here we might say that the negation is *internal* to the picture. A definitive feature of an elementary proposition is that it does not admit of an internal negation. This also means that at the fundamental level of representation, *negation does not appear as a picturing element*.

Returning to those things that puzzled us earlier, we can say that an elementary proposition and its denial correspond to the *same* reality; in one case, however, the depiction is used to exhibit an agreement with reality; in the other case it is used to exhibit a disagreement with reality. Furthermore, if negation is not an element *within* the picture, then we are not confronted with the specter of some *thing* being annihilated when two negations "cancel each other out."

In an attempt to bring these ideas together, we can notice that the picture theory of proposition meaning is under pressure from two directions. Most obviously, the propositions of our everyday language do not seem sufficiently like regular pictures to give the theory much initial plausibility. To solve this problem, we first give a highly abstract account of depicting: in a picture the elements are placed in relationships that are supposed to represent the way a set of proxied objects stand to one another. Elementary propositions satisfy this abstract standard for pictures. Then in order to show that the propositions of everyday language are themselves pictures, we need only show how they are based upon elementary propositions. It is this construction (via truth functions) that we are now in the midst of examining.

A more subtle pressure comes from a different direction. We might put it this way: regular pictures are not well behaved relative to the demands of logical theory. In particular, they are not correctly structured to capture the central idea that we can construct a set of *mutually independent* propositions that represent mutually independent states of affairs. One way to represent a combination of objects (Harold lying on his bed) will be incompatible with another way of representing their combination (Harold standing on his bed). In fact, these two pictures have an internal structure such that they are *contraries* of one another. It is very hard to think of any ordinary picture that does not have this feature of having other pictures as logical contraries. Elementary propositions, however, are not like this. They are perfect. They have all the structure needed for depiction, but no further structure that can cause interference. They seem too good to be true, or, at least, too sublime to be pictures. The process of making pictures suitable for logical purposes seems to bring the notion of a picture itself to the verge of total attenuation. This inability to reconcile the demands of the picture theory with the demands of logical theory is, I believe, one of the central problems of the *Tractatus*.

To return to the main topic, we are now in a position to define negation relative to elementary propositions, or rather, we are now in a position to convince ourselves that what we write down is a proper definition. The negation of an elementary proposition is *that* proposition which is false just in case the original is true, and true just in case the original is false. That there is exactly one proposition that is excluded if and only if an elementary proposition is true is guaranteed by the fact that the internal structure of an elementary proposition is compatible with *every* possible way that objects may be disposed to one another save one: that the objects do not stand to each other as they are *said* to stand to each other.

2
Logical "connectives"

It seems natural to treat such binary connectives as conjunction and disjunction as representatives of relations between facts. Viewed this way, these terms serve as names for logical objects. From this it is an easy extension to think of logical truths as pictures of logical facts. We have already seen that it is the "fundamental idea" of the *Tractatus* to reject this notion.

As we explore the Tractarian system more deeply, we shall see that its entire structure stands opposed to logical objects and logical facts.

But even at this stage we can see that these ideas are incompatible with Wittgenstein's atomism and his central ideas about a picture. If there are logical facts, then the propositions expressing them will mutually imply each, and they will be implied by every proposition whatsoever. Thus the doctrine of independence is lost. Again, if there were logical facts, then the pictures of these facts would be true *a priori*, but we already know that there are no pictures true *a priori*.[1] In sum, the apparent existence of logical terms, logical propositions, and, hence, logical facts, presents a fundamental challenge to Wittgenstein's working out of a picture theory of proposition meaning within the framework of his atomistic system.

Wittgenstein's solution to this problem involves what I shall call a *disappearance* theory of logical constants. He offers a method for analyzing expressions containing logical terms that simply eliminates these apparently referring expressions without replacing them with other referring expressions. In this respect, Wittgenstein's treatment of logical constants mimics Russell's treatment of the apparently referring expression "the present King of France" in the assertion "The present King of France is bald."

We can begin the exposition of Wittgenstein's constructive account of logical terms by examining the symbolism he employs. The common practice in introductory logic texts is to present the truth-table definition of, say, *material implication* in the way shown in Figure IV.1:

p	q	p $\supset$ q
T	T	T
F	T	T
T	F	F
F	F	T

Figure IV.1

Here we are given the independent expression "(p$\supset$q)" and the truth-table lays down its truth-conditions. Wittgenstein's format is significantly different (Figure IV.2):

"p	q	p"
T	T	T
F	T	T
T	F	F
F	F	T

Figure IV.2

Here instead of specifying the truth-conditions of the sign "(p⊃q)," the table *itself* is presented as a propositional sign. This is the significance of the quotation marks bracketing the entire truth-table. Thus the whole structure within the quotation marks—including the Ts and Fs—corresponds to the more familiar expression "(p⊃q)."

Since the truth-table format is unwieldy, Wittgenstein introduces the following abbreviative technique. We can stipulate that the columns on the left side of the truth-table are always written out in the same way, i.e.:

p	q
T	T
F	T
T	F
F	F

It is easy enough to stipulate a rule for cases involving more than two variables. Now if this portion of the truth-table is fixed in this way, we do not have to repeat it, and we need refer only to the right-hand column—the one in the box in Figure IV.3—in giving a full specification of the truth-table definition.

"p	q		
T	T		T
F	T		T
T	F		
F	F		T

Figure IV.3

We can transform this into a horizontal array as follows:

$$\text{"(TT\ T)\ (p,q)"}$$

or more explicitly:

$$\text{"(TTFT)\ (p,q)"}^2$$

This is more than a stylistic variation on standard notation, since it is important for Wittgenstein's program to show that propositional signs can be formulated in this way where the apparent logical connectives disappear altogether, not to be replaced by anything that even looks like the name for some substantive relation.

4.441 It is clear that a complex of signs "F" and "T" has no object (or complex of objects) corresponding to it, just as there is none corresponding to the horizontal and vertical lines or to the brackets.—There are no "logical objects".

Of course the same applies to all signs that express what the schema of "T"s and "F"s express.

The final sentence tells us that even if certain notations suggest, through their use of substantive-like expressions, the existence of logical objects, the elimination of these expressions in a notation that is both theoretically adequate and conceptually perspicuous shows this suggestion is an illusion. Using Russell's terminology, we might say that logical constants are *incomplete symbols*.

Given the propositional sign "(TTFT) (2 + 2 = 5, 2 + 2 = 7)," we see that it is idle to ask why a proposition formulated in this way is true given that the propositions in the right-hand parentheses are (as it turns out) both false. The notation contains (in the left-hand parentheses) the specification that the proposition is true whenever the constituent propositions (in the right-hand parentheses) are both false. To ask *why* the proposition is true under such circumstances is to misunderstand the point of the notation. This much is given by stipulation, but it is Wittgenstein's further claim that the logical constants of our everyday language admit of an analysis of the kind we are examining. Thus it must be equally idle to ask why the *conjunction* of two propositions is false whenever at least one of them is false. There is no back-up reason for this, for it is precisely the function of the conjunction sign to generate propositions defined under the schema: "(TFFF) (p,q)."

Given this account of the status of logical constants, we can now complete the analysis of the non-elementary proposition P left hanging at the close of Chapter III. Using Wittgenstein's more compact notation, we can express the notions of negation and logical product in the following way:

Negation $\quad$ (FT) (p)
Logical product $(T_1F_2 \dots F_{2n}) (P_1 \dots P_n)^3$

We know that every proposition that *expresses a thought* (or *has a sense*) represents a possible situation in logical space—the possibility of the existence and non-existence of states of affairs. Furthermore, we have already seen how all possible situations in logical space may be represented using only a set of elementary propositions and the notions of negation and logical product. Finally, given the truth-functional analysis of logical constants, we are in a position to make the following claim:

Every proposition with a sense is a truth function of elementary propositions.

3
Logical truths

In section 2 we came close to formulating one of the fundamental theses of the *Tractatus:*

5 A proposition is a truth-function of elementary propositions.

We fell short of this proposition only by limiting the thesis to propositions *with a sense*, i.e., propositions that depict arrangements of existing and non-existing states of affairs. It might seem that this limitation is no limitation at all, for if every proposition is a picture, then, for that reason alone, every proposition has a sense. But there are the propositions of logic to consider, and it is still not clear how to treat them within the picture theory of propositional meaning.

In fact, Wittgenstein was pulled in opposite directions concerning the propositions of logic. He seemed faced with two live options. He could hold fast to the picture theory and deny propositional status to the (so-called) truths of logic. Alternatively, he could admit that there are propositions of logic, but then modify the picture theory to accommodate them.

In the period preceding the final composition of the *Tractatus*, Wittgenstein was strongly tempted in the first direction. Thus, in the *Notebooks*, we find entries of the following kind:

"p.qv~q" is NOT dependent on "q"!
Whole propositions vanish:
    The very fact that "p.qv~q" is independent of "q" although it obviously contains the sign "q", shews us how signs of the form nv~n can apparently, but still only *apparently*, exist.
    This naturally arises from the fact that this arrangement "pv~p" is indeed externally possible, but does not satisfy the conditions for such a complex to *say something* and so be a proposition. (10.6.15)

At another place he remarks:

There are no such things as analytic *propositions*. (Wittgenstein's italics) (29.10.14)

Furthermore, echoes of this earlier position appear in the *Tractatus* itself. Consider the following propositions:

4.06 A proposition can be true or false only in virtue of being a picture of reality.
4.462 Tautologies and contradictions are not pictures of reality.

From this it follows that tautologies and contradictions are neither true nor false, and this, if taken seriously, forces a choice between the following positions:

(i) Tautologies and contradictions are not propositions.
(ii) Certain propositions (e.g., tautologies and contradictions) are neither true nor false.

Actually, Wittgenstein does not accept either of these options; instead, he retreats from 4.06. This, I believe, is due to a pressure coming from a different direction, i.e., his theory of *truth-functionality*. We have seen that we can generate new propositional signs (and thus formulate new propositions) simply by making truth-functional assignments for the various possible truth-conditions of constituent propositions. Thus we can generate a proposition by means of the following stipulation: (FTFF)(p,q). But we are equally free to make stipulations of the following kind: (TTTT)(p,q). This is a proposition that is true no matter what values "p" and "q" might take, i.e., it is a tautology built upon "p" and "q" as constituent propositions. Similarly, we can make the following assignment: (FFFF)(p,q), thereby generating a contradiction out of the base propositions "p" and "q." There seems to be no reason to make a special fuss concerning these assignments over any others.

It now seems that two parts of Wittgenstein's theory are pulling in opposite directions. From the standpoint of the picture theory, tautologies and contradictions should be excluded from propositional status for they are not "pictures of reality." Yet from the standpoint of the theory of truth-functionality, the particular specifications of truth values for tautologies and contradictions are on a par with any other specification. Wittgenstein attempts to reconcile these competing ideas in the following passage:

> 4.46 Among the possible groups of truth-conditions there are two extreme cases.
> In one of these cases the proposition is true for all the truth-possibilities of the elementary propositions. We say that the truth-conditions are *tautological*.
> In the second case the proposition is false for all the truth-possibilities: the truth-conditions are *contradictory*.
> In the first case we call the proposition a tautology; in the second, a contradiction.

Finally, then, it is the theory of truth-functionality that prevails, and we arrive at the position that tautologies and contradictions are, indeed, propositions and as propositions may be assigned truth-values.

Yet this final position is not accepted without grumbles from the side of the picture theory:

> 4.466 . . . Tautology and contradiction are the limiting cases—indeed the disintegration—of the combination of signs.

There is only a short distance between saying flatly that tautologies and contradictions are *not* propositions and saying, instead, that they are the *disintegration* of a combination of signs. What is important, however, is the reference to *limiting cases*. Tautologies and contradictions are truth-functions of *significant* propositions. Beginning with the proposition "it is raining" which does depend for its truth upon the state of the world, we can construct another proposition, "it is raining or it is not raining" which does not depend for its truth upon the state of the world. All the same, in an indirect way, tautologies and contradictions *do* depend upon the picturing mechanisms of our language. For Wittgenstein, the notions of truth and falsity are fundamentally tied to the idea of a picture agreeing or disagreeing with reality. Given the bit of nonsense "(^%^)," the following is not a tautology:

$$(^\wedge\%^\wedge) \ v \sim (^\wedge\%^\wedge)$$

The truths of logic do not, then, simply depend upon the pure interaction of logical terms. That there are truths of logic ultimately depends upon there being truths that are not truths of logic, i.e., elementary propositions.[4] By exhibiting tautologies and contradictions as limiting cases of propositions that *are* pictures, the picture theory and the theory of truth-functionality are brought into systematic connection. It is through this systematic connection that contradictions and tautologies are granted propositional standing.

4
The general form of the proposition

At 4.4 Wittgenstein says:

> 4.4 A proposition is an expression of agreement and disagreement with truth-possibilities of elementary propositions.

He goes on to elucidate this claim using the truth-tabular notation we have examined. This culminates with the explicit treatment of tautologies and contradictions, i.e., the theory is fully developed to encompass both those propositions that express a sense and those that do not. It is precisely at this point that Wittgenstein makes the following pronouncement:

> 4.5 It now seems possible to give the most general propositional form: that is, to give a description of the propositions of *any* sign-language *whatsoever* in such a way that every possible sense can be expressed by a symbol satisfying the description, and every symbol satisfying the description can express a sense, provided that the meanings of the names are suitably chosen.

It is clear that *only* what is essential to the most general
propositional form may be included in its description—for
otherwise it would not be the most general form.

The existence of a general form is proved by the fact that there
cannot be a proposition whose form could not have been foreseen
(i.e., constructed). The general form of a proposition is: This is how
things stand.

At least initially, it is hard to read this passage without feeling let down.
Indeed, given the elaborate wind-up, it may even seem a joke. (Cf. "It
is now possible to give the most general form of a departure; that is, to
give a description that every departure must satisfy and such that
anything satisfying this description must be a departure. It is clear that
the most general form of a departure cannot mention any particular
destination, etc., etc., etc. The general form of a departure is: GOING
OUT.")

Wittgenstein, of course, is dead serious. To begin with, it might
seem automatic that the general form of a proposition—just in being
general—will mention no particular objects and, *eo ipso*, make no definite
assertions about objects. But in fact it is possible to maintain that there
is some object (the THING) that must be referred to in order to refer
to anything at all. It is also possible to maintain that there is some
situation (the CIRCUMSTANCE) that must be pictured in order to
picture anything at all. It should be clear, however, that such views run
counter to Wittgenstein's commitment to the radical contingency and
independence of object-combinations. Beyond this, the general propositional form cannot be one wholly general proposition rather than
another, e.g., "(x)(F)Fx" rather than "~(x)(F)Fx." Although a perfectly
general proposition involves no particular reference, we are still dealing
with one proposition amidst others, and this one proposition does not
give the form for all the rest. Thus the general propositional form cannot
be a proposition:

4.53 The general propositional form is a variable.

We might also state matters this way: the general propositional form is
not a proposition, but a schema for propositions. This schema is given
in the construction: *This is how things stand.*

I think it is possible to misunderstand this construction through a
failure to see how the demonstrative works. We can imagine someone
pointing to something (perhaps the rioting masses in the streets) and
saying, "This is how things stand." We can then think of ourselves going
through the world uttering this formula and, except for some peculiar
cases, always getting things right. Taken this way, "This is how things
stand" would have much the same quality as "It is now" or "I am here."

But I think that it must be a mistake to take the formula in this way. Demonstratives are used to pick things out, but facts, situations, and states of affairs are not things, and just as they cannot be named, but only described, they cannot be picked out by a demonstrative. Whatever is picked out by a demonstrative can also be given a name.

We can get a correct idea of the role of demonstratives in the formula at 4.5 by considering first elementary propositions. An elementary proposition is simply a set of names going proxy for a set of objects, exhibiting in *their* structure the supposed form of the combination of proxied objects. To return to an image used earlier, we imagine names in an elementary proposition saying (in chorus): the things that *we* proxy stand to each other as *we* stand to each other. My suggestion is that the "this" in Wittgenstein's formulation operates in the same way as the "we" in my formulation. Taken this way, the formula "This is how things stand" does not have the unfortunate property of having as its instances propositions that always turn out to be true except in some strange circumstances.

Now let us suppose that the formula "This is how things stand" encapsulates the way in which *elementary propositions* work; why at 4.5 is Wittgenstein willing to say that it *"now* seems possible to give the most *general* propositional form" (my italics)? Here the trick is not to make something very simple seem complicated. Wittgenstein makes this remark after he has completed his discussion of the way in which "logical constants" operate. Logical constants produce truth-functions of other propositions, and this is done by a *stipulation* of values for the various truth possibilities. Given the elementary propositions "ABC" and "FGH," we can manufacture another proposition of the following kind:

$$(FFTF)(ABC,FGH)$$

This proposition is true just in case "ABC" is true and "FGH" is false, and it is false otherwise. Now whether the expressions "ABC" and "FGH" are themselves propositions will (ultimately) depend upon a relationship between their terms and objects in the world. The crucial point is that this kind of question does not arise *anew* when these propositions are embedded in: "(FFTF)(ABC,FGH)." Here the relationship between the constituent propositions and the world remains the same, for it is only our manner of making truth-value assignments that is at issue. By neither adding to nor subtracting from the picturing character of the base propositions—which ultimately must be elementary propositions—a truth-function of propositions preserves their fundamental character. Elementary propositions say *this is how things stand*, but since elementary propositions constitute the sole content of propositions, this is what every proposition says. A proposition is just a set

of pictures together with an assignment of truth values for the combinations of agreement and disagreement with reality.[5]

One final worry is that calling *this is how things stand* the general
form of a proposition, seems to ignore negation. Sometimes we want to
say that things do not stand in a certain way. Here, however, we must
recall that a proposition and its denial correspond to the same reality
and to negate a proposition is simply to present it under the stipulation
that it will be assigned the value true just in case the picture disagrees
with reality. This is equally a way of saying how things stand.

5
Logical inference

If every proposition is a truth-function of elementary propositions (a
result lifted to prominence at proposition 5), then, in Russell's words,
"we arrive at an amazing simplification of the theory of inference, as
well as a definition of the sort of propositions that belong to logic"
(TLP, Introduction, p. xvi.). Having discussed Wittgenstein's account
of the propositions of logic, we may now turn to his treatment of logical
inference.

Philosophers have often been attracted by the metaphor that the
validity of an inference from p to q depends upon the meaning of q
being *contained within* the meaning of p. Wittgenstein takes over this
traditional idea:

> 5.122 If p follows from q, the sense of "p" is contained in the sense
> of "q".

Wittgenstein unpacks this metaphor using the idea of *truth-grounds*.

The technical details can be spelled out quickly. By the truth-grounds
of a proposition, Wittgenstein means 'those truth-possibilities of its truth
arguments that make it true' (5.101). Thus we can read off the truth-
grounds for conjunction and disjunction from their truth-tables:

p	q	(p & q)	(p v q)
T	T	T	T
F	T	F	T
T	F	F	T
F	F	F	F

The truth-grounds for (p & q) are: (TT), and the truth-grounds for (p
v q) are: (TT), (TF), (FT). Now the theory of logical inference is
explained in these words:

> 5.11 If all the truth-grounds that are common to a number of
> propositions are at the same time truth-grounds of a certain

proposition, then we say that the truth of that proposition follows
from the truth of the other.
5.12 In particular, the truth of a proposition "*p*" follows from the
truth of another proposition "*q*" if all the truth-grounds of the
latter are truth-grounds of the former.

Thus (p v q) follows from (p & q), since all of the truth-grounds of the
latter (i.e., just (TT)) occur in the list of the truth-grounds of the former
(i.e., (TT), (TF) and (FT)). The inference does not hold in the other
direction since the disjunction contains two truth-grounds ((TF) and
(FT)) that are not truth-grounds of the conjunction.

6
Probability

Having explained how one proposition can *follow* from another, Wittgenstein turns his attention to the related topic of how one proposition
can give another a certain *degree of probability*. His fundamental thesis
about probability is given in these words:

5.15 If T_r is the number of the truth-grounds of a proposition "*r*",
and if T_{rs} is the number of the truth-grounds of a proposition "*s*"
that are at the same time truth-grounds of "*r*", then we call the ratio
$T_{rs} : T_r$ the degree of *probability* that the proposition "*r*" gives to
the proposition "*s*".

We can notice in the first place Wittgenstein here defines a *relation*: i.e.,
the degree of probability that one proposition *gives* another. He does
not speak of the probability of a proposition in isolation. Indeed, he
states quite explicitly that it makes no sense to assign a probability to a
proposition in isolation:

5.153 In itself, a proposition is neither probable nor improbable.
Either an event occurs or does not: there is no middle way.

Probability involves a relationship among structures of propositions; it
does not involve a relationship among propositions and certain special
features of the world:

5.1511 There is no special object peculiar to probability propositions.

It is clear, then, that Wittgenstein's approach to probability mirrors his
previous treatment of the proposition of logic. The technical aspects of
Wittgenstein's method are easily sketched. The basic numerical assignment is derived from the independence of elementary propositions. Given
one elementary proposition, we have no basis for deciding whether
another elementary proposition is true or false. Each alternative is equally
likely, so:

5.152 (b) Two elementary propositions give one another the probability ½.

The explanation of the basic proposition 5.15 is now straightforward. Again we can examine the relationship between the conjunction (p & q) and the disjunction (p v q), where the constituent propositions are elementary, thus guaranteeing that each line is equally likely:

p	q	(p & q)	(p v q)
T	T	T	T
T	F	F	T
F	T	F	T
F	F	F	F

To determine the probability the conjunction gives the disjunction, we take the ratio of the shared truth-grounds (T_{rs}) and the truth-grounds of the supporting proposition (T_r). In the present case, the conjunction and disjunction have only one truth-ground in common (i.e., (TT)) and the conjunction, which is the supporting proposition, has only a single truth-ground in its own right (again (TT)). The ratio, then, of T_{rs} to T_r is 1:1. Thus the conjunction gives the disjunction the degree of probability 1. This is what we expect, since the conjunction entails the disjunction.

Looking at the support relationship going the other direction, again the shared truth-grounds (T_{rs}) equal one, but the truth-grounds of the disjunction, which is now the supporting proposition, number three. Thus the ratio of T_{rs} to T_r equals 1/3, and this is the degree of probability that the disjunction gives the conjunction. More generally, it is not difficult to show that Wittgenstein's procedures will underwrite the axioms for a standard *a priori* probability calculus.

As noticed, Wittgenstein treats probability as a relationship between propositions, but there is a way of mimicking the idea of an absolute probability in his system. The value for the absolute probability of a proposition is just the value for the degree of probability that a tautology will bestow upon it. Thus the absolute probability of the conjunction (TFFF)(p,q) is 1/4, because this is the degree of probability bestowed upon it by the tautology (TTTT) (p,q). Reasoning in this way, we are led to assign an absolute probability of 1 to tautologies and an absolute value of 0 to contradictions. Perhaps it was a systematic connection of this kind that led Wittgenstein to view the scale of propositions from contradictions through tautologies as the basis for a theory of probability. Remarks to this effect occur at 5.1, 4.464 and again at 5.152:

5.152(c) If *p* follows from *q*, then the proposition "*q*" gives to the proposition "*p*" the probability of 1. The certainty of logical inference is a limiting case of probability.

(Application of this to tautology and contradiction.)

In a canonical notation we can simply read off the value of what I am calling a proposition's absolute probability by examining the left-hand parentheses and taking the ratio of *Ts* to *Ts and Fs*.

In assessing Wittgenstein's treatment of probability, we can notice, on the positive side, that it generates a standard probability calculus. More interestingly, it exploits the notion of the independence of elementary propositions to provide a theoretical basis for this construction. So the discussion of probability is not only consistent with the main theses of the *Tractatus*, but develops naturally from them.

The difficulties with Wittgenstein's account of probability are of two kinds. First, the view inherits all the difficulties inherent in any *a priori* account of probability. In particular, it is difficult to see how this approach can be extended to a theory of *confirmation:* Max Black puts the matter succinctly:

> Inferences from samples to "populations" are among the most
> common instances of the application of the probability concepts.
> A theory that is silent about the logic of sampling cannot be regarded
> as adequate.[6]

A second difficulty with Wittgenstein's treatment of probability is symptomatic of a shortcoming of the entire Tractarian approach. Notice that if we *could* fully analyze our everyday propositions into truth-functions of elementary propositions, then by putting them into a canonical form (i.e., with a string of Ts and Fs in the left-hand parentheses and a string of elementary propositions in the right-hand parentheses), it would be a wholly mechanical procedure to determine the degree of probability that one proposition gives another. This is an exciting result, but we must occasionally remind ourselves that Wittgenstein has given us no indication how this might be done for the propositions that we encounter in science and in everyday life.

V

Generality

1
The problem of general propositions

At proposition 5 Wittgenstein declares that a proposition (i.e., *every* proposition) is a truth-function of elementary propositions. A first reaction is that this claim is premature, since Wittgenstein has hardly canvassed the full range of things normally considered propositions. Most notably, he has yet to give an account of *general* propositions.

The expositional point is easily answered: we need only remind ourselves that the explanation and elucidation of a major proposition are usually subsumed under that proposition. In line with this, we find the exposition of generality, for the most part, in the propositions following 5. But there are also systematic reasons for doubting that Wittgenstein can give a proper account of general propositions. These doubts can be expressed naively. Thus far we have dealt only with logical relations between propositions taken as a whole, yielding the so-called propositional logic. But if we use just these resources in dealing with a standard syllogism, we get the following result:

All animals are mortal.	p
All men are animals.	q
∴ All men are mortal.	r

Thus the translation into propositional logic does not reveal the structure upon which the obvious validity of this argument rests.

The modern treatment of such arguments—which Wittgenstein attempts to take over—depends upon the use of *functions* for analyzing the internal structure of propositions. The argument is symbolized in the following way:

$$(x)(Ax \supset Mx)$$
$$\underline{(x)(Hx \supset Ax)}$$
$$\therefore (x)(Hx \supset Mx)$$

This symbolization is part of standard quantification theory in which the validity of this argument is easily shown. We shall examine Wittgenstein's attempt to introduce this portion of logic into the Tractarian system in two stages: (i) we shall first examine his treatment of functions, and then (ii) describe his method of extending his truth-functional techniques to propositions analyzed along functional lines.

2
Functions and expressions

As just noted, a fundamental idea of modern logic is to treat the internal structure of propositions on a function-argument model. Thus Frege, to whom this basic insight is often credited, would decompose the singular proposition "Smith is grave" into two components:

"   is grave"   and   "Smith"

In the unified sentence "Smith is grave," the argument expression "Smith" completes the functional expression "   is grave." This mathematical analogy is carried over to the notation where "Smith is grave" is translated "Gs." Frege gave a realistic account of these various kinds of expressions. Function names name functions; argument names name arguments (objects) and, consistent with this, the functional expression as a whole names its *value*. Thus "Smith is grave," if true, names the truth-value the true. For reasons that are not difficult to find, Wittgenstein cannot take over Frege's approach as a whole. We already know that Wittgenstein will not allow propositions to have a reference and, as we shall shortly see, he will not allow functional expressions to have a reference either. Wittgenstein takes over the functional analysis of propositions, but offers an alternative interpretation to that given by Frege.

We have gotten in the habit of representing an elementary proposition as a concatenation (not a list) of names, e.g.,

ABCD

Comparing "Gs" with "ABCD," we first see that the former expression contains two kinds of symbols whereas the latter expression contains only one kind of symbol. Using Frege's realistic language, "Gs" contains both a *function* name and an *object* name. It is a central feature of the Tractarian analysis that an elementary proposition contains only *object* names. So, unlike Frege, Wittgenstein does not provide himself with

55

functional expressions straight off by simply making them basic constituents of propositions. Let us examine what he does instead.

Wittgenstein presents his theory of functional expressions in a compact set of propositions headed by 3.31:

> 3.31 I call any part of a proposition that characterizes its sense an expression (or a symbol).
> (A proposition is itself an expression.)
> Everything essential to their sense that propositions can have in common with one another is an expression.
> An expression is the mark of a form and a content.

This may seem obscure, but the elucidatory propositions that follow are helpful:

> 3.313 . . . an expression is presented by means of a variable whose values are the propositions that contain the expression.
> (In the limiting case the variable becomes a constant, the expression becomes a proposition.)
> I call such a variable a "propositional variable."
> 3.315 If we turn a constituent of a proposition into a variable, there is a class of propositions all of which are values of the resulting variable proposition.

That is, if we begin with an elementary proposition "ABCD," we can replace one of its constituents by a variable, producing, for example, "AxCD." Doing this produces what Wittgenstein calls a *propositional variable* or what we now call a *propositional function*. The values of this function will be just those propositions we get by replacing the variable with a name.

Now that we see how functional *expressions* are introduced into the Tractarian system, let us consider *functions* themselves. We can begin by asking what the expression "Ax" *stands for;* what does it *represent?* Frege, as noted, said that functional expressions name functions. This, however, cannot be Wittgenstein's position, since a genuine name relation exists only among *simple* signs and objects. Functional expressions are not simple signs; they have an articulated structure. Neither propositions nor propositional variables enter into a name relation.[1] Do functional expressions then *picture* the world? The answer to this must be no, but functional expressions provide a prototype for a set of pictures of the world. They are proto-pictures.

A beautifully compact and clear summary of Wittgenstein's analysis of functions was offered by F. P. Ramsey in *The Foundations of Mathematics:*

A propositional function is an expression of the form "fx̂", which is such that it expresses a proposition when any symbol (of a certain appropriate logical type depending on *f*) is substituted for (x̂). Thus "x̂ is a man" is a propositional function. We can use propositional functions to collect together the range of propositions which are all the values of the function for all possible values of x. Thus "x̂ is a man" collects together all the propositions "a is a man", "b is a man", etc. Having now by means of a propositional function defined a set of propositions, we can, by using an appropriate notation, assert the logical sum or product of this.[2]

By making everything explicit, this interpretation shows that Wittgenstein's account of the explicit quantification over *objects* turns upon an implicit quantification over *propositions*. It further suggests that this quantification over propositions depends, in its turn, upon an implicit quantification over propositional *signs* and names. Let me explain. We use the propositional function "x̂ is a man" to collect *all* the propositions that are in the range of this function for values of *x*. It is not altogether clear how these propositions are themselves generated, but something of the following sort is demanded. We know that a proposition is a "propositional sign in its projective relation to the world" (3.121). It thus *seems* that in order to generate all propositions of a certain class, we will have to generate all the corresponding propositional *signs* of a corresponding class (i.e., the set of propositional signs which, in virtue of the projection rules of the system, *express* these propositions). In order to obtain all such propositional signs we must successively fill the gaps in the functional signs with all those *names* appropriate to the functional sign. Thus, at the end of the road, we find *something like* a *substitutional* theory of quantification emerging.

3
Functions and type theory

In giving a broad account of Wittgenstein's treatment of functions, I have glossed over some of its obscure features. Suppose I have generated the function *AxCD* from the elementary proposition ABCD; what limits are placed on the range of arguments that I may substitute for the variable? Wittgenstein answers this question unambiguously:

> 3.316 What values a propositional variable may take is something that is stipulated.
> The stipulation of values *is* the variable.

In other words, we define the propositional function *AxCD* just by stipulating what sorts of propositions can be constructed through filling its argument place.

What form should this stipulation take? A natural suggestion, which attracted both Russell and Ramsey, is this: In the proposition "ABCD," the name "B" stands for a thing of a certain *kind;* we may therefore substitute for it the name of anything else of that same kind. Substitutions outside this range will generate nonsense. Developing a theory along these lines, we might say that "Smith is grave" yields the function "x is grave," and we will get a genuine proposition whenever we substitute for "x" the name of something that is of a kind with Smith. "Jones is grave" is all right, but "14 is grave" is not.

A central feature of Wittgenstein's treatment of functions is that he flatly *rejects* this natural suggestion:

3.317 And the *only* thing essential to the stipulation is *that it is merely a description of symbols and states nothing about what is signified.*

How the description of the propositions is produced is not essential.

Obviously any talk about the kind or type of thing referred to by a group of symbols is excluded by this ruling.

What is the point of this? To begin with, a proposition saying what sorts of objects are appropriate to what sorts of functions would use so-called *formal* concepts, and they cannot appear in a language that only shows how objects are in fact combined. Yet this is not a special embarrassment for Russell's way of speaking for, on the contrary, virtually every sentence of the *Tractatus* contains formal concepts, and thus fails to have a propositional status. We must, therefore, look further to discover Wittgenstein's special complaint against the use of a language of types (or kinds) in logic.

The key, I think, is a doctrine that we will examine in closer detail later on:

6.126 One can calculate whether a proposition belongs to logic, by calculating the logical properties of the *symbol.*

If a proposition expresses a "truth of logic," this can be determined by purely calculative procedures, that is, without raising the question whether the proposition *squares with reality.* In the same way, whether a given expression can serve as an argument for a particular function is not something that can be said and is therefore not something that can be established through a comparison with reality. It must, instead, be something that can be settled through examining symbolism alone.

We are now in a position to see how Wittgenstein's position resembles formalism and also see how it differs from it. Whether a functional expression is properly formed is something established by a stipulation concerning symbols and therefore may be checked through an examination of the symbols alone.

> 3.33 In logical syntax the meaning of a sign should never play a role. It must be possible to establish logical syntax without mentioning the *meaning* of the sign: *only* the description of expressions may be presupposed.

This expresses the formalist's working rule. Wittgenstein's divergence from formalism is revealed in the following passage:

> 3.328 If a sign is *useless*, it is meaningless. That is the point of Occam's maxim.
>
> (If everything behaves as if a sign had meaning, then it does have meaning.)

Wittgenstein's view, then, seems to be this: we stipulate rules for sign combination, and, by other stipulations, names are correlated with objects. This raises an obvious question: what guarantees that the *permitted* name-combinations of the language match *possible* object-combinations in the world? To answer this question, Wittgenstein appeals to the *application* or *use* of the symbolism. If a sign combination finds no employment then, for that very reason, it is *meaningless* (3.328). More strikingly, this appeal to application is ultimate, for "if everything behaves as if a sign had meaning, then it does have meaning" (3.328). Thus if our symbolism finds employment, this will show that our linguistic rules mirror the categorial structure of the world.

Returning to the question of formalism, we can see how Wittgenstein's standpoint differs from stricter versions of that position. In the development of a proper symbolism, all the formalistic rules are in force. We must be able to determine everything of *logical* significance through an examination of the symbolism alone. At the same time, the construction of the symbolism will be an idle ceremony if it finds no application picturing the world. Wittgenstein does not believe that logic is the study of sign manipulation, but he does believe that, in a properly constructed language, all logical questions can be *settled* without an appeal beyond the syntax of the symbols themselves. We thus have an image of a formalistic system gaining its significance through *mirroring* the structure of the world. This is one central idea of the *Tractatus*.

In this same context Wittgenstein attacks Russell's notion of a *hierarchy* of types. His criticism depends upon his idea that the propositional function (variable) provides a *prototype* for those propositions that are its values. For Wittgenstein, a proposition cannot refer to itself, for to do so, the propositional *sign* must occur in an argument place properly within itself (3.332). Wittgenstein adds, parenthetically, that this "is the whole of the 'theory of types' " (3.332). In 3.333, Wittgenstein argues, or seems to argue, that any attempt to take a function as its own argument is bound to fail since such a substitution will always yield a *new* and *different* function:

> For let us suppose that the function $F(fx)$ could be its own argument: in that case there would be a proposition "$F(F(fx))$", in which the outer function F and the inner function F must have different meanings, since the inner one has the form $\phi(fx)$ and the outer one has the form $\psi(\phi(fx))$.

Wittgenstein adds that these considerations "dispose of the Russell paradox" (3.333).

The difficulty with this suggestion is that nothing is worked out in detail. We know that paradoxes arise with the unrestricted introduction of higher-order notions—functions of functions, classes of classes, properties of properties, and the like. Invoking his idea that a function provides the prototype for its values, Wittgenstein diagnoses the Russell paradox as the vulgar mistake of trying to identify a whole with one of its proper parts. It is in virtue of this diagnosis that he dismisses the Russell paradox in an offhand manner. But in fact, Wittgenstein has given no account of higher-order functions (classes, etc.), nor shown how his own account of functions as prototypes applies to them. Only when this is done can we assess the force of Wittgenstein's metaphor—which he takes so seriously—of the impossibility of symbolic self-containment.

4
Generality and the operation N

Although I do not find my account of Wittgenstein's treatment of functions altogether satisfactory, I must now turn to the total expression "$(x)Fx$," i.e., I will now examine how Wittgenstein handles general *propositions*.

In his introductory essay, Russell speaks of "Mr Wittgenstein's theory of the derivation of general propositions from conjunctions and disjunctions" (TLP, Introduction, p. xvi). What Russell has in mind is the identification of the universally quantified expression $(x)\ Fx$ with the conjunction:

$$Fa\ \&\ Fb\ \&\ Fc\ \&.\ .\ .\ .$$

and the identification of the existentially quantified expression $(Ex)\ Fx$ with the disjunction:

$$Fa\ v\ Fb\ v\ Fc\ v.\ .\ .\ .$$

The idea, then, is that we can construct these quantified statements by constructing the appropriate conjunction or disjunction out of *all* the values of the function *Fx*.

Turning to the text, we find the following passage on this subject:

5.521 I dissociate the concept *all* from truth-functions. Frege and Russell introduced generality in association with logical product or logical sum. This made it difficult to understand the propositions "(E*x*).*fx*" and "(*x*).*fx*", in which both ideas are embedded.

The situation is curious: Russell credits Wittgenstein with the "theory of the derivation of general propositions from conjunctions and disjunctions," whereas Wittgenstein, on his side, attributes the view to Frege and Russell, and speaks of its shortcomings. In fact, I think that here Russell has simply gotten Wittgenstein wrong, for Wittgenstein is consciously attempting to construct an alternative to the theory that *derives* general propositions from conjunctions and disjunctions. This becomes clear when we look at the technical development of his position.

In his account of general propositions, Wittgenstein employs a *truth-functional operation* he labels *N*. In general, an operation takes us from a base to a result. For example, doubling is an operation that takes us from the base 2 to the result 4. Operations are expressed in the form of a variable-constant combination. The operation of doubling can be expressed as "2x." Operations are iterable, i.e., they can be embedded in one another. We can double the result of doubling something ("2(2x)"). Operations of one kind can be embedded in operations of a different kind. We can triple the result of halving something ("3(x/2)"). With a *truth-functional* operation we start with a set of base propositions and generate a result that is a definite truth-function of these base propositions. Wittgenstein says that negation, logical addition, logical multiplication, etc., are operations of this kind (5.2341). Logical multiplication (or taking a logical product) works in the following way: given a set of propositions, this operation generates a single proposition that is true just in case all the base propositions are true; it is false otherwise.

Since it is easy to see how to construct the counterpart operation for the so-called "logical constants" we have examined thus far, the following claim should raise no new difficulties:

5.234 Truth-functions of elementary propositions are operations with elementary propositions as bases. (These operations I call truth-operations.)

But according to proposition 5, every proposition is a truth-function of elementary propositions, so we may derive the conclusion that "all propositions are results of truth-operations on elementary propositions" (5.3). Furthermore, Wittgenstein places a restriction upon these constructions that will play a decisive role in our discussion later on. The

61

construction of a proposition from elementary propositions may not involve the super-task of completing infinitely many (or endlessly many) steps:

5.32 All truth-functions are results of successive application to elementary propositions of a finite number of truth operations.

Given all this, we can now cast our question concerning general propositions in the following way: how is it possible to construct general propositions through finitely many applications of truth-operations on elementary propositions?

Unfortunately, it is not altogether easy to extract from the text a transparent answer to this central question. In the first place, Wittgenstein introduces a symbolism of his own whose explanation, as Russell remarks, "is not fully given in the text" (TLP, Introduction, p. xv). On top of this, Wittgenstein's treatment of general propositions is embedded in a discussion of how *all* truth operations may be derived from a single truth operation discovered by Peirce and later rediscovered by Sheffer. Since there is no way around this thicket, we must go through it.

Proposition 6 is stated as follows:

6 The general form of a truth-function is $[\bar{p}, \bar{\xi}, N(\bar{\xi})]$.
This is the general form of a proposition.

The terms in the ordered triple $[\bar{p}, \bar{\xi}, N(\bar{\xi})]$ are explained as follows. $\bar{p}$ stands for all atomic propositions. $\bar{\xi}$ stands for a selection of propositions that may include elementary propositions and propositions already constructed. $N(\bar{\xi})$ stands for the operation used successively to construct the series of propositions. Given a set of propositions, it generates a proposition that is true just in case all the base propositions are false, and it generates a false proposition in all other cases.

In the simplest case, the construction proceeds in the following way: we are given set $\bar{\xi}$ by enumeration, say (P, Q, R). $N(P, Q, R)$ is a proposition (not a set), that is true just in case all the propositions in $\bar{\xi}$ are false. In other words $N(P, Q, R)$ *is equivalent to the joint denial of the three propositions in the set* $\bar{\xi}$. Since the operator N is mimicking the so-called Sheffer stroke, it is clear that the logical constants of the propositional logic can be defined using it alone.

The treatment of quantificational formulas is more complex. Here the set $\bar{\xi}$ is specified by giving "a function fx whose values for all values of x are the propositions to be described" (5.501). For example, we can construct the formula "$(Ex)fx$" in the following way. We let $\bar{\xi}$ have as its members the values of the function fx for all values of the variable x, i.e., it is the set of propositions fa, fb, fc, etc. Now $N(fx)$ *is a proposition that is true just in case all the propositions in the set* $\bar{\xi}$ *are false.* It is thus equivalent to the joint denial of these propositions, i.e., *~fa & ~fb &*

~fc. . . . . This, in turn, is equivalent to the proposition $(x)\text{-}fx$. The next step is to let ξ be this single proposition. Applying N to this set yields the denial of this proposition, i.e., $\sim(x)\text{-}fx$, and that, under standard interpretations of quantifiers, is equivalent to $(Ex)(fx)$. In sum, in the Tractarian notation, "$(Ex)(fx)$" is represented as "$N(N(fx))$."
Russell's summary passage gets things exactly right:

> Wittgenstein's method of dealing with general propositions [i.e.,
> "$(x).fx$" and "$(Ex).fx$)"] differs from previous methods by the fact
> that the generality comes only in specifying the set of propositions
> concerned, and when this has been done the building up of truth-
> functions proceeds exactly as it would in the case of a finite number
> of enumerated arguments p, q, r. . . . (TLP, Introduction p. xv)

This, I think, is the whole story of Wittgenstein's account of general propositions: generality comes *only* in specifying the set of propositions concerned by means of a propositional function. All the rest is technical detail.

Although the text is compact, I think that we can find three reasons why Wittgenstein favors this account of general propositions. (i) It is part of a single uniform method for introducing all needed logical notions. (ii) It avoids some of the most obvious difficulties associated with the theory that derives general propositions from conjunctions and disjunctions. (iii) Most importantly, it makes clear the logical form of a quantified statement by bringing into prominence the role of a *variable*.

(i) We have already seen that Wittgenstein has a sharp eye for cases where it is assumed, without explanation, that a single item can occur in different roles.[3] For this reason, Wittgenstein insists that the basic notions of logic be introduced in a manner that at once covers all the settings in which they appear.

> 5.451 . . . If a primitive idea has been introduced, it must have been
> introduced in all the combinations in which it ever occurs. It cannot,
> therefore, be introduced first for *one* combination and later re-
> introduced for another. For example, once negation has been
> introduced, we must understand it both in propositions of the form
> "$\sim p$" and in propositions like "$\sim(p \ v \ q)$", "$(Ex).\text{-}fx$", etc.

I think that this statement is clear as it stands, but it may not be clear that Wittgenstein's own procedures meet the demands laid down in it. For example, Wittgenstein first uses the operation N on enumerated propositions. In this way, he can generate "$(\sim p \ \& \ \sim q)$ by applying the operation N to the propositions p and q, i.e., $N(p, q)$. But if we are trying to construct the proposition "$\sim(Ex)(Fx \ \& \ Gx)$" the use of the operation has a very different appearance, i.e.:

$$N(Fx \ \& \ Gx)[4]$$

What shall we say about the sudden appearance of a functional sign under the operation N? That, after all, seems like a new departure. The answer is that it is still only propositions that are brought under the scope of logical operations; it is only the method of *stipulation* or the method of *description* that has changed. The central point is this: the operation N takes a set of propositions and generates from them their joint denial. For this to take place, these propositions have to be specified, described or picked out in one way or another, but the manner in which they are presented is wholly irrelevant to the employment of the *truth-functional* operation N. So, for Wittgenstein, the operation N has the same employment in generating the formulas of the propositional logic and the formulas of quantification theory.

(ii) There are strong logical instincts that support the idea that universal propositions are associated with conjunctions and existential propositions are associated with disjunctions.

$$(x)Fx = Fa \ \& \ Fb \ \& \ Fc \ \& \ . \ . \ . \ .$$
$$(Ex)Fx = Fa \ v \ Fb \ v \ Fc \ v \ . \ . \ . \ .$$

There is even a temptation to treat the expressions on the right as the proper analysis or definition of the expressions on the left. When this is done we arrive at the theory that derives "general propositions from conjunctions and disjunctions." This, as we saw, is a view that Russell attributes to Wittgenstein, and Wittgenstein, returning what he thinks a disfavor, imputes to Frege and Russell.

Wittgenstein begins this disclaimer with the following obscure remark:

5.521 I dissociate the concept *all* from truth-functions.

To see what he is probably getting at in this sentence we can notice that the general form of the logical product analysis of "$(x)Fx$" is:

$$(T_1, F_2, \ . \ . \ . \ F_2{}^n)(Fa_1, Fa_2 \ . \ . \ . \ . \ Fa_n)$$

If we substitute for n the number of things there are, then "$(x)Fx$" is defined as a specific truth-function.[5] Yet it seems wholly uncharacteristic for a logical issue to turn upon the question of *how many* things there are and Wittgenstein insists—on three different occasions—that logic has no privileged numbers.[6] One good reason, then, for Wittgenstein to dissociate the concept *all* (as he phrases it) from truth-functions is that there is no particular truth-function with which it can be associated without admitting extra-logical considerations into logic.

(iii) Although Wittgenstein begins by dissociating the concept *all* from truth-functions, he does acknowledge, in criticizing Frege and Russell, that there is some close connection between generality and the truth-functional notions of a logical product and a logical sum:

5.521 I dissociate the concept *all* from truth-functions. Frege and Russell introduced generality in association with logical product or logical sum. This made it difficult to understand the propositions '(Ex).*fx*' and '(x).*fx*', in which both ideas are embedded.

The claim that the ideas of logical product and logical sum are embedded in (*beschlossen liegen*) these general propositions is metaphorical, but I think what Wittgenstein has in mind is this: each of the individual conjuncts or disjuncts (Fa, Fb, etc.) counts as an *instance* of these general formulas. It is just this relationship between the general proposition and its instances that demands explanation. Now I think we can see the thrust of Wittgenstein's complaint against the theory (attributed to Frege and Russell) that "introduces generality in association with logical product and logical sum." These logical products and logical sums are themselves constructed out of *instances* of the general proposition. Thus the relationship most in need of explanation—how general propositions are related to their instances—is simply taken for granted by Frege and Russell.

Wittgenstein's own account of this relationship returns to the idea—first introduced in his discussion of functions—that a propositional function provides a prototype for those propositions that are its values:

5.522 What is peculiar to the generality-sign is first, that it indicates a logical prototype, and secondly, that it gives prominence to constants.
5.523 The generality-sign makes its appearance as an argument.

5.523 certainly sounds peculiar, for it seems to say that the existential quantifier (for example) should appear as the argument of a function in the following way: "F(Ex)." But this cannot be Wittgenstein's intention, for, not only is this idea ridiculous in itself, it is something that he explicitly rejects (at 4.0411). So when Wittgenstein speaks about the generality-sign he is not referring to the quantifiers "(x)" and "(Ex)." Using the standard notation "(x)Fx," it is clear that it is the second occurrence of the letter "x" that Wittgenstein calls the generality-sign, for it does make its appearance as an argument. So Wittgenstein's basic idea is that *generality* comes with the occurrence of a *variable*.

This whole approach depends, of course, upon the idea that propositional functions (variables) serve as prototypes for the propositions that are its values. A general proposition exhibits the logical form of its instances. The particular quantifiers (the universal quantifier and the existential quantifier) specify a definite truth operation of those propositions that are the values of the propositional functions they govern. It is in this way that Wittgenstein attempts to bring general propositions under the dictum that every proposition is a truth-function of elementary propositions.

5
Fully general propositions

Wittgenstein's treatment of general propositions concludes with a discussion of what he calls *fully* general propositions. In a fully generalized proposition, all of the non-logical constants are replaced by bound variables. For example, starting from the singular proposition "Cain is angry," we can construct the fully generalized proposition "$(Ex)(E\phi)\phi x$." If we allow ourselves the use of formal concepts, we could render this latter expression as: "There is at least one thing having at least one feature."

Few problems gave Wittgenstein more difficulties than offering a correct account of fully general propositions. In the *Notebooks* we find him agonizing over this problem in the following words:

> The proposition is supposed to give a logical model of a situation. It can surely only do this, however, because objects have been arbitrarily correlated with elements. Now if this is not the case in the quite general proposition, then it is difficult to see how it should represent anything outside of itself.
>
> In the proposition we—so to speak—arrange things experimentally. . . . But if the quite general proposition contains *only* "*logical* constants", then it cannot be anything more to us than—simply—a logical structure, and cannot do anything more than show us its own logical properties.—If there are quite general propositions—*what* do we arrange experimentally in them? (NB, 15.10.14)

This passage turns upon an assumption that may, at first, seem central to the Tractarian framework as well: in order for a proposition to picture the world, it must contain names that have been arbitrarily correlated with objects. Wittgenstein seems to make a further assumption: since fully general propositions cannot picture the world, they must be propositions of logic.

Wittgenstein finally came to the conclusion that this second assumption is false:

> "$(E\phi):(x).\phi x$"—of this proposition it appears almost certain that it is neither a tautology nor a contradiction. Here the problem becomes extremely sharp. (NB, 16.10.14)[7]

In other words, here we have a proposition that is wholly general but does not fall within the domain of logic. A day later he won through to the position adopted in the *Tractatus:*

> If there are quite general propositions, then it looks as if such propositions were experimental combinations of "logical constants". (!)
>
> But is it not possible to describe the whole world completely by means of completely general propositions? (The problem crops up on all sides.)
>
> Yes the world could be completely described by completely general propositions, and hence without using any sort of name or other denoting signs. And in order to arrive at ordinary language one would only need to introduce names, etc., by saying, after an "(Ex)", "and this x is A" and so on.
>
> Thus it is possible to devise a picture of the world without saying what is a representation of what. (NB, 17.10.14)

This final claim is repeated in the *Tractatus:*

> 5.526 We can describe the world completely by means of fully generalized propositions, i.e., without first correlating any name with a particular object.

Thus Wittgenstein came to abandon an assumption that seemed wholly evident to him at one time, namely, that picturing depends upon setting up names as representatives or proxies for objects. How then does a fully general proposition describe the world? Wittgenstein's answer is that a fully generalized proposition can describe the world in virtue of its articulated or composite structure:

> 5.5261 A fully generalized proposition, like every other proposition, is composite. (This is shown by the fact that in "$(Ex,\phi).\phi x$" we have to mention "ϕ" and "x" separately. They both, independently, stand in signifying relations to the world, just as is the case in ungeneralized propositions.)

Although Wittgenstein does not say this explicitly, the mechanism for correlating the individual components of the proposition is given in the phrasing for the quantifiers, e.g., "there is at least one x such that. . . ."

This account of fully generalized propositions raises a number of questions that are difficult to answer. (i) The most obvious objection is that fully generalized propositions cannot possibly say everything that can be said with propositions containing names, just because a fully general proposition does not say *of a particular thing* that it has some feature. (ii) A more subtle objection comes from the other direction. F. P. Ramsey suggested that if the world contains only finitely many

67

objects, then we seem able to say *more* with fully generalized propositions than we can with elementary propositions. Roughly, we can construct a general proposition containing more distinct variables than there are things in the world. I shall state Ramsey's criticism more carefully later on.

(i) Since the *Tractatus* is silent about the way we picture the world using only fully generalized propositions, we must turn to the *Notebooks* for help. Continuing the entry for 17.10.14, where it was left off above, Wittgenstein says:

> Let us suppose, e.g., that the world consisted of the things A and B and the property F, and that F(A) were the case and not F(B). This could also be described by the following propositions:

$$(\exists x,y).(\exists \phi). x \neq y.\phi x. {\sim}\phi y : \phi u.\phi z. \supset_{u,z}. u \ = \ z$$
$$(\exists \phi).(\psi).\psi = \phi$$
$$(\exists x,y).(z).z = x v z = y$$

Idiomatically (or more or less idiomatically) the first proposition tells us that the world contains *at least* two things and at least one property; *at least* one of these things possesses this property and *at least* one of these things lacks this property; and, finally, *at most* one thing possesses this property. The second and third propositions indicate, in turn, that the world contains *exactly* one property and *exactly* two things. Wittgenstein's thesis is that this world description using only fully general propositions is as complete as the world description using individual and predicate constants.

Yet it seems obvious that the world description containing only fully generalized propositions lacks something present in the world description using names. Naively, we want to say that the fully general description does not tell us *which* things are *what* way. More carefully, the general descriptions do not distinguish between two different and, indeed, incompatible worlds. In one world—the one we started with—we have the two things A and B and the property F, where A possesses this property and B does not. In a second world we have the same basic furniture, but this time A lacks the property and B possesses it. Wittgenstein's set of general propositions equally describes each of these worlds.

If Wittgenstein has an answer to this criticism it must, I think, proceed along the following lines. In fact, something *is* lost when we pass from a language using names to a language in which names no longer appear: we are no longer saying *of a thing* that it has a feature or lacks it. Yet on the Tractarian account, nothing *descriptive* has been lost. Naming (real naming) is not a kind of describing, and so identifying what does what in the world does not extend the description of the world. This may seem a strange position, especially if we identify names with the names of our everyday language. Wittgenstein, of course, would consider the names of our everyday language implicit descriptions, but if we hold strictly to the Tractarian notion of names, it is clear that this position follows directly from central features of the Tractarian system. On the side of language, it is connected with the idea that genuine names have only a reference and no sense, for, if proper names had a sense, then saying who did what would extend our knowledge of the world. From the side of the world, it is connected with the claim that objects are, in a manner of speaking, colorless (2.0232). Objects, being simple, cannot be described.

(ii) The second criticism, noted above, was first formulated by F. P. Ramsey.[8] It raises the possibility that a system of fully generalized propositions may have a *greater* descriptive potential than the total set of elementary propositions. Once more we can consider a world consisting of two objects, A and B, and a single property F. What shall we say about the wholly general proposition that at least three things possess at least some property? It seems that however the property F is distributed in the world, this proposition must be false in asserting the existence of more objects than actually exist. But if we take this line we must decide whether it is *contingently* false or *necessarily* false. Each option leads to unacceptable results. If the proposition is contingently false then its truth is a possibility and, as Anscombe has remarked, "the completely generalized propositions will allow more play to the facts than the totality of elementary propositions."[9] We should also notice that if this proposition is considered contingently false, then Wittgenstein must abandon a central feature of his picture theory of meaning and acknowledge the existence of a contingent proposition that does not depend for its truth upon the combination and separation of objects *within* logical space. Thus there are strong systematic reasons behind Ramsey's suggestion that we must treat this proposition as a *necessary* falsehood—and for the *Tractatus* that means treating it as a contradiction. But even if Ramsey's suggestion is systematically well-motivated, it can hardly be introduced into the Tractarian framework without causing profound disruption. It is a central idea of the *Tractatus* that logic must take care of itself, i.e., that we should never have to go beyond the symbols in settling logical issues.

> 5.551 Our fundamental principle is that whenever a question can be decided by logic at all it must be possible to decide it without more ado.
>
> (And if we get into a position where we have to look at the world for an answer to such a problem, that shows that we are on a completely wrong track.)

But if a necessary truth depended upon the number of objects in the world, then this principle is violated.

I think that an answer is forthcoming to these difficulties if we return to Wittgenstein's basic idea concerning the character of general propositions. Since Russell's phrasing hits the mark exactly, I shall repeat it:

> Wittgenstein's method of dealing with general propositions . . . differs from previous methods by the fact that the generality comes *only in specifying the set of propositions concerned.* (my italics, TLP, Introduction, p. xv)

The method of specification involves the use of a propositional function (variable) that provides a prototype for those propositions which are its values. Given this set of propositions, truth-functions of them are constructed in the normal way through the use of truth-operations. But now it should be obvious how to deal with the case where our commitment to distinct things through existential quantifiers outstrips the number of objects in the world. In this case the propositional function will have *no* values, i.e., no base propositions to serve as grist for the truth-operational mill. There is no *application* for a general proposition of this kind; it is *useless;* and for that reason *meaningless* (5.47321).

There is, however, a technical difficulty here. The standard translation for "At least three things possess some property" is this:

(i) $(Ex)(Ey)(Ez)(E\phi)[\phi x \ \& \ \phi y \ \& \ \phi z \ \& \ x \neq y \ \& \ y \neq z \ \& \ x \neq z]$

Suppose, now, we make the following substitutions:

$$
\begin{array}{ccc}
a & \text{for} & x \\
b & \text{for} & y \\
b & \text{for} & z \\
F & \text{for} & \phi
\end{array}
$$

This yields the self-contradictory instance:

$$Fa \ \& \ Fb \ \& \ Fb \ \& \ a \neq b \ \& \ b \neq b \ \& \ a \neq b$$

Of course, all substitutions in the model world will be self-contradictory. But this does not give us the result we want; indeed, it leads us right back to the result we are trying to avoid, namely, Ramsey's suggestion that a formula whose existential commitment outstrips the number of objects in the world is self-contradictory. The conclusion we are trying to reach is that such a formula generates no proposition at all.

At this point we are getting interference from the occurrence of an *identity-sign.* The contradiction arises because there is no way of making a substitution into the schema without saying that something is not identical with itself. In section 6 we shall see that Wittgenstein excludes a sign for identity from a proper symbolism. His own procedure is to *show* the identity of objects through the identity of signs and to *show* the difference in objects through a difference in signs. The same issues arise concerning Wittgenstein's treatment of identity that are worrying us now, so we cannot quit this subject until we examine Wittgenstein's treatment of identity. For the moment, however, we can examine the results of adopting Wittgenstein's conventions concerning identity.

Instead of using (i), we drop all the reference to identity and just write:

$$\text{(ii) } (Ex)(Ey)(Ez)(E\phi)[\phi x \ \& \ \phi y \ \& \ \phi z]$$

The systematic difference between these approaches comes out in the following way:

$$\text{Fa \& Fb \& Fb \& } a{\neq}b \text{ \& } b{\neq}b \text{ \& } a{\neq}b$$

is an instance of the first formula. It is self-contradictory and for the model world we have envisaged, all substitutions will be self-contradictory. In contrast,

$$\text{Fa \& Fb \& Fb}$$

is *not* an instance of the second formula, since our model world is incapable of providing instances for this formula. We thus arrive at a nice result. If we employ standard symbolism containing identity, a formula with an existential commitment outstripping the number of objects in the world is self-contradictory. This, as we have seen, would be an embarrassment for the *Tractatus*. In contrast, if we adopt Wittgenstein's conventions that exclude an identity-sign from the symbolism, we arrive at the conclusion we want: a formula whose existential commitment outstrips the number of objects in the world will find no *application*, and therefore be a *useless* expression formulating no proposition.

Writers on Wittgenstein do not usually stress the role of the *application* or *use* of language in the *Tractatus*. Some, I think, are merely diffident about projecting back upon the *Tractatus* doctrines thought characteristic of Wittgenstein's later writings. Others wish to maximize the distance between the *Tractatus* and Wittgenstein's later writings in order to make the transition more dramatic. In fact, the notion of application is central to the *Tractatus*, for it is only through the application of language that we are able to resolve many questions that defy proper formulation within our language.

6
Identity[10]

Although I have not dwelt upon this subject, it is important to remember that the *Tractatus* was written under the dominating influence and impact of Whitehead and Russell's *Principia Mathematica*. To go further, I do not think we grasp the full intent of the *Tractatus* unless we see that one of its pretensions—perhaps its chief pretension—was to serve as a replacement for *Principia Mathematica*.

In that work Whitehead and Russell attempt to complete the logistic program initiated by Frege, i.e., they tried to show how arithmetic (in particular) could be reduced to logic. Certain features of *Principia Mathematica* attracted immediate questioning. The *theory of types*, which was Russell's way around the antinomy he had found in Frege's system, struck many as both arbitrary and overly restrictive. We have already remarked upon Wittgenstein's vaunting rejection of type hierarchies in favor of his own prototype theory of functions. A second area that drew criticism concerned some of the axioms used by Russell which seemed either dubious in their own right or contrary in their content to the demands of the logistic program. For example, the Axiom of Infinity provides a way of saying (in effect) that the world contains infinitely many things (objects, individuals). Whether this axiom is true or not may be hard to say, but even granting its truth, it seems hardly a truth of *logic*. This was Wittgenstein's position, for he thought that it was the very essence of logic not to get involved with such commitments about the world. Logic must take care of itself. Wittgenstein's prototype theory of functions serves as his alternative to type theory; his treatment of identity, as we shall now see, gives his alternative to the Axiom of Infinity.

The connection between identity and the Axiom of Infinity is mentioned in an early entry in the *Notebooks:*

> The question about the possibility of existence propositions does not come in the middle but at the very beginning of logic.
>   All the problems that go with the Axiom of Infinity have already to be solved in the proposition "$(Ex)x = x$". (NB, 9.10.14)

On Wittgenstein's account, a truth of logic is a tautology, that is, it can *say* nothing about the world. Yet the formula "$(Ex)x = x$," which is a logical truth in the system of *Principia Mathematica*, does seem to say something, namely, that the world contains at least one thing having a specific property, i.e., self-identity.

But Wittgenstein's worries are not restricted to the emergence of such a formula as a *truth* of logic; the sheer possibility of constructing such a formula runs counter to Tractarian principles. Earlier in the *Tractatus*, Wittgenstein makes the following remark:

> 4.1272 . . . one cannot say, for example, "There are objects", as one might say "There are books". And it is just as impossible to say "There are 100 objects", or "There are $\aleph_0$ objects."

Since we have gone over similar ground before, it is easy to see why such remarks as "There are objects," "There are 100 objects," etc., must be placed on the Index. It does not seem plausible to treat them as truths or falsehoods of logic, i.e., as tautologies or contradictions. Yet they cannot be treated as contingencies either, since it hardly makes sense to treat the claim that the world has 100 objects as an assertion that the objects of the world stand to one another in some determinate relationship. Given these considerations, it will not be sufficient to block such assertions from the status of truths (or falsehoods) of logic; instead, in a proper conceptual notation, such assertions should not be allowed to arise at all.

It should now be clear why a language containing a sign for the identity of individuals raises troubles in the Tractarian system. Given this resource, it seems that we *are* in a position to formulate proscribed propositions. Here is how we say that there is exactly one thing:

$$(Ex) (y) (y = x)$$

Wittgenstein's solution to this problem is to banish the offending symbol from the language. In a proper conceptual notation a sign for the identity of individuals does not occur.[11]

Before commenting upon the plausibility of this move, we can see how it works in detail. Here is Wittgenstein's general strategy:

> 5.53 Identity of object I express by identity of signs, and not by using a sign for identity. Difference of objects I express by difference of signs.

This procedure allows us to eliminate some window-dressing uses of the identity-sign. Thus instead of writing "f(a,b). a = b," we write "f(a,a)" (5.531). This is not an interesting shift, since this is not a case where the Russell notation *requires* the use of the identity-sign; "f(a,a)" is all right in the Russell notation as well. The crucial cases arise where the Russell notation requires the use of the identity-sign for the formulation of undeniably legitimate propositions. Consider the claim that there are *at least* two things that are F—where F is some such material feature as being a book. Russell would formulate this proposition in the following way:

$$(Ex)(Ey)(Fx \ \& \ Fy \ \& \ (x \neq y))$$

Wittgenstein's formulation is simply:

$$(Ex)(Ey)(Fx \ \& \ Fy)$$

Table V.1 gives some other examples patterned after those given in 5.531, 5.532 and 5.5321:

Table V.1

English	Russell	Wittgenstein
Somebody likes somebody.	(Ex) (Ey) [Px&Py&Lxy]	(Ex) (Ey) [Px&Py&Lxy] v (Ex) [Px&Lxx]
There are at most two books on the table.	(x) (y) (z) [(Bx&By&Bz) ⊃((x=y) v (x=z))]	~(Ex) (Ey) (Ez) (Bx&By&Bz)

It seems obvious—though a proof for this is needed—that Wittgenstein's method can shadow Russell's, making numerical assignments to things already described under some other non-logical predicate. But Wittgenstein's procedures will not produce counterparts for what we might call *pure* occurrences of the identity-sign, i.e., occurrences of the identity-sign governing individuals not previously qualified by some non-logical predicate. It thus seems that the only occurrences of an identity-sign that are not eliminable by Wittgenstein's procedure arise in expressions that Wittgenstein wishes to exclude from the language. This brings us to the following conclusion:

5.533 The identity-sign, therefore, is not an essential constituent of conceptual notation.

Thus in a correct conceptual notation "pseudo-propositions like 'a = a,' . . . , '(Ex).x = a,' etc. cannot even be written down" (5.534). With this move, the employment of the identity-sign to formulate existence propositions is blocked. Since they cannot be written down, problems about them can no longer arise. The discussion concludes on a characteristic Tractarian note:

5.535 All the problems that Russell's "axiom of infinity" brings with it can be given at this point.
     What the axiom of infinity is intended to say would express itself in language through the existence of infinitely many names with different meanings.

Here, using the subjunctive, Wittgenstein leaves open the question whether any correct conceptual notation must satisfy this demand.

7
Propositional attitudes

At proposition 5, Wittgenstein states that every proposition is a truth-function of elementary propositions. At proposition 6 he makes the stronger claim—using his own commentary at 6.001—that every proposition is a result of successive applications to elementary propositions of the operation $N(\xi)$. In between these two propositions Wittgenstein is largely engaged in the project of showing that certain kinds of propositions *are* truth-functions of elementary propositions through showing how they may be constructed using truth-functional operations. The development of a theory for general propositions is the most important feature of this part of the text. Wittgenstein has, however, a back-up strategy when these constructive efforts fail: independent grounds are presented showing that the proposition is, after all, a pseudo-proposition and therefore ought *not* to occur in a correct symbolism. The apparent significance of these so-called pseudo-propositions is typically—though not always—explained by saying that they are mistaken attempts to say that which can only be *shown*.

There is at least one case where it is not clear which of these strategies Wittgenstein adopts. The occurrence (or apparent occurrence) of propositions in belief statements seems to be an exception to the principle that one proposition can occur in another only truth-functionally:

5.541 At first sight it looks as if it were also possible for one proposition to occur in another in a different way.
Particularly with certain forms of proposition in psychology, such as "A believes that p is the case" and "A has the thought p", etc.
For if these are considered superficially, it looks as if the proposition p stood in some kind of relation to an object A.

Specifically, if we treat belief statements as asserting a relationship between a person (an object A) and a proposition (p), then it is evident that the truth of the belief statement is not a function of the truth of the proposition believed.

Wittgenstein's solution to the problems concerning the logical status of belief statements is given in a single sentence:

5.542 It is clear, however, that "A believes that p", "A has the thought p", and "A says p" are of the form " 'p' says p": and this does not involve a correlation of a fact with an object, but rather the correlation of facts by means of the correlation of their objects.

As a first approximation, Wittgenstein seems to be saying this: when a person believes something, he constructs a picture of a fact, putting elements of his picture into correlation with elements of the fact. A picture, however, is itself a fact. We therefore have a "correlation of facts by means of the correlation of their objects." He compares belief statements, in this respect, with statements like " 'Greenland is cold,' says that Greenland is cold." Here, according to Wittgenstein, we are correlating the elements of the propositional *sign* (which is a picture) with the elements of a fact. More carefully, the elements in the propositional sign are correlated with objects in the world, and the mode of their combination in the proposition is used to represent the way these objects are themselves combined.

The above gives a schematic account of Wittgenstein's treatment of belief statements. Unfortunately, Wittgenstein's own account hardly goes further, and it is very difficult to determine what his position comes to. Here are two possibilities. (i) The proposition "John believes that Greenland is cold," admits of an analysis that both eliminates the apparent occurrence of a proposition in a non-truth-functional setting and exhibits how such propositions can be constructed as the result of truth operations on elementary propositions. (ii) These apparent occurrences of propositions in a non-truth-functional setting arise because we are attempting to *say* something that can only be *shown*. We are trying to talk about a correlation of facts by means of a correlation of objects, but this cannot be done. In our effort to make such a claim we convert the *picturing fact* and the *pictured fact* into bogus substantivals and assert a relationship between them. The advantage of the first approach is that it preserves the idea that the proposition "John believes that Greenland is cold" is a contingency. Yet if this is Wittgenstein's position, we should wonder why he has not sketched the method for constructing these propositions as the result of truth-operations on elementary propositions. This is something he did attempt for general propositions and for those Russellian identity statements he thought worth saving. The second reading is reinforced by other portions of the text where Wittgenstein proscribes second-order talk about meanings. Black develops this theme in the following words:

> It should be noticed that on W's principles the meaning of a sentence can only be shown (4.022a). So the proper verdict is that *p* does not occur at all in "A believes *p*" (which is *not* a truth function of p). A cannot *say* that he believes *p*, but he shows that he does by uttering a certain sentence; and we show that we take him to be believing *p* by treating him as asserting *p*, e.g., by contradicting him or agreeing with him.[12]

Black's reading is persuasive, but it is tempered by two considerations: (i) Wittgenstein nowhere *says* that belief statements are attempts to say things that can only be shown, and (ii) the view is not persuasive in its own right. Belief propositions seem to be part of everyday language and thus in perfect order just as they stand (5.5563). In general, Wittgenstein does not banish utterances of the vulgar tongue as pseudo-propositions.[13] Anyway, judgments ascribing beliefs certainly seem to be empirical and to the extent that we are impressed with this, the showing account must seem implausible.

It thus seems that Wittgenstein's analysis of belief statements involves only a first step that allows two very different completions. He certainly holds that the proposition p does not occur at all in the proposition "A believes p." It is also clear that the proposition concerns a correlation between elements in a picture and objects in a fact pictured. What is left unclear is whether this correlation can be expressed in a truth-functional language or must, instead, be treated as something that makes itself manifest in the employment of a truth-functional language. I do not think that the text settles this issue.

VI

The Naive Constructivism of the *Tractatus*

1
A fundamental error in the logic of the Tractatus

In the first edition of this work I argued that the logic of the *Tractatus* is fundamentally flawed, a claim since challenged by Peter Geach and Scott Soames.[1] As the heading of this section indicates, I remain unrepentant on this matter, but I have come to see that the issues here are much more complex and far-reaching than I had previously supposed. The disputed point concerns the expressive capacity of the operator *N* introduced at proposition 6. In the previous chapter we saw how the *N* operator is used to construct quantified expressions. Here I shall ask whether Wittgenstein's procedures are adequate to construct all formulas of a standard first-order quantificational theory. It is easy to show that, *given the procedures explicitly stated in the Tractatus*, it is not.

To make good this claim, we need only examine the following family of formulas:

1	(x) (y) fxy	5	(x) (y)~fxy
2	(Ex) (Ey) fxy	6	(Ex) (Ey)~fxy
3	(x) (Ey) fxy	7	(x) (Ey)~fxy
4	(Ex) (y) fxy	8	(Ex) (y)~fxy

(To facilitate comparisons, we shall adopt the convention that negation signs be driven inward as far as possible. This way, we will not be distracted by such formulas as "~(x)~(Ey)~fxy.")

To construct such multiply-general propositions we let ξ have as its values the values of the function *fxy* for all values of *x* and *y*, i.e., *faa*, *fab*, *fba*, *fac*, etc. Since *N(fxy)* gives the joint denial of all those propositions that are the values of the propositional function *fxy*, it is evident we have produced a proposition equivalent to "~(Ex) (Ey) fxy." Driving the negation sign inward brings us to the canonical proposition 5:

"(x) (y)~fxy." We can next bring this resulting proposition under the operator N, i.e., just deny it, and this gives us a result equivalent to proposition 2: "(Ex) (Ey)fxy." This road now becomes sterile, since any further applications of the operator N generate results that flip-flop back and forth between propositions equivalent to propositions 2 and 5. A parallel result emerges if we employ the propositional function—*fxy*. Here we can generate propositions 1 and 6, but the application of the operator N becomes sterile beyond this. We can, if we like, construct various truth functions of the propositions constructed—for example, we might conjoin propositions 2 and 6 and then negate that result—but such procedures will be of no help in constructing the four remaining multiply-general propositions in the initial family of eight. We now see that if we begin with the functions *fxy* or ~*fxy* and apply the operator N directly to them, four members of the family of multiply-general propositions can be generated, four of them cannot.

It is easy enough to diagnose the present difficulty. When we apply the operator N to the propositions that are the values of the function *fxy*, both argument places under the function are handled at once in the same way, i.e., both variables are captured. So whatever kind of quantifier emerges governing one of the variables, that same kind of quantifier must emerge governing the other. It is for this reason that we are able to construct the *homogeneous* multiply-general propositions 1, 2, 5 and 6, but we cannot construct the *mixed* multiply-general propositions 3, 4, 7 and 8.

This much is clear; given the explicitly stated notational procedures of the *Tractatus*, there is no way of constructing mixed multiply-general propositions and therefore the system of the *Tractatus* is expressibly incomplete. Neither Geach nor Soames, whose suggestions I will examine in a moment, denies this. A second question is this: can the system of the *Tractatus* be made whole by extending its notational resources? The answer to this, as Geach and Soames have shown, is yes. The third, and deepest, question is whether this extension can be made within the constraints of the *Tractarian* system? I do not know the answer to this, but it is clear to me that the suggestions offered by Geach and Soames do not satisfy this requirement.

Here is how Geach proposes to extend the notation of the *Tractatus* in order to make mixed multiply-general propositions expressible:

> To bring out in full the way Wittgenstein's N operator works, we need (something he does not himself provide) an explicit notation for a class of propositions in which one constituent varies. I shall write "$N(x{:}fx)$" to mean the joint denial of the class of propositions got by substituting actual names for the variable in the propositional function (represented by) "*fx*". Thus "*(Ex)fx*" and "*(x)fx*" will

come out in a Wittgenstein notation as "*N(N(x:fx))*" and "*N(x:N(fx))*" respectively. The first is the denial of the joint denial of a class of propositions saying that such-and-such is *f*, and thus says that something or other is *f*: the second is the joint denial of the class of propositions saying that such-and-such is *not f*, and this amounts to saying that nothing is not *f*, i.e. that everything is *f*.

Geach concludes by showing that the mixed multiply-general proposition "*(Ex) (y) (fxy)*" can be represented in his Wittgenstein-style notation as "*N(N(x:N(fxy)))*".[2] It seems, then, that Geach has found an ingenious way of doing precisely what I said cannot be done.

As it turns out, we do not have to reach multiply-general propositions to formulate the correct response to Geach's suggestion. (We do, however, have to reach such propositions to offer a fundamental criticism of the Tractarian system itself.) Troubles begin even with his account of the singly quantified formula "*(x)fx*" which Geach renders as "*N(x:N(fx))*". On the surface, it may seem that this expression indicates two successive applications of the operator *N*, but here the symbolism is completely misleading. The expression "*(x:N(fx))*" specifies (or is shorthand for) a set of propositions that is the result of possibly infinitely many (unordered) applications of the operator *N* to a possibly infinite set of propositions. This stands in contrast with Geach's representation of "*(Ex)fx*", which has the following form: "*N(N(x:fx))*". Here we do have two successive applications of the operator *N* on sets of (possibly) infinitely many propositions. I think that it is easy to become confused concerning the semantic difference between these two methods of representing sets because of a natural tendency to treat the operator *N* as equivalent to the standard negation sign "~". Thus the expression *N(~fx)* will generate propositions from a set of (possibly) infinitely many propositions through a single application of the operation *N*. Here the symbol for negation is treated as a constituent of the propositional function used to generate the set of propositions. By way of contrast, the inner-most "*N*" in Geach's *N(x:N(fx))* is not a constituent of a propositional function at all, and to think otherwise is to misunderstand its role entirely. In sum, Geach's notation tends to disguise the difference between "the performance of *one* operation on a (possibly) infinite class of operands with the performance of an infinite number of operations."[3] Once we understand the semantic content of Geach's notational innovation, we see that his construction of universally quantified propositions stands squarely at odds with the following central tenet of the *Tractatus*:

5.32 All truth-functions are results of successive applications to elementary propositions of a finite number of truth-operations.

Not only does Geach's notation disguise the occurrence of infinitely many applications of the operation N, it also violates the demand for successiveness. If the set of base propositions is infinite, then nothing will count as the immediate predecessor of the final application of the operation N in the construction of a universally quantified proposition.

Earlier I remarked that we did not have to reach mixed multiply-general propositions in order to respond to the Geach-Soames suggestions for enriching the notational power of the *Tractatus*. Even for singly general propositions, their extension of the symbolism runs counter to fundamental features of the Tractarian system. There are, however, ways of correcting this flaw that do not have this result. One solution is to consider the denials of elementary propositions as themselves elementary propositions. Although this suggestion runs directly counter to the letter of the *Tractatus*, a strong internal case can be made for revising the Tractarian system along these lines. Although I have defended such a position elsewhere,[4] it would probably be a mistake to introduce such a far-reaching revision to deal with an essentially trivial problem. Our difficulty is just that we have been let down by the operator N. We know exactly what truth-functional operation we need to construct the proposition "$(x)fx$," using the values of the function fx for our base; i.e., *logical product*. Obviously the best solution to this problem is to add the operation of logical product to the system straight off. Indeed, we should feel quite free to add whatever truth-operations are needed for our purposes. The operation N was given a preferred position in the system of operations on the mistaken assumption that all other truth-operations could be constructed from it. Since it is clear that this is not true, we can simply drop proposition 6 and move up proposition 5.3 into a position of prominence:

5.3 All propositions are results of truth-operations on elementary propositions.

I think that we can now see why the counter-examples generated by mixed multiply-general propositions exhibit a fundamental flaw in the Tractarian system rather than simply a correctable hitch. Here we can enrich our stock of truth-operations in any way we please, and we will still be unable to construct the proposition "$(x)(Ey)fxy$" in finitely many applications of these truth-operations to elementary propositions. It seems evident that the relevant truth-operations here are logical product (associated with the variable x) and logical sum (associated with the variable y). Yet if we employ either of these truth-operations directly to the set of propositions that are the values of the function fxy for all values of x and y, we capture both variables generating either a double universal or a double existential proposition. It is clear that the *Tractatus* contains no explicit means for resolving this problem. Furthermore, if my arguments are correct, then solutions of the kind suggested by Geach and Soames are not available either, since they conflict with basic tenets of the Tractarian system.

This last remark raises a different kind of question that cannot be easily settled. Unlike Geach, Soames states explicitly that his extension of the Tractarian symbolism is incompatible with other aspects of the *Tractatus:*

> Fogelin is right to insist, in his reply to Geach, that the *Tractarian* commitment to a decision procedure conflicts with the adoption of a rich logical symbolism. However, this does not show that the *Tractatus* excludes [such a rich symbolism]; it shows that the *Tractatus* is inconsistent. Fortunately, much of interest remains after the commitment to decidability is given up. This would not be so if the *Tractatus* were denied the power of [such a symbolism].[5]

For Soames, a notation for quantification theory that is expressibly incomplete would contain "an elementary logical blunder"[6] that would deprive the system of all its interest. If avoiding this result means that Wittgenstein will have to give up his demand for a decision procedure, then, for Soames, this is clearly a price worth paying.

My instincts are the opposite of this: I am willing to attribute a logical blunder to Wittgenstein in order to preserve what I take to be the central features of the Tractarian system. Wittgenstein has told us that his "fundamental idea is that the 'logical constants' are not representatives"(4.0312). This is related to his claim that the propositions of logic are not true in virtue of picturing logical facts. Propositions of logic do not picture, and there are no logical facts. How, then, is logical truth determined? Wittgenstein answers that "one can calculate whether a proposition belongs to logic, by calculating the logical properties of the *symbol*" (6.126) Or again:

> Our fundamental principle is that whenever a question can be decided by logic at all it must be possible to decide it without more ado.

These remarks, together with many others (including the sequence 5.2 through 5.4), plainly indicate that Wittgenstein is committed to a decision procedure for propositions of logic. Furthermore, I consider Wittgenstein's account of the status of logical propositions central to the vision of the *Tractatus*. That this vision eventually proved incapable of realization does not diminish its significance. Indeed, the theorems of Gödel and Church are important precisely because they deny an idea of great profundity. A *Tractatus* containing an expressibly complete symbolism, but lacking decidability, may, as Soames suggests, still be of much interest, but it would be a system with a wholly different philosophical tendency.

2
Proposition 5 and proposition 6

I have offered two criticisms of proposition 6. One is that the operator *N* is not adequate to the task allotted to it; the other, more important, criticism is that no system of truth-operations will be adequate for generating all the formulas of the first-order functional calculus out of elementary propositions. Here I shall only note that these criticisms of proposition 6 leave proposition 5 untouched.

Proposition 5 is worded in the following way:

5 A proposition is a truth-function of elementary propositions.

This proposition tells us that the truth of any proposition is ultimately dependent upon the truth of elementary propositions.[7] But proposition 5 does not say that every proposition can be *constructed* as a truth-function of elementary propositions, and it carries no implication that there is a decision procedure connecting every proposition with those elementary propositions that are its truth-grounds. It is clear, then, that proposition 6 makes a much stronger claim than proposition 5.

It seems that Wittgenstein merely assumed that propositions 5 and 6 match each other; that is, he did not see that a price must be paid for constructability. Constructability is an important but a naively developed theme of the *Tractatus*. But it is one of the themes that carries over into Wittgenstein's later writing and ultimately becomes part of a fundamental revision of Tractarian ideas.[8]

3
Numbers and equations

Wittgenstein's account of mathematics is clear in what it says and baffling in what it leaves unsaid. He uses an operation to define the integers:

6.03 The general form of an integer is $[0, \xi, \xi + 1]$.

Here 0 is the first member of the series, ξ is a typical member of the series and $\xi + 1$ is the operation that takes one from one member of the series to the next. That is, we start with 0 and generate the integers by repeated use of an operation that generates a successor. This is what Wittgenstein has in mind when he says, at 6.021, that "a number is the exponent of an operation." Having said little more than this, he tosses off the following criticism:

6.031 The theory of classes is completely superfluous in mathematics.
    This is connected with the fact that the generality required in mathematics is not *accidental* generality.

He then moves on to another topic.

Reflecting upon these passages, Russell makes the following remark:

> There are some respects, in which, as it seems to me, Mr Wittgenstein's theory stands in need of greater technical development. This applies in particular to his theory of number (6.02 ff.) which, as it stands, is only capable of dealing with finite numbers. No logic can be considered adequate until it has been shown to be capable of dealing with transfinite numbers. I do not think there is anything in Mr Wittgenstein's system to make it impossible for him to fill this lacuna. (TLP, Introduction, p. xx)

Here I think that Russell is too sanguine, for it is the essence of Wittgenstein's position that a *number is the exponent of an operation*, and the repetition of an operation will not take us beyond the finite.

The most surprising feature of this discussion is that Wittgenstein doesn't mention transfinite numbers at all. Wittgenstein was, of course, aware of the theory of transfinite cardinals.[9] Both Frege and Russell made a particular point of saying that their definitions of numbers at once covered finite and transfinite cardinals. Wittgenstein certainly knew this material and understood the significance of the claim. So the question arises again: how could Wittgenstein offer a general theory of numbers that covers only finite numbers without giving a word of explanation?

The answer is that Wittgenstein does give a word of explanation—a very bare word. His dismissal of the theory of classes as entirely superfluous in mathematics is obviously an attack upon the works of Cantor, Frege, Russell, *et al.*, i.e., it is an attack upon the classical approach to the foundations of mathematics. The backing for this sweeping indictment is restricted to the single remark that "the generality required in mathematics is not *accidental* generality." Presumably, the opposite of accidental generality is some form of *rule-governed* generality, in particular, the kind of rule-governed generality exhibited in Wittgenstein's own definition of numbers. Mathematics is not concerned with mere collections of things, it is concerned with internally related series of things where one item is derived from another. So Wittgenstein is invoking some kind of constructivist ideal and dismissing the classical works in the foundations of mathematics because they fail to meet it. But what sort of constructivism is this? How can the definition of the integers be used to construct wider portions of mathematics? How much of classical mathematics can be encompassed by these procedures? And so on. Until we have answers to questions of this kind, we have no idea what Wittgenstein's position comes to.

Turning now to Wittgenstein's treatment of mathematical *equations*, we find ourselves back on familiar ground. Wittgenstein patterns his treatment of equations (e.g., "2 + 5 = 7") on his earlier treatment of tautologies. Mathematics is a logical method (6.2), i.e., not an empirical method, and

6.22 The logic of the world, which is shown in tautologies by propositions of logic, is shown in equations by mathematics.

An equation, like a tautology, does not have a sense, and hence, does not express a thought (6.21). Equations, being empty of content, are really of no interest in themselves. This is adumbrated in the following remarkable passage:

6.211 Indeed, in real life a mathematical proposition is never what we want. Rather, we use mathematical propositions *only* in inferences from propositions that do not belong to mathematics to others that likewise do not belong to mathematics.

This passage casts a long shadow forward to Wittgenstein's later position that equations are not even *attempts* at formulating propositions, but are, instead, expressions of rules.

In the *Tractatus*, however, Wittgenstein is still fascinated with the idea that tautologies, though they do not *say* anything, are still able to *show* something about the structure of the world. It is this comparison with tautologies that dominates the discussion of equations and leads finally to incoherence. Given the tautology $p \ v \ {\sim}p$ we may notice that its logical constants also find employment in *non*-logical propositions. It is precisely through this connection with non-logical propositions that tautologies are themselves counted as genuine—though queer—propositions. As Wittgenstein describes the situation, the sign for equality has an altogether different standing: it *never* occurs in a genuine proposition. It seems, then, that our language contains a symbol whose *sole* function is to formulate propositions that attempt to say something that can only be shown. Of course, it is very hard to make sense of misfiring attempts to employ a symbol when there is no such thing as a proper employment of that symbol.

I think that Wittgenstein's discussion of equations shows that he is already on the road that leads to his later view of mathematical expressions. The whole system of propositions under the 6.0s, the 6.1s and the 6.2s burgeons with the constructivist themes that are characteristic of Wittgenstein's later conception of mathematics and logic. Unfortunately, these themes are muted (and not thought through) because they are dominated by the idea that logic and mathematics present an "infinitely fine network, the great mirror" of reality. If propositions devoid of sense (tautologies) and pseudo-propositions (equations) can do this, it hardly seems necessary to find some further employment for them.

VII

Necessity

1
Necessity and the doctrine of showing

At 6.1 Wittgenstein declares that the propositions of logic are tautologies and therefore "say nothing" (6.11). Wittgenstein's truth-functional analysis of propositions is intended both to explain and justify this key doctrine. The question next arises why anyone should be interested in the propositions of logic if, as Wittgenstein maintains, they are empty of sense. Wittgenstein's extraordinary answer is that we are interested in such tautologies precisely *because* they say nothing. That symbols can be combined in such a way that their representational capacity cancels out reveals something important about the character of these symbols. But an insight into the basic operation of our symbolism must at once give us an insight into the fundamental structure of the world. Our language, Wittgenstein seems to reason, finds application to the world and therefore must share a common structure with it.

> 6.12 The fact that the propositions of logic are tautologies *shows* the formal—logical—properties of language and the world.
>
> The fact that a tautology is yielded by *this particular way* of connecting its constituents characterizes the logic of its constituents.

We have met the doctrine of *showing* before, but this is its most important occurrence. The basic reasoning goes something like this:

(i) The underlying form of our language must match (a word that needs explaining) the underlying form of the world.

(ii) In a tautology the underlying form of language is made manifest through a combination of signs that completely cancels out the significance of material content. (At 6.121 Wittgenstein speaks of this as a "zero-method.")

86

(iii) In line with (i), that which shows us the underlying form of language must *eo ipso* reveal the underlying form of the world.

Here Wittgenstein says (perhaps for dramatic effect) that "the propositions of logic *describe* the scaffolding of the world," but immediately cancels the suggestion that propositions of logic have content by saying, rather, that they "*represent* it" (6.124, both italics mine).

Whatever our ultimate judgment, the doctrine that tautologies show the formal (logical) properties of language and the world is not without initial plausibility. This initial plausibility appears almost entirely on the side of language. The proposition "It is raining or it is not raining" is not *about* the logical constants "or" and "not," but Wittgenstein seems right in suggesting that the very fact that this proposition says *nothing whatsoever* reveals something about these logical constants. Where the content has been bleached out, the form becomes manifest. Of course, Wittgenstein wants to say more than this; in particular, he holds that that which is shown (but not said) by a tautology cannot be said by *any* proposition whatsoever (4.121). This, of course, is tied to his special theory that the only thing that can be said is that certain contingent combinations of objects do in fact obtain. Logic has nothing to do with such contingencies.

Turning to the formal properties of the world, though it is not an evident principle, it is at least a persistent idea in philosophy that thought, to be correct, must somehow be congruent with reality. The *Tractatus* works out this congruence at three levels: (i) names (simple signs) *go proxy* for objects (simple things); (ii) elementary propositions *picture* states of affairs, and (iii) the formal properties of our language *mirror* the formal properties of the world. In the *Tractatus*, none of these relations (i.e., proxying, picturing and mirroring) can count as a genuine relation—as a relation that can be expressed or asserted in a proposition. In one way or another each must make itself manifest or show itself in the operation or employment of language.

In the context of Wittgenstein's theory of a threefold parallelism between language and reality, it follows at once that, in manifesting formal features of its own structure, language can manifest formal features of the world. But Wittgenstein employs the notion of showing in another way that is more problematic: our language can show us something about the formal or logical properties of the world when we recognize that a sign combination is not simply devoid of sense (*sinnlos*), but actually non-sensical (*unsinnig*). Although Wittgenstein does not dwell on this point, equations seem to fall into this category (6.22). A second area where the recognition of nonsense shows us something about the "logic of the world" pertains to the pseudo-propositions that are used to formulate the Tractarian system itself. Wittgenstein is absolutely clear in saying that these propositions are not merely devoid of sense (*sinnlos*), but non-sensical (*unsinnig*) and, apparently, it is through a recognition of this that one can come to "see the world aright" (6.54). It is this last use of the notion of showing that is most controversial, and it is a topic that I shall consider in detail in Chapter VIII.

2
Are there non-tautological necessary propositions?

By now we know that the answer to this question must be no—a point that is made explicit in these passages:

6.1 The propositions of logic are tautologies.
6.37 The only necessity that exists is logical necessity.[1]

But aren't there obvious counter-examples to this claim? Wittgenstein recognizes this challenge, and the 6.3s are largely dedicated to meeting it. The form of the question gives the possible answers to it. Presented with a reputed non-tautological necessary proposition, Wittgenstein can argue: (i) that it is, in fact, tautological, (ii) that it isn't necessary but rather contingent, or finally, (iii) that it is not a proposition at all. Wittgenstein employs all three strategies.

The discussion is carried out largely in a series of proclamations. The first is this:

6.31 The so-called law of induction cannot possibly be a law of logic, since it is obviously a proposition with a sense.—Nor, therefore, can it be an *a priori* law.

It is not clear exactly what Wittgenstein has in mind under the heading "law of induction," but presumably he is thinking of the claim that regularities that have held in the past will continue to hold in the future; in short, nature is uniform. Wittgenstein seems to take it for granted that this is a *contingent* hypothesis (thus adopting the first strategy), and no explanation is given why others may have thought differently. This dogmatism is not characteristic of the remainder of the discussion.

The treatment of the law of causality—together with the principle of sufficient reason, laws of least action, continuity in nature, etc.—is more interesting:

6.34 All such propositions . . . are *a priori* insights about the forms in which the propositions of science can be cast.

The expressions "law of causality," "law of continuity," etc., are not names for specific laws that govern nature; instead, they are ways of characterizing *kinds* of laws:

6.321 "Law of causality"—that is a general name. And just as in mechanics, for example, there are "minimum principles", such as the law of least action, so too in physics there are causal laws, laws of causal form.

In sum, the law of causality does not give us *a priori* knowledge that the world must be disposed in a certain way, but instead, we demand that laws take certain forms; our *a priori* insight is that such forms are possible (6.33). For this set of cases, then, we have a diagnosis of the confused thought that leads to the belief in necessary structures in nature. For whatever reason, we accept the demand (for example) that laws of nature employ continuous, but never discontinuous, functions. We then project this demand concerning the form that laws must take upon nature itself. This projection illicitly converts our *a priori* knowledge concerning the *possible* form of a law into an *a priori* belief concerning the actual disposition of objects that fall under a law. Once these confusions are unraveled, we see that "what is certain *a priori* proves to be something purely logical" (6.3211), for the question of what propositions are possible does fall into the domain we have sketched for logic.

Notice that Wittgenstein does not suggest that any of these laws are tautologies. Instead he adopts the third strategy noticed above and claims that they are pseudo-propositions:

6.36 If there were a law of causality, it might be put in the following way: There are laws of nature.

But of course that cannot be said: it makes itself manifest. This, of course, is something of a conversation-stopper. When Wittgenstein argues that a tautology, just in saying nothing, shows the logical properties of language and the world, we can at least dispute the claim that the proposition in question is tautological. When we try to decide what a pseudo-proposition might show, we seem forced back to brute intuition.

Wittgenstein illustrates these ideas using an extended analogy concerning the application of variously constructed nets to describe black spots on a surface. Of course, the character of the description—its simplicity, etc.—will be a function of the structure of the net and the kinds of spots that appear on the surface. If we now think of various physical theories (for example, in mechanics) as alternative networks for description, we can then say the following:

6.35 Laws like the principle of sufficient reason, etc., are about the net and not about what the net describes.

This means that the principle of sufficient reason, the laws of causality, continuity, least action, etc., are *not* themselves networks for the description of nature. They stand once removed from nature; they are, to use

Wittgenstein's metaphor, "about the net and not about what the net describes." Since these propositions are about the net (i.e., about modes of description), they have an *a priori* status, but, for the same reason, these laws do not govern objects in the world.[2]

Most of the present discussion is highly abstract, but Wittgenstein considers two concrete examples of apparently non-tautological necessary propositions and gets into difficulties with each. The first (introduced at 6.36111) concerns Kant's famous discussion of *incongruous counterparts*. Kant held that it must be a *synthetic a priori* truth that a right-hand glove cannot be made to coincide with a left-hand glove, for this is surely an *a priori* truth and not a tautology. Wittgenstein's reply is strange indeed. He first notices that the same problem exists in one-dimensional space.

$$- - - 0\!\!-\!\!-X - - - X\!\!-\!\!-0 - - -$$
$$ab$$

Here the diagrams *a* and *b* cannot be made to coincide unless they are rotated out of the line. If we hold to the standard idea that congruence involves the possibility of making figures coincide, then we can conclude that in a one-dimensional space these diagrams are incongruent. But Wittgenstein adopts the opposite tactic. He sticks with the claim that these diagrams *are* congruent and declares it simply irrelevant that they cannot be made to coincide. His solution to Kant's problem is then given in these words:

> 6.36111 . . . The right hand and the left hand are in fact completely congruent. It is quite irrelevant that they cannot be made to coincide.
>
> A right-hand glove could be put on the left hand, if it could be turned round in four-dimensional space.

So Wittgenstein solves the problem of incongruous counterparts by denying that the counterparts are incongruous.

This is one of the few arguments in the *Tractatus* that strikes me as just awful. It is surely obvious that Kant's central point is that a right-hand glove and a left-hand glove cannot be made to *coincide* in a three-dimensional space. For this reason he calls them incongruent. Here it will not help to offer—as Wittgenstein does—an alternative definition of congruency. We want to know the status of the proposition that these two gloves cannot be made to coincide. It seems to be a *necessary* proposition, but not—even on Wittgenstein's broad use of this notion—a *logically* necessary proposition. Wittgenstein does suggest that our inability to make the two gloves coincide is just a contingency, for "a right-hand glove could be put on the left hand, if it could be turned round in four-dimensional space," but this is again an *ignoratio elenchi*.

How does this new claim settle the status of the proposition that the gloves cannot be made to match in three-dimensional space, and what shall we say about this new claim itself that they can be made to match in a four-dimensional space? Instead of eliminating a synthetic *a priori* proposition, Wittgenstein seems to have turned up a new one. One way out of these difficulties is to adopt a position later championed by the positivists: propositions of *pure* geometry are merely axioms or theorems of a deductive system and thus may be considered analytic; propositions of an *interpreted* geometry are contingent and empirical. I do not find this position in the *Tractatus*, and, anyway, examples like Kant's incongruous counterparts make it hard to accept.

The most famous counter-example to Wittgenstein's thesis that the only necessity is logical necessity was presented by Wittgenstein himself. It is not worded as a counter-example; indeed, it is given as an *illustration* of the thesis that the only necessity is logical necessity.

> 6.3751 For example, the simultaneous presence of two colours at the same place in the visual field is impossible, in fact logically impossible, since it is ruled out by the logical structure of colour.

What gives this example its peculiar interest is that it concerns ordinary empirical predications. If a patch is colored brown, this excludes the possibility of its being colored blue.[3] Furthermore, the exclusion is not contingent or accidental. It might turn out that nothing brown smells of hyacinth and tastes like cream (this could follow from laws of nature), but the incompatibility of colors is not like this. The simultaneous predication of distinct colors to the same point (at the same time, etc.) yields a proposition that is *necessarily* false. Wittgenstein never considers denying this. Nor does Wittgenstein argue that such an assertion is a pseudo-proposition, presumably because the predicates involved (being brown and being blue) are not formal concepts. So Wittgenstein has only one line open to him: he must show that the proposition is contradictory. His attempt to do so takes the following form:

> 6.3751 . . . Let us think how this contradiction appears in physics: more or less as follows—a particle cannot have two velocities at the same time; that is to say, it cannot be in two places at the same time; that is to say, particles that are in different places at the same time cannot be identical.

The difficulty here is precisely the same as that which arose in Wittgenstein's treatment of incongruous counterparts: rather than exhibiting the necessity of color incompatibility as a *logical* necessity, he has merely exchanged this sort of necessity for another that is equally in need of explanation. As Ramsey remarked, the necessary connections within the color system are explained by reference to the necessary connections within space and time, but no argument is presented that shows that these spatio-temporal necessities are themselves logical.[4] The lapse in argument is quite remarkable and can be explained, I think, only with reference to Wittgenstein's vaunting confidence that the *truth* of his thoughts was "unassailable and definitive" (Preface, p. 5). The antecedent confidence that detailed applications will be forthcoming when needed does not encourage making them.

Later Wittgenstein returned to the problem of color incompatibilities and found the account in the *Tractatus* unsatisfactory. In "Some remarks on logical form" he saw that any quality that admits of *degree* raises problems for the Tractarian system, for an object that possesses a quality to one degree cannot possess it to another degree. In this 1929 essay Wittgenstein already sees that these material incompatibilities force fundamental changes in the Tractarian system. By the summer of 1930, when he prepared the material published as his *Philosophische Bemerkungen*, he had won through to some striking conclusions: our color predicates form a connected system related in such a way that to apply one color predicate is, *eo ipso*, to exclude all others. He illustrates this by a new use of the ruler metaphor. If a ruler assigns a length of three inches to a stick, that at once excludes the assignment of any other length. In the same way—though the details are not worked out—our system of color measurement is so constituted that it can yield only a single value when applied (see PB, 76).

This is not the place to comment upon the plausibility of the *Bemerkungen* approach, but we can notice—and Wittgenstein saw this clearly—that a move in this direction completely subverts some central features of the Tractarian system. In the *Tractatus* we have elementary propositions (combinations of names) correlated with states of affairs (combinations of objects). On this new approach we have systems of propositions with elementary relationships between them. With this the central notion of independence is compromised and the very idea of an elementary proposition has been profoundly altered. In Wittgenstein's words:

> The concept of an "elementary proposition" now loses its former meaning altogether. (PB, 83)

The point of the present discussion is not to hold up Wittgenstein's later views as criticism of the *Tractatus;* the discussion of color incompatibility in the *Bemerkungen* has troubles of its own. The fundamental consideration is that the *Tractatus* contains no plausible account of color incompatibilities, and it is difficult to see how this omission can be made good.

VIII

My World, Its Value, and Silence

1
Solipsism

The keynote for this portion of the text (which I have taken up slightly out of order) is given by the claim that "the limits of my language mean the limits of my world" (5.6). A problematic feature of this discussion is the sudden appearance of the personal pronoun "*my.*" Exactly how personal this pronoun is is itself unclear.

> 5.62 The world is *my* world: this is manifest in the fact that the limits of *language* (of that language which alone I understand) mean the limits of *my* world.

The parenthetical clause has been read in two ways: (1) it refers to a private language, a language that I alone speak; (2) there is no reference to privacy, but merely a reference to that one and only language I speak. On the first reading there is a direct connection with Wittgenstein's talk about solipsism which, after all, is pretty straightforward, e.g.:

> 5.621 The world and life are one.
> 5.63 I am my world. (The microcosm.)

Later on these solipsistic themes are picked up in an ethical context, e.g.:

> 6.431 So too at death the world does not alter, but comes to an end.

One line, then, is that Wittgenstein is really a solipsist with the caveat that what he means to say is unsayable. I think that this is the most straightforward reading of the text, but it raises an objection: where does Wittgenstein establish the essential privacy of each person's representation of the world? I do not think such an argument is found in the text and, more importantly, I do not think that there is anything in the Tractarian system that demands this conclusion.

On the second reading, no implications of privacy are read into the text. My world is limited to that world that my language represents. Others might speak this same language and be subject to the same limitations. This approach has two advantages. (i) It gains some support from the exact wording of the text, for the German reads "der Sprache, der allein ich verstehe" which more naturally translates "the language which alone I understand" rather than "the language which I alone understand."[1] (ii) It also has the advantage of giving the text an austere reading that does not saddle it with an unsubstantiated doctrine of privacy. Unfortunately, this second advantage has difficulties of its own in not explaining the point of those seemingly solipsistic passages we have noticed.

The situation is made more difficult, rather than resolved, when Wittgenstein denies that solipsism is a substantive alternative to realism:

5.64 Here it can be seen that solipsism, when its implications are followed out strictly, coincides with pure realism. The self of solipsism shrinks to a point without extension, and there remains the reality co-ordinated with it.

The reason that the solipsistic self shrinks to a point without extension is that there really is no such thing as the thinking or representing subject (*das denkende, vorstellende, Subjekt*) (5.631). This goes back to a theory about the nature of belief propositions that Wittgenstein was anxious to reject. He rejected any theory that conforms to the following general pattern.

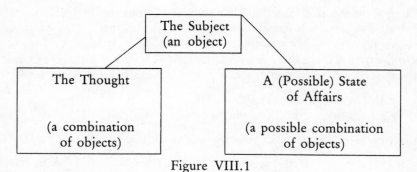

Figure VIII.1

Here the subject employs the thought in order to represent reality. Wittgenstein's original reason for rejecting any theory of this kind is that it generates an occurrence of a proposition (i.e., a thought) in a non-truth-functional setting (5.54 ff.). There are, however, other reasons why such a theory is incompatible with the basic structure of the *Tractatus*. Suppose the subject were another object in the world which, through thinking, puts a set of objects (the thought) into representational relationship with the world. If this were the case, the meaning of every proposition would depend upon the truth of another, for it would be a contingency that the required relationship obtains between the subject (one object in the world) and the thought (another set of objects in the world).

In support of this interpretation, we may note that Wittgenstein explicitly says that the exclusion of the thinking subject from the world "is connected with the fact that no part of our experience is at the same time *a priori* . . . " for "whatever we can describe at all could be other than it is" (5.634). I think that this is just a transposition of the reasoning sketched above. I suggested that if the thinking self *were* part of the world, then it would stand in a contingent relationship to its thoughts. Wittgenstein argues that if the thinking self were part of the world, then there would be necessary connections within the world, for the relationship between the thinking self and its thoughts cannot be contingent. We thus have an inconsistent triad of propositions:

(1)   The thinking self is in the world.
(2)   All relationships within the world are contingent.
(3)   The relationship between the thinking self and the objects in the world it thinks about is not contingent.

Since (2) and (3) are important Tractarian commitments, (1) must be rejected.

We can now return to the equation of solipsism with "pure realism." The world is just the totality of facts. Some of these facts (pictures) are put into correlation with the world. What carries out this process of putting parts of reality into projective relationship with other parts of reality? The traditional answer is the thinking subject. But we have now learned that the thinking subject cannot be part of the world. The postulation of a thinking *thing* to do the thinking is an error. By thus expunging the solipsistic self as a thing, solipsism is made to coincide with pure realism.

It is obvious that there is no place within the Tractarian system for a thinking subject that enters into intentional relationships with other things in the world. What is unclear is whether Wittgenstein still helps himself to this notion in some indirect way. The final equation of solipsism with pure realism points in one direction, but the continued use of solipsistic language (especially in the ethical sphere) points in the other. Wittgenstein was unquestionably attracted by the solipsistic standpoint and saw at the same time that his own position precluded its formulation. Is solipsism true or not? For Wittgenstein, even the question does not exist. This sounds tough-minded, but, combined with the doctrine of showing, it provides a perfect insulation for a deeply held belief.

2
Values

Wittgenstein's leading pronouncement on values takes the following form:

6.4 All propositions are of equal value.

This means it is a matter of ethical indifference whether this or that contingency holds. The realm of value and the realm of facts are wholly separated, for matters of fact are accidental and values have nothing to do with the accidental.

6.41 . . . If there is any value that does have value, it must lie outside the whole sphere of what happens and is the case; for all that happens and is the case is accidental. What makes it non-accidental cannot lie within the world, since if it did it would itself be accidental.

It is now a short road to the conclusion that "it is impossible for there to be propositions of ethics" (6.42). Propositions express contingencies or (in the limiting cases) tautologies and contradictions. In the passages cited above, Wittgenstein rejects the option that value judgments express factual contingencies, and, of course, there is no plausibility in the idea that every value judgment is either a tautology or contradiction. Values are not concerned with anything *within* the world; instead they are concerned with the character of the world as a whole. This, I think, gives the main features of Wittgenstein's treatment of values.

We can notice in the first place that this reasoning depends upon an antecedent rejection of *naturalism* in ethics. Furthermore, nothing in the Tractarian account of propositions forces a rejection of naturalism in ethics. The truth of a strict hedonism is, for example, compatible with Wittgenstein's treatment of propositions. For the strict hedonist, value propositions are simply psychological propositions. Of course, Wittgenstein would retort that psychological propositions have no place in a philosophical discussion, but the hedonist would hardly blush at this result.

For reasons that I do not understand, naturalism in ethics is still widely rejected, and for those who share this view the above remarks may not seem important. But I am making a systematic point. There seems to be nothing within the Tractarian account of propositions that excludes value judgments from being contingent propositions. This demand is introduced for external reasons. Yet once this decision is made, the Tractarian system forces other decisions. Certainly Wittgenstein assumes that value judgments have import or significance. They cannot be significant in what they *say*, since as pseudo-propositions they say nothing. They then must be significant in what they show—or significant in their attempt to say something that can only be shown. This is undoubtedly Wittgenstein's general approach.

When we reflect upon the things that can be shown but not said, we notice that they concern the form of the world as a whole—its underlying structure within which all contingencies obtain. Tautologies, equations, and pseudo-propositions containing formal concepts all provide ways of mirroring—though not talking about—these underlying formal structures. In parallel fashion, value judgments are connected with the world as a whole:

> 6.43 If the good or bad exercise of the will does alter the world, it can alter only the limits of the world, not the facts—not what can be expressed by means of language.

In short, the effect must be that it becomes an altogether different world. It must, so to speak, wax and wane as a whole. So Wittgenstein takes essentially the same approach to problems of logic and problems of value. Neither concerns the merely contingent; instead they concern necessary structures within which contingency obtains. In the Kantian sense, both logic (6.13) and ethics (6.421) are *transcendental*.

I think that it would be a mistake to try to say more about the substantive content of Wittgenstein's views concerning ethical and aesthetic values. They clearly derive from Kant and Schopenhauer, but they are gnomic even by Tractarian standards. A more interesting question is whether Wittgenstein, given the limitations imposed by the *Tractatus*, has the right to favor any one ethical standpoint over another. I shall turn to this question at the close of this chapter.

3
The insignificance of the sayable

Wittgenstein makes the following declaration:

> 6.54 My propositions serve as elucidations in the following way: anyone who understands me eventually recognizes them as nonsensical, when he has used them—as steps—to climb up beyond them. (He must, so to speak, throw away the ladder after he has climbed up it.)

The conceptual situation is clear: the theory of proposition meaning in the *Tractatus* is self-destructive. What remains unclear is the source of Wittgenstein's equanimity—even pride—given this result. Of course, it has *something* to do with the doctrine of showing, but saying this does not solve our problem; it only points us in the direction of more obscurity.

Before talking directly about the doctrine of showing, I wish to point to some reasons why Wittgenstein would not be upset with the result that his own remarks lack propositional status. I do not think that Wittgenstein viewed this as a defect in his work; on the contrary, I think that he considered it one of its merits. This comes out when we notice Wittgenstein's attitude toward what *can* be said. We can begin by recalling the concluding paragraph of his Preface:

> [The] *truth* of the thoughts that are here set forth seems to me unassailable and definitive. I therefore believe myself to have found, on all essential points, the final solution of the problems. And if I am not mistaken in this belief, then the second thing in which the value of this work consists is that it shows how little is achieved when these problems are solved. (TLP, p. 5)

The first two sentences may seem an extraordinary example of hubris, but we can let that go; it is the third sentence that is interesting. We might view this as a small dash of humility intended to counterbalance the pride expressed in the first two sentences, but nothing of the sort is going on. What are the problems that Wittgenstein thinks he has solved? Roughly speaking, he thinks that he has given the correct characterization of the general form of a proposition and thereby solved the whole family of problems that surround it. This was the task of the *Tractatus*—a task that Wittgenstein thought he had completed in all but minor details. Is Wittgenstein then saying that solving these problems was itself a small achievement? I do not think that there is any such false modesty here. What he is saying, I think, is that once we understand the general form of a proposition, we recognize the *insignificance* of anything that can be said.

This theme of the *insignificance of the sayable* appears at various places in the text, but gets its clearest expression in passages near the close of the book. Here are some samples:

> 6.432 *How* things are in the world is a matter of complete indifference for what is higher. God does not reveal himself *in* the world.
> 6.4321 The facts all contribute only to setting the problem, not to its solution.

Or as noticed earlier:

> 6.41 If there is any value that does have value, it must lie outside the whole sphere of what happens and is the case.

The domain of how things are—of fact, of what happens, of what is the case—is precisely the domain of that which can be put into words. The irrelevance of this domain to anything important (or beautiful) is made abundantly clear. If the task of the *Tractatus* is to reveal the foundations

98

of the Tower of Babel, its point is to show the insignificance of that structure.

I think that Wittgenstein welcomed the result that his own theory of meaning was meaningless because it put it in good company with the aesthetic and the ethical. But why was he pleased with the outcome that aesthetic and ethical utterances are meaningless? The answer is that it put both beyond the reach of language. Here is how he explained this to the publisher Ludwig von Ficker:

> . . . my work consists of two parts: of the one which is here, and of everything which I have *not* written. And precisely this second part is the important one. For the ethical is delimited from within, as it were by my book; and I'm convinced that, *strictly* speaking, it can only be delimited in this way. In brief, I think: all of that which *many* are babbling today, I have defined in my book by being silent about it.[2]

The central point of the *Tractatus* is to place limits upon language to protect the ethical from babbling—particularly the babbling that takes place in sophisticated circles. Paul Engelmann captured the force of this position when he remarked that "ethical propositions do not exist; ethical actions do exist."[3] (110)

I think we must go outside the framework of the *Tractatus* to understand why this was an important motive in Wittgenstein's philosophy. Wittgenstein came to the *Tractatus* with certain ethical and aesthetic commitments that were not, after all, demanded by an inquiry into the general form of the proposition. These commitments came from various sources which have been discussed by Engelmann among others. Here I shall mention only one influence, that of Tolstoy.

Wittgenstein read and was deeply impressed by Tolstoy's *What is Art?*, and he accepted much of the ethical and aesthetic ideals put forth in it. The ethical ideal was one of simplicity, austerity, honesty, and humanity. Art should be a reflection of the ethical life: free of artifice and sophistication, and unembarrassed in its appeal to common emotions. For Tolstoy—and Wittgenstein largely agreed—a work of art should be intelligible to the simplest peasant.

Of course, if Wittgenstein is right, we are already going wrong in trying to express these ethical and aesthetic ideals in words—again we are talking nonsense. Perhaps we can do better by looking briefly at a short story that exemplifies this attitude: Tolstoy's "Three Hermits." We know that Wittgenstein particularly admired it.[4] In bare outline it has the following form: A bishop encountered three hermits living together on an island: "a tall one with only a piece of matting tied around his waist; a shorter one in a tattered peasant coat, and a very old one bent with age and wearing an old cassock—all three standing hand in hand." Discovering that the hermits did not know their prayers, the bishop spent the rest of the day teaching them, with great difficulty, the Lord's Prayer.

That night as the ship sailed from the island, the steersman saw a bright light rapidly approaching the stern of the boat.

> "Look there, what is that, my friend? What is it?" the Bishop [asked the steersman], though he could now see plainly what it was—the three hermits running upon the water, all gleaming white, their grey beards shining, and approaching the ship as quickly as though it were not moving.
>
> . . . .
>
> Before the ship could be stopped, the hermits had reached it, and raising their heads, all three as with one voice, began to say:
>
> "We have forgotten your teaching, servant of God. As long as we kept repeating it, we remembered, but when we stopped saying it for a time, a word dropped out, and now it is all gone. We remember nothing of it. Teach us again."
>
> The Bishop crossed himself, and leaning over the ship's side, said:
>
> "Your own prayer will reach the Lord, men of God. It is not for me to teach you. Pray for us sinners."

For Wittgenstein, the ethical ideal, which cannot be stated directly, shows itself in simple tales of this kind.

4
A critique of showing

The conceptual situation is clear: given Wittgenstein's account of propositions, it is impossible to express the essential character of language or the world in a proposition. These essential features can only show themselves or make themselves manifest. In the *Tractatus* there seem to be four such appeals to showing:

(1) Our regular propositions, which embody underlying logical structures, make them manifest in concrete application.

(2) Tautologies, just in saying nothing, show the logical properties of language and the world.

(3) The pseudo-propositions of logic (i.e., propositions containing formal concepts) show something just in being nonsensical, i.e., in having no application to the world.

(4) Expressions concerning values and life are also literally meaningless, but this meaninglessness shows us something about value and life.

I shall consider these cases one at a time.

(1) On the assumption that our language does possess essential features, it does not seem implausible that these features would reveal themselves in the actual employment of our language. Each actual use of language is a particular embodiment of these underlying structures. It remains an open question how manifest these structures are and Wittgenstein, in fact, holds a rather ambiguous position in this respect. At one point he makes the following claim:

> 4.002 Language disguises thought. So much so, that from the outward form of the clothing it is impossible to infer the form of the thought beneath it, because the outward form of the clothing is not designed to reveal the form of the body, but for entirely different purposes.

In a logically perspicuous language, a difference in logical function would be reflected in a difference in symbolic form. Everyday languages are not perspicuous in this way. But even if the symbolism of our everyday language does not reflect the underlying structure of language, this structure emerges in the actual employment of this symbolism:

> 3.262 What signs fail to express, their application shows. What signs slur over, their application says clearly.

I confess to being rather taken with this modest use of the doctrine of showing. For one thing, it has some clear empirical analogies. The underlying grammar of our language shows itself in our willingness to employ certain word combinations but not others even though (superficially) the word combinations seem similar.

(2) What I have said about everyday propositions pretty much carries over to tautologies. In the Tractarian system, a tautology represents a limiting case of the application of language to the world. Just the fact that certain sign combinations yield tautologies (i.e., truth-functions that are devoid of sense) shows something about the signs so combined. I see nothing objectionable in this, since degenerate cases are often illuminating just in their degeneracy. Of course, we can accept Wittgenstein's opinions concerning what the emptiness of certain sign combinations shows about our language without accepting his further claim that this emptiness also shows something about the *a priori* structure of the world mirrored in our language.

(3) Wittgenstein's claim that the senselessness of his formal propositions also shows us something about the logic of language and the structure of the world seems different from the previous two claims. When we appeal to the use of an everyday proposition to show something, then this proposition will be about some particular subject matter (perhaps the sudden increase in tent caterpillars), but it will show something about an entirely different domain (it might show that general

101

propositions are possible). With respect to tautologies, a similar division takes place. A tautology is not about any subject matter at all, so, quite trivially, it must show something other than what it says. But now consider the status of pseudo-propositions that employ formal concepts or speak of formal properties. Since virtually any proposition from the *Tractatus* will serve, we can take one that is short:

3.25 A proposition has one and only one complete analysis.

This proposition seems to be about propositions, and it says of them that they have one and only one complete analysis. We can call this the *manifest* content of the proposition—using this phrasing to leave open the question whether we have a genuine propositional content. We next notice that this proposition is quite literally nonsensical, but then this very recognition is supposed to show us something. The peculiarity of this situation is that what we are shown is just what was manifestly (though not genuinely) said, and this differentiates this case from the previous two.

We might say that the system of the *Tractatus* is reflexively self-destructive. In effect, Wittgenstein presents a metalanguage specifying the truth-conditions for a set of propositions that make up an object language. Matters are so arranged that the propositions in the metalanguage do not satisfy the conditions for propositions in the object language. In this way, standard paradoxes are avoided. If the complaint is now made that the object language is incomplete in not characterizing propositions of the kind that make up the metalanguage, Wittgenstein has a remarkable reply: although the propositions in the object language cannot say what the propositions in the metalanguage say, they make these things manifest simply by *embodying* the principles laid down in the metalanguage. So no loss occurs when these metapropositions are expelled from the language, for the propositions of the object language are able to make known, without saying, what these metapropositions attempt to say. Metapropositions are a temporary expedient. Modern logic has not followed this course, but it remains an idea of both depth and originality.

(4) Turning, finally, to Wittgenstein's remarks concerning values and life, we find another application of the doctrine of showing where the manifest content of a pseudo-proposition is important. Here is a specimen of such a remark:

6.43 The world of the happy man is a different one from that of the unhappy man.

This is a pseudo-proposition because its manifest content speaks of the world as a whole, and does not concern matters of fact within the world. The peculiarity of this proposition is that Wittgenstein seems to take sides on a transcendental issue. A competing sage might say that the world of the happy man is no different from that of the unhappy man (and this too has a ring of profundity). This second utterance is meaningless, and meaningless for precisely the same reasons that Wittgenstein's original is meaningless. As denials of each other, their meaninglessness should show the same thing, just as tautologies and contradictions show the same thing. Thus when speaking of values and life, Wittgenstein's preference for one manifest (pseudo) content over another is wholly arbitrary and has no place in the *Tractatus*. The ethical and mystical remarks toward the end of the *Tractatus* tell us something about the author of the *Tractatus*, and some may find these pronouncements moving. But in his own words, they should have been passed over in silence, and been part of the work that was *"not* written."⁵

PART TWO

WITTGENSTEIN'S LATER PHILOSOPHY

IX

The Critique of the *Tractatus*

1
The problem of interpretation

It was Wittgenstein's wish that the *Philosophical Investigations* be published in a volume containing his earlier work, the *Tractatus Logico-Philosophicus*. This suggests a close connection between these works, and this is immediately borne out upon examining the text. Given Wittgenstein's method of presentation, it is difficult to fix labels to various portions of the *Investigations*, for he continually drops hints concerning future topics and often circles back over previously discussed material, approaching it from different angles.[1] With this reservation in mind, I suggest that the first 137 sections of the *Investigations* are dominated by criticisms of those commitments that led to the Tractarian system.

In these sections two broad features of the Tractarian standpoint are subjected to attack:

(1) The particular picture of the essence of human language that holds that words stand for things and sentences are combinations of such words picturing, in their combination, how objects are combined.
(2) The doctrine that sense must be determinate.

We saw in the first part of this work that these two commitments gave the *Tractatus* much of its characteristic structure. When these commitments are exorcised, the drive in the direction of the Tractarian standpoint is removed.

When I say that the first 137 sections are dominated by criticisms of the Tractarian system, I do not mean that they contain a point-by-point criticism of the text. Although transparent allusions to the *Tractatus* occur throughout the *Investigations*, there are only four explicit references: one occurs in the Preface and the others in ## 23, 97, 114. It is the commitments that lie behind the text rather than the specific realization of them that is the subject of investigation and criticism. But this method of criticism, however searching, raises problems for the interpretation and assessment of Wittgenstein's work. Wittgenstein seems to view the *Tractatus* as a highly sophisticated development of naive themes that were uncritically accepted. This is Wittgenstein's general attitude toward philosophical positions, but, in attacking these underlying themes, he often seems utterly unfair to the philosophy under consideration.

I can illustrate this by citing his critique of a passage from St Augustine that Wittgenstein uses to open the *Investigations:* Wittgenstein begins by quoting a passage from St Augustine's *Confessions*:

> When they (my elders) named some object, and accordingly moved towards something, I saw this and I grasped that the thing was called by the sound they uttered when they meant to point it out. Their intention was shewn by their bodily movements, as it were the natural language of all peoples: the expression of the face, the play of the eyes, the movement of other parts of the body, and the tone of voice which expresses our state of mind in seeking, having, rejecting, or avoiding something. Thus, as I heard words repeatedly used in their proper places in various sentences, I gradually learnt to understand what objects they signified; and after I had trained my mouth to form these signs, I used them to express my own desires. (PI, #1)

Now compare this passage, with all its richness, with Wittgenstein's reflections upon it. He tells us that these words "give us a particular picture of the essence of human language:"

> [T]he individual words in language name objects—sentences are combinations of such names. . . . Every word has a meaning. This meaning is correlated with the words. It is the object for which the word stands. (PI, #1)

Here Wittgenstein neglects some important features of the Augustinian original. Nothing is said about those "bodily movements" which are, as it were, "the natural language of all peoples." Later Wittgenstein himself will say that "words are connected with the primitive, the natural, expressions of *[a]* sensation and used in their place" (PI, #244). For Wittgenstein, it is important that language arises through shaping various "primitive and natural" human responses, but a similar notion in the Augustinian passage is ignored. Nor does Wittgenstein notice Augustine's reference to the use of these words "in their proper places in various sentences" even though a parallel idea was important to him throughout his philosophical development. Instead, Wittgenstein simply discusses "a particular picture" that this passage suggests—a picture more naive than the view actually presented by Augustine. In the same way, if we suppose that Wittgenstein is citing this passage from Augustine as a way of alluding to the *Tractatus* (and surely this is true), then a similar problem presents itself. The view of language developed in the *Tractatus* is nowhere as simple as the picture of language that Wittgenstein here invokes. We need only recall that it was one of the leading ideas of the *Tractatus* that certain signs (e.g., logical constants and numerals) do *not* go proxy for objects.

But if the picture that Wittgenstein invokes is not adequate to the passage he cites nor to the text that concerns him most deeply (the *Tractatus*), what is the point of introducing it and why, for our part, should we take it seriously? This brings us at once to one of the major problems in interpreting and assessing the *Philosophical Investigations*. Time and again Wittgenstein expends enormous energy exorcising philosophical commitments which—as it seems—no one has held. To the critic he seems only to attack straw men. Indeed, one natural response to Wittgenstein's whole approach is to feel that it is mere trifling (*leere Spielerei*, Z, #197). Russell, for example, who valued the early writings of his former student and colleague, had no such opinion of his later writings.[2] Yet the overriding fact is that Wittgenstein has had enormous impact upon the development of philosophy in the middle decades of this century, and any treatment of his work that makes this unintelligible must itself be suspect.

I think there is a straightforward reason why Wittgenstein operates in the way that he does and why his approach can generate such differing responses. Quite simply, Wittgenstein holds that philosophers come to their tasks with a certain conception of how things must be. This picture lies in the background, unexamined, and dictates the questions asked and specifies the form the answers will take. *One* such picture concerns the essence of language: Words stand for things—these things being their meanings—a sentence is a combination of such words. This is not the stated position of the *Tractatus*, for, as we know, the *Tractatus* is a highly sophisticated synthesis of a number of themes. Yet, if Wittgenstein is correct, the *Tractatus* was constructed under the domination of this image, and this is not an implausible suggestion. Of course, the claim that logical constants do not represent objects departs from the primitive picture that Wittgenstein has sketched, yet it does so in a way that provides a perfect realization of this primitive picture where it counts—in the notion of an *elementary proposition*. Elementary propositions provide the basic mechanism for representation, and here we find words standing for objects, combined to show how their corresponding objects are combined. Looked at this way, the *Tractatus* emerges as a highly sophisticated theory intended to meet a primitive demand. Now the critique of "the particular picture of the essence of human language" with which the *Investigations* begins, far from being unfair and superficial, goes to the heart of the Tractarian system by challenging its motivation.

This does not mean that Wittgenstein had no concern for the technical and detailed difficulties of the Tractarian system. For example, in "Some remarks on logical form" he is concerned with the threat to his doctrine of independence posed by the existence of continuous magnitudes. He saw at once that an adjustment in this area would have far-reaching consequences for the entire Tractarian system. Yet these criticisms, however deep, did not force the abandonment of the Tractarian standpoint. As long as one is convinced of the basic soundness of a position, problems will appear as difficulties to be straightened out—perhaps by others—later on. Of course, the persistence of unresolved problems can contribute to the abandonment of a general standpoint, and this is certainly true of Wittgenstein's ultimate rejection of some of the basic features of the Tractarian system. Yet even if Wittgenstein took such criticisms seriously at one point in his career, they had largely fallen into the background by the time he was writing the *Philosophical Investigations*. This work is not primarily an attack upon particular solutions to philosophical problems, but an inquiry into the moves that initiate philosophical reflection; for the most part it is not a criticism of the results of philosophizing, but an interrogation of its source.

We can also say that in the *Investigations* Wittgenstein attempts to *persuade* us that certain pictures are one-sided, distorted and incomplete. Persuasion is sometimes effected through argument, but often—perhaps more often—it consists of getting people to take acknowledged facts seriously.[3] It brings about a reorientation in our sense of *importance*. Thus, when Wittgenstein wrote the *Tractatus*, he knew as well as anyone that there was a great disparity between the essence of language as he described it and the appearance of language as we all encounter it. For a variety of reasons, this acknowledged difference was not allowed to matter.

How are we to evaluate a method that aims at persuasion? The only way is to read the material and see if, in fact, it persuades—and continues to persuade under critical examination. I shall therefore not attempt a rational reconstruction of the *Philosophical Investigations*, but rather take things as they come and comment upon their import and plausibility.

2

The motley of language

The *Investigations* begins with an examination of a particular picture of the essence of human language: "the individual words in language name objects—sentences are combinations of such names. . . . Every word has

110

a meaning. . . . It is the object for which the word stands" (PI, #1). As the text unfolds, various aspects of this view of language come under scrutiny, but in a general way, the criticism of this picture passes through two stages. Wittgenstein first points out that this conception of language, with its one-sided emphasis upon the use of names to formulate descriptions, gives a distorted image of language through ignoring the wide variety of other ways we use language. Even a casual survey of our everyday linguistic behavior reveals a motley of activities that can hardly be captured under the paradigms of naming and describing. This theme dominates the first twenty-four sections of the *Investigations* and will be the subject of the present section. The second stage of Wittgenstein's criticism goes deeper by challenging the account of names itself. Wittgenstein tries to show that the surrogate theory of meaning—the idea that words stand for things or take their place—is an inadequate account even for names. Thus the full indictment of this particular picture of language comes to this: it involves the projection of an *inaccurate* account of one *portion* of language on the whole of language.

In order to exhibit the multiple ways that words function, Wittgenstein invents a simple language-game. Here a person is given a slip marked "five red apples." He has been trained to bring this slip to a drawer marked apples, match the apples against a sample on a color chart, and then count out five apples. Here it is immediately evident that the words "five," "red" and "apples" play roles of very different *kinds*. In contrast with this first language-game, Wittgenstein constructs a second where, as he says, "the description given by Augustine is right" (PI, #2). A builder calls out the words "block," "pillar," "slab" or "beam," and the assistant, who has been trained to do so, brings the appropriate object.[4] The striking difference between language-game 1 and language-game 2 is that words function in a variety of ways in language-game 1 but in only a single way in language-game 2. Of course, when the builder calls out "pillar" he is not doing the same thing as when he calls out "slab" (he is calling for a pillar, not a slab), yet the similarity between the uses of "pillar" and "slab" becomes evident when we compare them with the contrasting uses of "apples" and "five" in language-game 1. So the initial contrast between language-games 1 and 2 is that in the first the uses of words are diverse; in the second they are, by contrast, uniform. And the same comparison holds between natural language and the conception of language Wittgenstein attributes to Augustine. An inspection of our actual language reveals a wide variety in the employment of words, whereas Augustine's view acknowledges relatively few. Wittgenstein draws this moral explicitly:

Augustine, we might say, does describe a system of communication; only not everything that we call language is this system. (PI, #3)

Wittgenstein pursues this point in #8 by constructing yet a more complex language-game using the pillar-slab game of #2 as his base. The original language-game is extended to include numerals, the demonstratives "this" and "there," and a set of color samples.[5] The builder can now say things like: "d—slab—there" while simultaneously showing his assistant a color sample and pointing to a particular place. The worker then gets d slabs ("d" functions as a numeral) of the indicated color and puts them where the builder points. Again it is evident that we are dealing with symbols with a variety of employments, a fact that Wittgenstein underscores by remarking on the differences in the training appropriate to each. With the numerals, a set of symbols is learned by heart in a given order. Then a particular training is needed to master the employment of these symbols. Having learned to recite numerals, the assistant is taught how to use them to count objects. The techniques for teaching the assistant the employment of the words "slab," "pillar," etc., has a different form. Again there can be a preparatory activity of learning certain words, but learning them in a particular *order* need not, at least in any obvious way, form part of this training. Furthermore, in the two cases, the point of correlating these words with objects is different, and this too will be seen in the training appropriate to each, for example, in the patterns of mistake and correction. The demonstratives will be taught in yet a different way exhibiting the following distinctive feature:

> Imagine how one might perhaps teach their use. One will point to places and things—but in this case the pointing occurs in the *use* of the words too and not merely in learning the use. (PI, #9)

Pointing is part of the employment of these symbols, not something we merely use in preparing for their employment and discard later.

Here one should not put the wrong construction on Wittgenstein's reference to *training*. We look to the training in the use of a symbol because the character of that training will often bring into prominence distinctive features of the use itself. This is not surprising since training shapes behavior, often breaking it down into constituent parts. (First we learn to recite numerals, then we learn to count.) Yet it remains a matter of fact whether an appeal to training will be illuminating with respect to the character of the linguistic skill it generates. If a person could acquire the skills of another by devouring him—I understand something like this happens with worms—then an appeal to the way the skill is acquired will presumably not tell us much about the character of the skill itself. The primary way of understanding the use of a symbol is to examine its application, not its origin. Sometimes an appeal to training will give guidance in this.

Returning to the main point, Wittgenstein exhibits the motley of language by constructing and contrasting a series of simple language-games. For "it disperses the fog to study the phenomena of language in primitive kinds of application in which one can command a clear view of the aim and functioning of the words" (PI, #5). In these primitive language-games it becomes evident that words function in very different ways, but once our attention is drawn to this diversity, we cannot fail to notice a similar diversity in the language we actually speak. Yet, according to Wittgenstein, this is something we ignore or do not take seriously enough, especially when doing philosophy. Why is this? What is the source—or what are the sources—of this pressure in the direction of assimilating various uses of language under one or a few simple paradigms?

One answer that Wittgenstein gives is that we are confused by "the uniform appearances of words when we hear them spoken or meet them in script and print" (PI, #11). This echoes a passage in the *Tractatus*:

> 3.143 For in a printed proposition, for example, no essential difference is apparent between a propositional sign and a word.
>
> (That is what made it possible for Frege to call a proposition a composite name.)

The words in our language are like the handles in the cabin of a locomotive. They all look more or less alike, which is natural "since they are all supposed to be handled" (PI, #12).

I confess that I do not find this line of reasoning particularly persuasive. It is hard to believe that philosophers have been misled—and deeply misled—by the mere look (or sound) of language. A person who has never operated a locomotive could be misled by the outward similarity of its handles, but we are not amateurs with respect to the language we employ. The locomotive cab analogy suggests that we don't know how to use the words of our language and therefore are misled by surface similarities into supposing that they all work in the same way. That, however, is simply wrong. The fact is, we do know how to use the words in our language, but are misled none the less. The trouble is that our language does not always contain explicit markers indicating differences in use. Admittedly some of these differences are reflected in surface grammar through moods, inflections, punctuation, and so on. We also have a battery of useful terms that serve to clarify the situation when genuine misunderstanding arises. Thus we can say "I am not asking you to leave, I'm ordering you to leave" or "I wasn't proposing, I was just wondering what you think about marriage." Yet for the most part our everyday language does not flag differences in employment with explicit markers. This sometimes causes confusion in everyday life, but is more apt to confuse the philosopher whose activities are often detached from the first-level employment of words. The philosopher wondering about promising is not actually making a promise and therefore the constraints and, indeed, the point of this activity can easily slip from sight. Perhaps the claim is best made in a negative way: our language does not always contain sufficient devices to block the unwarranted assimilation of diverse uses of language.

Wittgenstein next argues, I think more strongly, that our language contains terms which, when misunderstood, invite the unwarranted assimilation of different uses of language. Given any word—with the possible exception of a proper name—we can always ask about its meaning. Somewhat differently, we can usually ask what a word signifies. Thus we can say that certain names signify hurricanes and that numerals signify numbers. Since both proper names and numerals signify things, we may now be tempted to ask about this signifying relationship shared in these two cases. Wittgenstein's strategy is to attack this development before the deeper move takes place:

> But assimilating the descriptions of the uses of words in this way
> cannot make the uses themselves any more like one another. For,
> as we see, they are absolutely unlike. (PI, #10)

Perhaps Wittgenstein goes too far in declaring that these uses are *absolutely unlike*, for it is also possible to discover (and dwell upon) similarities between different uses of language. Yet Wittgenstein's central point is surely correct: noting that various kinds of words all *signify* something does not show that they function in the same way.

It is in the present context that Wittgenstein first introduces his famous comparison between *words* and *tools*, saying that "the functions of words are as diverse as the functions of these objects" (PI, #11). Again, we may be tempted to assimilate the various uses of tools by bringing them under a formula: "All tools serve to modify something" (PI, #14). Here we are probably thinking of a saw, hammer, or screwdriver. But what does a plumb bob modify? Does it modify our previous knowledge concerning the perpendicular from a point above the earth? In fact, we *could* say this, and we would even understand it if we did. Yet it is hard to see the point of manipulating things so that our description of the use of a plumb bob looks as similar as possible to our description of the use of a saw.

Of course, Wittgenstein is not attacking the words "signify" or "modify." The word "signify" has an honest employment in our language. For example, if someone does not know that in language-game 8 we use letters as numerals, we can tell him this by saying that they signify numbers. Notice that this is a high-level statement, since the explanation presupposes knowledge of the *employment* of numerals of some other kind. But the explanation does not presuppose that these words stand for or represent objects. *Sometimes* we explain the meaning of a term by pointing to the thing that it signifies, but linguistic explanation need not take this form. To suppose the contrary merely takes it for granted that the name relation is the model for the way all words signify. One of the main tasks of the opening paragraphs of the *Investigations* is to break the spell of this tacit assumption.

"But isn't all this obvious?" Wittgenstein would welcome an affirmative answer to this question. "But what is the point of it all; what philosophical positions are refuted by the considerations Wittgenstein has presented?" To answer this question, we can take a specific case: do Wittgenstein's remarks refute the Platonic doctrine that numerals are the proper names of abstract particulars? The answer to this is no. The Platonist also recognizes important differences between numerals and, say, ordinary proper names. He chooses to explain this difference by locating it in the character of the things referred to. We might put it this way: the Platonist is parsimonious in the number of uses of language he acknowledges, and then makes up for this by being profligate in his ontology. Wittgenstein is profligate in the number of uses of language he admits,[6] but this, in itself, relieves the pressure to explain differences in meaning by reference to differences in *things* signified. This, of course, does not refute the Platonic move, but it does show it for what it is: one answer amidst others, and an answer that is probably given before the question itself is subjected to scrutiny.

3
The critique of ostensive definition

"One thinks that learning language consists in giving names to objects" (PI, #26). Wittgenstein's first criticism of this conception is, as we have seen, that it ignores the diverse ways in which words in our language function. Wittgenstein never tires of insisting upon this—drawing our attention to the motley of language is a persistent theme in the *Investigations*. Wittgenstein now deepens his criticism of this particular picture of the essence of human language by attacking another of its key features: the idea that a meaning can be assigned to a word *merely* through an act of ostensive definition.

Taking Wittgenstein's own example, suppose we try to teach someone the meaning of the word "two" in the following way: we point at a pair of nuts and say this is called "two." Obviously, he can take this definition in various ways. He might, for example, treat it as a proper name for this particular group of nuts. In the same way:

. . . he might equally well take the name of a person, of whom I give an ostensive definition, as that of a colour, of a race, or even of a point of the compass. That is to say: an ostensive definition can be variously interpreted in *every* case. (PI, #28)

In sum, the mere act of pointing at something and saying that it is called a ϕ leaves open endlessly many interpretations of the way in which "ϕ" should be used. This leads to the conclusion, which I shall first state incautiously, that an ostensive definition (i.e., pointing to something and saying it is called a such and such) can never, by itself, fix the meaning of a word.

This way of phrasing the conclusion is incautious because instead of sounding like a truism—which I think it is—it seems to express an obvious falsehood. Walking through the woods, I point to a mushroom and say "That's called The Old Man of the Woods." My companion, with no further ceremony, catches my meaning and in the future refers to the mushroom this way. This sort of thing commonly happens, but it is useful to fill out some of the details of the scene that this remark invokes. Presumably my companion has some acquaintance with plants and knows, for example, that they are classified into kinds. This is important for him to know, but it is such a general fact that we tend to pass it by unnoticed. It is also important for him to know that we do not, in general, give plants proper names, although the General Sherman tree in Sequoia National Park is an exception to this. It is against the general background of a great many assumptions of this kind that an ostensive definition can (and often does) secure immediate uptake. In Wittgenstein's words, "the ostensive definition explains the use—the meaning—of the word when the overall role of the word in language is clear" (PI, #30).

Here it will be helpful to contrast two different ways in which someone might misunderstand an ostensive definition. The most obvious kind of misunderstanding will show itself in an inability to identify another mushroom as an Old Man of the Woods. Here the person either succeeds or fails in playing the ostensive definition game correctly. Of course, no matter how many times he succeeds in playing this game, it remains an abstract possibility that he has not mastered it. That is, however many successes he has in a row, we can always imagine some surroundings that would lead us to suspect his ability. Perhaps, like Clever Hans, his ability is based upon subliminal clues. Perhaps he is telepathic, etc. Now just because doubt is always imaginable it doesn't mean that we are always going to doubt. Nor does our ability to imagine a doubt *justify* our doubting. The move from imagined doubt to dubitability is the way of *general scepticism*. It is essential to see that this is *not* a pattern of argument adopted by Wittgenstein at this point.[7]

A second way that an ostensive definition might be misunderstood need not reveal itself in the ostensive definition game. My companion might think, somewhat plausibly, that I am referring to the distinctive pattern on the cap of the mushroom when I say "That's called the Old Man of the Woods." Since the standard way of identifying this mushroom is to notice this particular pattern on its cap, this misunderstanding could easily go unnoticed in the game of What's That Called? Though abstractly possible, this misunderstanding could hardly go undetected when we step outside the ostensive definition game and employ the name in regular discourse. We know something has gone wrong if our companion is utterly baffled when told that the Old Man of the Woods, though not poisonous, has a woody and unpleasant taste. Or he might say that the Old Man of the Woods is indistinct when the mushroom first pushes up through the ground. This brings us to the decisive point: a person does not understand the meaning of a term unless he can use it correctly in regular discourse, that is, *beyond* the ostensive definition game. We have now, I think, arrived at a truism: an ostensive definition does not fix the meaning of a term by itself, for the ability to answer the question "What's that called?" does not settle how a term will be used in further discourse.

"We name things and then we talk about them: can refer to them in talk."—As if what we did next were given with the mere act of naming. (PI, #27)

Of course, none of this goes against the obvious fact that people often learn the meaning of a word simply by being told that it is called a such-and-such. Here, however, the person already possesses linguistic skills and these skills, when applied in the context of an ostensive definition, will often settle the question of meaning straight off. At other times, we guard against confusion by indicating the place that the word will function in our language. We say, for example, that this *color* is called sepia. But this remark only helps if the person is already familiar with color words. And the situation is the same even if we do not say explicitly that this *color* is called sepia, for in order for the person to understand the meaning of the word "sepia," he must be able to use it in color ascription:

One has already to know (or be able to do) something in order to be capable of asking a thing's name. (PI, #30)

What is it that someone has to know?

We may say: only someone who already knows how to do something with it can significantly ask a name. (PI, #31)

The most striking passage occurs a bit later in the text:

For naming and describing do not stand on the same level: naming is a preparation for description. Naming is so far not a move in the language-game—any more than putting a piece in its place on the board is a move in chess. We may say: *nothing* has so far been done, when a thing has been named. (PI, #49)

117

Wittgenstein is now in a position to complete the criticism of the particular picture of the essence of human language that he found latent in Augustine's writings:

> And now, I think, we can say: Augustine describes the learning of human language as if the child came into a strange country and did not understand the language of the country; that is, as if it already had a language, only not this one. Or again: as if the child could already *think*, only not yet speak. (PI, #32)

The point behind this striking metaphor is simple: if we take ostensive definition as the *fundamental* method of assigning meanings to words, we have failed to realize that the activity of giving an ostensive definition makes sense only within the context of a previously established linguistic framework. Such an account of language acquisition presupposes that the learner already possesses a language; that is, it presupposes the very phenomenon it is intended to explain.

4
Inner acts of ostention

Wittgenstein considers a criticism of his view as sketched in the previous section.

> Suppose, however, someone were to object: "It is not true that you must already be master of a language in order to understand an ostensive definition: all you need —of course!—is to know or guess what the person giving the explanation is pointing to. That is, whether for example to the shape of the object, or to its colour, or to its number, and so on." (PI, #33)

Again there is a truth hovering in the region of this protest, for we do sometimes guess what a person giving an ostensive definition is pointing to. But what is involved in pointing to a shape rather than to a color? The natural answer is that we concentrate our attention upon the color rather than the shape. But what is involved in *concentrating our attention* upon the shape rather than the color? This last may seem a strange question, for isn't concentrating one's attention upon something a common phenomenon? Of course it is, and Wittgenstein does not deny this. He only wishes to attack a certain conception of this phenomenon, i.e., that concentrating one's attention is a specific mental act—an act of private pointing.

Returning to the theme of diversity, Wittgenstein first attacks the idea that attending (for example, to the color of a thing) is a quite *specific* act. Here he invites the reader to imagine various cases, citing a few examples of his own:

"Is this blue the same as the blue over there? Do you see any difference?"—
You are mixing paint and you say "It's hard to get the blue of this sky."

Or again:

"Look what different effects these two blues have."
"This blue signal-light means. . . ." (PI, #33)

In each case we are attending to the color, but the cases themselves show we are dealing with a diverse system of phenomena. At least the manifest diversity of these cases should block the facile assumption that we are dealing with a simple phenomenon with which we are all familiar.

But Wittgenstein has a deeper criticism in mind, for someone might grant that attending to a color forms a diverse system of mental activities and say that we employ one or another of these ways of attending when we fix the meaning of a word through an ostensive definition. To set aside the question of diversity, let us suppose then that there is a single psychological characteristic associated with attending to a color. The person who *intends* his definition to be a definition of a color does so by attending to it in this way. The person who *interprets* the definition correctly does so through a similar act of attention. How either comes to be in this particular frame of mind is, we shall suppose, beside the point. Can this be a correct account of intending and interpreting a definition? The answer to this is no! Suppose the teacher intends his ostensive definition to be a definition of the color sepia. Couldn't the student be in any state of mind at all and still not be able to use the word "sepia" correctly? A *necessary* condition for understanding the meaning of the word "sepia" is the ability to use it correctly in identifying colors. Of course, the student need not be unerring in his use of this word, but his level of success must be high enough so that his failures will count as *mistakes* rather than random responses. So the student's interpretation of the definition will come out in his activities *after* he has received the definition and is not established by the state he is in at the time he receives it. The same thing can be said about the original *intentions* of the teacher. The way he intends the definition is not settled by his mental state at the time he offers the definition, but by the way he employs this word "sepia," for example, in encouraging and correcting the student's attempted use of this word. These are the reasons that lie behind the following claim:

For neither the expression "to intend the definition in such-and-such a way" nor the expression "to interpret the definition in such-and-such a way" stands for a process which accompanies the giving and hearing of the definition. (PI, #34)

In the present context, Wittgenstein is primarily concerned with attacking the appeal to *mental* states in the explanation of meaning. This is entirely natural, since there has been a long tradition of invoking inner acts of the mind for such explanations. But it is important to see that the present attack is not directed at the *mentality* of these acts. No accompanying process, be it *mental* or *physical*, constitutes intending a definition in a certain way or interpreting it in a certain way.

Yet it remains a fact that ostensive definitions sometimes succeed. Wittgenstein's account of this, as we have seen, is that the ostensive definition takes place against the background of other linguistic skills that have already been mastered. Now it follows on this account that not all of these background skills could be acquired through ostensive definitions, so it is natural to ask how they can be acquired at all. Actually, the form of the problem gives us its answer. Since an ostensive definition will not, by itself, determine the use of an expression, we will need some other form of training that does determine the use. Nothing could be better than a direct training in the use itself. This is the situation envisaged in the primitive language-games that appear at the beginning of the *Investigations*, for here there is no institution of asking the name of something. These primitive language-games do not contain the ostensive definition game. The helper is taught the use of a word by being taught how to use it.

The idea that the meaning of terms can be introduced through using expressions that employ them actually goes back to the *Tractatus*.

> 3.263 The meanings of primitive signs can be explained by means of elucidations. Elucidations are propositions that contain the primitive signs. So they can only be understood if the meanings of those signs are already known.

At first this passage is puzzling, for it seems to say that the meaning of a primitive sign (i.e., a sign that is not capable of definition) will be explained through the employment of a proposition containing it where the understanding of this proposition will, in turn, depend upon the understanding of the term being explained. But the apparent circularity of this passage is not vicious. I think what Wittgenstein is saying is this: we learn the meaning of primitive terms by learning how to employ these terms in propositions, but a condition for understanding a proposition is to grasp it as an articulated structure. That is, to understand a proposition, we must see how it is related, by way of its constituent expressions, to the world and to the entire system of propositions in logical space.

When we come to the *Investigations*, much of the background of the Tractarian system has been abandoned; for example, the notion of primitive signs (at least in the Tractarian sense) is given up. Yet the fundamental idea that the meaning of a term is specified through its employment in a wider setting is carried over from one period to the other. I think that Wittgenstein alludes to this similarity in this passage cited, in part, earlier:

> We may say: *nothing* has so far been done, when a thing has been named. It has not even *got* a name except in the language-game. This was what Frege meant too, when he said that a word had meaning only as part of a sentence. (PI, #49)

In his later writings the looser notion of a language-game replaces the tighter notion of a proposition as the setting in which a term can have a meaning. But in both periods Wittgenstein insists that the meaning of a term has not been fixed until its use in a broader setting has been established. The burden of the present argument is that this cannot be identified with being in a particular mental state (or undergoing a particular mental process) at a particular point in time, for example, on the occasion of an ostensive definition.

5
A remark on meaning and use

The asserted connection (almost identity) between the notions of meaning and use constitutes a central theme in the *Philosophical Investigations*. In the present context Wittgenstein has only argued that knowing how to use an expression is a *necessary* condition for knowing its meaning. Later (at #43) Wittgenstein comes close to saying that knowing how to use an expression constitutes both a *necessary and sufficient* condition for knowing its meaning. I think it is important not to mix up the weaker and stronger claim, for to do so invites a misguided attack upon Wittgenstein's "theory of meaning" as a response to his particular criticisms.

Wittgenstein has assumed that knowing how to use an expression is a necessary condition for understanding its meaning. On the basis of this assumption, he has argued that it is not sufficient to correlate a word with a thing in order to fix the sense of that word. Given this correlation, it still remains an open question whether the word is used to name the object, ascribe a feature to it, greet it or sound a warning of its presence. It is only when this correlation is embedded in some wider context that these further determinations are made.

I do not think that anyone will deny that a necessary condition for understanding the meaning of a word is the ability to use it outside of the ostensive definition game. The difficulty here is to understand the range and content of this dictum. Think of various constructions we can put upon the phrase "the use of a word in the language." Here examples help:

I can use the word "chukker" to:

speak about a chukker;
make a statement about a polo match;
ask a question about a polo match;
tell someone what a period is called in polo;
show off my familiarity with polo;
distinguish it from "chukka";
give a pass word;
frighten someone by shouting it in his ear.

Pretty clearly, it is the examples at the top of this list that point to the kind of use in question when Wittgenstein relates use to meaning. But even these examples are heterogeneous. First we speak of the use of a *word* to refer to something, then we speak about the use of *sentences* employing this word, then we speak about the effect—or intended effect—of using the word in a given *context*. Very different considerations enter into the analysis of each of these uses. Which sort of use does Wittgenstein have in mind? The answer, I think, is that he really doesn't say. There is no articulated theory of meaning as use in the *Investigations*. Here we might try to make up for this lack by doing what Wittgenstein chose not to do: produce a careful taxonomy of the uses of language. Alternatively, we can simply rely upon context to settle what uses are relevant to a discussion. I shall adopt the second course, for the first is difficult and, anyway, would unavoidably saddle Wittgenstein with paraphernalia he chose not to develop.

6
Simples

We saw in Part One that the doctrine of *simples* played an important and problematic role in the Tractarian system. In Wittgenstein's eyes, the demand for simples was connected with the demand for *definiteness of sense* (TLP, 3.23). Against this I have argued that Wittgenstein did not show that the demand for definiteness of sense is itself legitimate nor did he show that the doctrine of simples is the only way to realize this demand. Although my own criticism of the doctrine of simples borrowed heavily from Wittgenstein's later criticisms, I did not, in Part One, actually present Wittgenstein's arguments. This is the task of the present section. Wittgenstein's critique of simples has two main parts: (i) an attack upon the view of language that leads us to posit simples; and (ii) a positive claim that the notion of a simple is always relativized to a particular framework of discourse (or language-game).

(i) Wittgenstein slides into a discussion of simples through reflection upon the treatment accorded to demonstratives by certain philosophers—presumably Russell in particular. Philosophers have sometimes treated demonstratives as names and, beyond this, as the only *genuine* names. Grouping demonstratives with names is sensible for some purposes, for they often play similar grammatical roles in sentences. Yet demonstratives are not names. When I speak of *this* thing I am not naming the object "this" (not even temporarily), and if I were to name an object "this," then this word would merely be a homonym for the demonstrative usually expressed by this word. But if demonstratives are not names, why have philosophers treated them as names, indeed, as the very paradigms of what a name should be? Wittgenstein answers:

> But why does it occur to one to want to make precisely this word into a name, when it evidently is *not* a name?—That is just the reason. For one is tempted to make an objection against what is ordinarily called a name. It can be put like this: *a name ought really to signify a simple*. (PI, #39)

What exactly is the objection against "what is ordinarily called a name"? The objection again has its source in a particular picture of the essence of human language: words stand for things—these things being the meanings of the words. It is plain that some words in our everyday language (including some names) do not stand for things. Just as important, for many names that *do* stand for things, it is wholly *contingent* that there is an object corresponding to them. This points to the conclusion, on this particular view of language, that it is contingent whether any particular proposition is meaningful or not. In the Tractarian period, Wittgenstein viewed this as an impossible result and took elaborate measures against it. He did not succumb to the temptation of invoking demonstratives as a foolproof method of securing reference;[8] instead, he argued that language must be based upon a system of absolutely simple signs correlated with absolutely simple objects. Wittgenstein illustrates this Tractarian way of reasoning with the following example:

> [I]f "Excalibur" is the name of an object, this object no longer exists when Excalibur is broken in pieces; and as no object would then correspond to the name it would have no meaning. But then the sentence "Excalibur has a sharp blade" would contain a word that had no meaning, and hence the sentence would be nonsense. But it does make sense; so there must always be something corresponding to the words of which it consists. So the word "Excalibur" must disappear when the sense is analysed and its place taken by words which name simples. It will be reasonable to call these words the real names. (PI, #39)

Wittgenstein loses no time in pointing out that this view is false, indeed, categorically false. It confuses the *meaning* of a name with the *bearer* of a name, a confusion that becomes manifest when we remember that it makes sense to say that the bearer of a name has died, but it makes no sense to say that its meaning has died. I think that Wittgenstein is obviously correct in saying this, but it is important to keep the object of Wittgenstein's criticism in sharp focus. He is attacking the theory that identifies the meaning of a name with its bearer, but his criticism does not touch the quite different view associated with John Stuart Mill, that proper names do not have a meaning (connotation or sense) but only serve to pick out (denote or refer to) objects. We can return to this position later when we consider certain criticisms of Wittgenstein's own account of the status of proper names in everyday language.[9]

Philosophers have been dissatisfied with everyday proper names largely because they can suffer from reference failure. Wittgenstein gives his discussion a nice turn by beginning with a case where a word *would* lose its meaning if its bearer were destroyed (PI, #41). Returning to the primitive language-game played between a builder and his assistant, the builder calls out the name of a tool and his assistant brings it to him. Suppose that the particular tool N is broken or lost, what meaning will attach to the word "N" under this circumstance? Given the specification of the language-game, there is no employment of the word "N" in circumstances where there is no tool bearing that name to be fetched. Since the existence of the tool is one of the conditions for the employment of the sign, this sign loses its significance (meaning) upon the destruction or loss of the tool. Yet we can also imagine this language-game enriched so that a significant response occurs when the tool is lost or broken. The assistant might be taught to shake his head in such cases—now the word "N" will continue to play a role in the language even when it lacks a bearer.

Wittgenstein goes on to imagine the possibility of a name "X" "which has never been used for a tool" (PI, #42). Could such a name also have a meaning? The answer to this depends upon the possibility of finding a use for such a word. Wittgenstein suggests, not very persuasively, that the assistant might also be trained to shake his head to mean no when the sign "X" is called out just as he shakes his head to mean no when the name of a broken tool is called for. This, Wittgenstein suggests, might be "a sort of joke between them." It is hard, however, to see how the assistant would recognize the point of this joke. Yet we do have institutions that employ proper names that never have (nor ever will have) a bearer. Each year the National Weather Bureau sets up a list of names for the year's hurricanes. In a given year there may not be enough hurricanes to get down to Katherine, yet the name "Katherine" loses none of its significance on this account. We can imagine someone saying, "Given the destruction Judy caused, we are lucky that she was not followed by Katherine." The moral to this is plain: we can construct language-games where a name has employment only in the presence of its bearer, and we can also construct language-games where a name has an employment in the absence of its bearer (PI, #44); therefore the meaning of a name cannot, in general, be identified with the bearer of that name.

(ii) There seem to be other, and perhaps deeper, reasons for setting aside our everyday names in favor of genuine names that stand for simples. Here Wittgenstein remarks on a passage from Plato's "Theaetetus" that expresses a view strikingly similar to that developed in the *Tractatus:*

> [T]here is no formula in which any element can be expressed: it can only be named, for a name is all there is that belongs to it. But when we come to things composed of these elements, then, just as these things are complex, so the names are combined to make a description (*logos*), a description being precisely a combination of names. (*Theaetetus*, 202)

Wittgenstein makes short work of this position which he found so attractive earlier in his career. Taking a chair as an example of something composite, Wittgenstein remarks that it makes "no sense at all to speak absolutely of the 'simple parts of a chair' " (PI, #47). What will count as a part of a chair, that is as one of its simple parts, will depend upon our choice of a system of classification. Whether the chair is said to be made up of legs, arms, seat, etc., or of pieces of wood, or of molecules, or atoms, etc., depends upon our particular interests at the time. The assumption that basic components (simples) must exist as the ultimate constituents of all complexes is itself unwarranted and is perhaps generated by the following illicit argument:

I   Every complex is made up out of simples.
II There are simples out of which every complex is made up.

Statement I, of course, is a truism, whereas II, on its most natural reading, is significant and unwarranted.

Yet certain things do seem to be absolutely composite, a chessboard for example. But if a chessboard is absolutely composite, what exactly is it a composite *of?*: thirty-two white squares and thirty-two black squares, a grid with black and white filling, a set of thirty-two dominoes—each half white and half black—or what? A chessboard seems absolutely complex because it is so easy to think of ways of describing it as a combination of elements. Yet there seems to be no way of settling upon which features of the chessboard are to count as basic elements and, with this recognition, the notion of a fixed and absolute complexity begins to fade. Furthermore, if we think of a chessboard as a distinctive pattern—just as we might think of a swastika as a distinctive pattern—it seems more natural to think of it as one of the simple or basic patterns rather than as a complex pattern built up from other patterns.

The point of this discussion is that "we use the word 'composite' (and therefore the word 'simple') in an enormous number of different and differently related ways" (PI, #47). In characteristic fashion, Wittgenstein attempts to establish this thesis by a series of examples:

> Is the colour of a square on a chessboard simple, or does it consist of pure white and pure yellow? And is white simple, or does it consist of the colours of the rainbow?—Is this length of 2 cm. simple, or does it consist of two parts, each 1 cm. long? (PI, #47)

By constructing contexts of various kinds, it is easy to imagine answering each of these questions in various ways. Furthermore, and this is important, a context in which one question is appropriate may be totally inappropriate for another. For example, we can imagine a circumstance where we would say that the square on the chessboard does consist of pure white and pure yellow—perhaps these are the colors of the paints used to mix the particular shade of ocher. Here it would be inappropriate to suggest that in the same sense pure white consists of all the colors of the rainbow. This helps to show that there is no simple hierarchy of complex entities with objects at each level composed of objects at some lower level. Indeed, the basic metaphor of *composition* does not seem essential for the distinction between complex and simple. Wittgenstein remarks that "the concepts of complexity might also be so extended that a smaller area was said to be 'composed' of a greater area and another one subtracted from it" (PI, #48). This may not seem persuasive, but, as Wittgenstein notices, examples of this kind actually exist:

> Compare the "composition of forces", the "division" of a line by a point outside it; these expressions show that we are sometimes even inclined to conceive the smaller as the result of a composition of greater parts, and the greater as the result of a division of the smaller. (PI, #48)

Earlier we noticed the (obvious) fallacy of arguing from the truism that every complex is composed of simples to the conclusion that there is some determinate set of simples out of which all complexes are ultimately composed. Pointing out this fallacy leaves open the possibility that it is still true that there are simples out of which all complexes are ultimately composed. Now I think we can say something stronger: once we see that complex-simple contrasts are introduced for widely different purposes and on categorically different grounds, it seems altogether *unlikely* that there is a single complex-simple contrast upon which all the rest ultimately depend. This doesn't show that an atomism of the kind developed in the *Tractatus* is false, but it does destroy all presumption in

126

its favor and thereby takes away the motive for making such a standpoint legislative for the organization of a theory.

7
Transcendental illusions surrounding the idea of simples

Here I shall examine a particular feature of the Socratic dream and examine Wittgenstein's comments upon it. It is part of the traditional doctrine of simples (and Wittgenstein takes this over in the *Tractatus*) that *nothing* can be properly attributed to them, not even existence ("for if it did not *exist*, one could not even name it and so one could say nothing at all of it" (PI, #50)). Where does such an idea come from? Certainly not from experience, for when we describe, say, the parts of a chair, it is always possible to give a further description of these parts. Yet there seems to be a strong demand to introduce elements which, by their nature, will not tolerate ascriptions (even of existence and non-existence). What is the source of the drive in this direction?

Wittgenstein answers this by considering what he calls an "analogous case."

> There is *one* thing of which one can say neither that it is one metre long, nor that it is not one metre long, and that is the standard metre in Paris.—But this is, of course, not to ascribe any extraordinary property to it, but only to mark its peculiar role in the language-game of measuring with a metre-rule. (PI, #50)

To begin with, it may not seem obvious that we cannot say of the standard meter that it is a meter long; indeed, we may be inclined to say the opposite, that it is the only thing that *really* is one meter long. But suppose, for a moment, we analyze the claim that x is a meter long as the assertion that x has the same length as the standard meter. In this case, the claim that the standard meter is a meter long amounts to saying that the standard meter is the same length as the standard meter. Thus our attempt to ascribe a length to the standard meter leads to the formulation of an empty tautology which, of course, does not attribute a length to a particular object.[10] Wittgenstein is making the same point later on when he says, "I know how tall I am" and then placing his hand on top of his head saying "this tall!" (PI, #279). Of course we can, and often do, use our bodies as standards of measure. We say that so-and-so comes up to here on me. But it is ludicrous to put a hand on top of one's head and say "And *I* come up to here on me!!" Why is it ludicrous? According to Wittgenstein, these curiosities arise because a particular object (a metal bar or my body) is employed in a special way as an "instrument of the language" for the ascription of length, and then misapplied back upon itself.

In this language-game it is not something that is represented, but is
a means of representation. (PI, #50)

So in particular language-games the standard meter or my body forms
part of an institution for the ascription of lengths. None of this makes
the objects themselves remarkable, for we can always remove something
from its position as standard and measure it against some other standard.
(I hold my hand at *my* chin and say "I come up to here on him.")
Curious illusions arise—and I do not think it is wrong to call them
transcendental illusions—when this procedure is applied back upon the
objects that are used as instruments in this institution.

What does this have to do with simples and, in particular, with the
idea that neither existence nor non-existence can be attributed to them?
The surface comparison should be obvious: we feel that we cannot
attribute existence or non-existence to *elements* for the same sorts of
reasons we feel that we cannot attribute a length to the standard meter.
The reason for this, and this is a bit more obscure, is that the things that
we are inclined to call elements are (like the rod that became the standard
meter) objects that have been taken up into the language as instruments
of representation. Here the object is assigned the special role as a standard
or paradigm in the language.

An example of something corresponding to the name, and without
which it would have no meaning, is a paradigm that is used in
connexion with the name in the language-game. (PI, #55)

So if a particular color term is introduced into the language using a single
color patch as a sample, then the significance of all talk employing this
color term will presuppose the existence of that sample. In certain language-games, then, the meaningfulness of a word will depend upon the
existence of a given object. When this phenomenon is seen out of focus,
it can look as though the very possibility of thought demands the existence of such objects.

What looks as if it *had* to exist, is part of the language. It is a
paradigm in our language-game; something with which comparison is
made. (PI, #50)

Here we arrive at one of the important ideas of the *Philosophical
Investigations:* philosophical misunderstandings arise when we misinter-
pret a role *assigned* to an object and treat it as a remarkable feature of
the object itself. When we describe something, certain things are set up
(perhaps tacitly) as elements of the description. These items are used in
the description and are not themselves further described—they are
assigned a particular role in the language-game of describing. Given the
job assigned to them they are, as it were, out of bounds to present

description. It is just this fact that can be misunderstood, for we can come to think that there are things which by their nature are not subject to description; they can only be named. The doctrine of simples as the indescribable elements that underlie all descriptions is the ontological crystalization of this fantasy.

This brings us to a fundamental difference between the Tractarian theory and the position developed in the *Investigations*. We saw that it was a central feature of the *Tractatus* that the meaningfulness of a proposition is a matter of necessity. It is a further feature of that system that the meaningfulness of a given proposition will depend upon the existence of a given object. These theses, taken together, yield the following valid argument:

1 Necessarily: if "ABCD" is meaningful, then it is necessarily meaningful.
2 Necessarily: if "ABCD" is meaningful, then an object corresponding to "A" exists.

Therefore:

3 Necessarily: if "ABCD" is meaningful, then an object corresponding to "A" *necessarily* exists.[11]

We have already seen that Wittgenstein abandoned the position expressed by the second premise of this argument. Whether a name has a meaning when there is no object corresponding to it is settled within the context of the language-game in which it is employed: it is not something settled by reflecting upon the nature of the name-relation. But I think that we see more deeply into the differences between the *Tractatus* and the *Investigations* when we recognize that Wittgenstein abandoned the first premise of this argument as well. The meaningfulness of a proposition is itself something contingent, not, as he held in the *Tractatus*, something necessary.

Wittgenstein makes this point in PT, #57, and I shall here expand somewhat on his reflections. We are inclined to think that the meaning of the term "red" would persist even if all red things were destroyed. Perhaps we would still remember things that were red and notice that none exist any longer. But suppose we all forget what it is like for things to be red, shall we still say that the word "red" has a meaning? Here we can say a number of things. We can say, quite indisputably, that we no longer know what the word *meant*. (The past tense here is important.) Yet how shall we choose between the two following formulations?

1 We no longer know what the word "red" means.
2 The word "red" no longer means anything.

I think that there is some temptation to adopt the phrasing in 1 because we, who are reflecting upon this case, *do* know that the word "red" has a meaning. But if we take the example seriously, the phrasing in 2 will seem more appropriate:

> When we forget which colour this is the name of, it loses its meaning for us; that is, we are no longer able to play a particular language-game with it. (PI, #57)

Once more Wittgenstein invokes the idea that (at least) a necessary condition for the meaningfulness of an expression is that it have an employment in some language-game. But whether an expression will find such employment turns upon matters of fact and therefore is contingent. This is a point that Wittgenstein insists on throughout the *Investigations*.

Here, then, is a fundamental contrast between the *Tractatus* and the *Investigations*. In the *Tractatus* we have a basic division between logical space with its crystaline purity and the system of wholly contingent facts embedded in it. In the *Investigations* the underlying scaffolding of necessary connections is abandoned in favor of a wholesale commitment to contingency. In the *Tractatus* the problem of meaning is related to this underlying structure of necessary connections. In the *Investigations*, this underlying structure is revealed as an illusion, and questions of meaning are settled by examining contingent facts of everyday life.

8
The attack on analysis

Wittgenstein raised the problem of analysis by asking the following question:

> When I say: "My broom is in the corner",—is this really a statement about the broomstick and the brush? (PI, #60)

It seems that we can replace the statement about the broom with another concerning the broomstick and the brush and their relationships to one another. Shall we then say that we have provided an analysis of the original statement in the sense of breaking its meaning down into its constituent parts? As soon as the question is made explicit, there is probably little temptation to answer it affirmatively. The assumption here is that, given the proposition *S is P*, a further description of the object named by "S" will give further knowledge of the meaning of the proposition concerning it. The assumption is incredible. A detailed knowledge of how the bristles are arranged in the brush will, of course, increase our knowledge of the *broom*, but it will not increase our understanding of the meaning of the assertion that the broom is in the corner.

But who, it might be asked, ever held a view subject to this criticism?

Well, G. E. Moore for one. In the first chapter of *Principia Ethica* he explains what he means by saying that good is indefinable. He tells us that in defining a horse we may present: (i) an "arbitrary verbal definition" (or stipulation); (ii) a "verbal definition proper" (or lexical definition); or (iii) "we may, when we define horse, mean something much more important."

> We may mean that a certain object, which we all of us know, is composed in a certain manner: that it has four legs, a head, a heart, a liver, etc., etc., all of them arranged in definite relations to one another.[12]

It is this final sort of definition that Moore finds philosophically interesting, and it is in this sense of a definition that Moore holds that good is indefinable.

It should also be clear that Wittgenstein held a sublime version of this view in the *Tractatus*. A proposition derives content through the name relationship, and this relationship obtains only between simple signs and objects. Again this implies that as we describe objects further, we increase our knowledge of the *meaning* of propositions that speak of them. More strongly, on the Tractarian account, a singular proposition must already contain all the information about any object it refers to, for this follows immediately from that picture of the essence of human language that holds that the meaning of a term *is* the object it stands for.[13]

Wittgenstein illustrates these points using a simple language-game. We are to imagine an assistant fetching things when they are requested by his superior. There are two ways of playing this game; in game 1 there are names for composite objects but no names for their parts, and in game 2 there are names for parts of objects but the wholes are not given names. Let us suppose that we can always use a description in game 2 to pick out anything named in game 1. Here Moore, at least given the passage just cited, would hold that the corresponding sentences in 2 constitute an analysis of the sentences in 1 and that furthermore the analyzed form given in 2 is more fundamental than the counterpart in 1. Speaking for a holder of such a view, Wittgenstein puts it this way:

> If you have only the unanalyzed form you miss the analysis; but if you know the analyzed form that gives you everything. (PI, #63)

But the task of analysis is to show how a particular expression derives its sense. Is this achieved by translating sentences of language 1 into sentences of language 2? More concretely,

> [D]oes someone who says that the broom is in the corner really mean: the broomstick is there, and so is the brush, and the broomstick is fixed in the brush? (PI, #60)

Of course, the person may have no such thought in mind when he says that the broom is in the corner and he may feel, *quite rightly*, that this is a very roundabout way of speaking of a broom. It might even turn out that our ability to grasp the point of an order in 2 would depend upon our prior understanding of 1: that is, we would only see the point of a remark about sticks and brushes when we recognized that it was *brooms* that were being discussed.

Here the correct thing to say is that 1 and 2 are language-games that intersect in various ways. By stipulation, every remark in 1 has a counterpart in 2, but not conversely. Yet this does not show that the counterparts in 2 offer an analysis of the respective sentences in 1, for a person could command the concepts of 1 without having any grasp—not even an implicit grasp—of the concepts in 2. Furthermore, as different language games, 1 and 2 will differ in the aspects of a situation that they can represent perspicuously. And it is not true that 2 will always have the advantage in this. Using 1 we might say that there are three more chairs in this room than tables; imagine what this will look like in its counterpart version in 2. Through attending to examples of this kind, we will give up the idea that understanding a language like 1 must always involve a (tacit) understanding of a language like 2. This amounts to rejecting the quest for analysis as it was understood during the heyday of logical atomism.

Yet it should also be added that Wittgenstein seems to have a one-sided view of the character and purpose of logical analysis. Analysis as he views (and rejects) it is an attempt to discover referential simples, i.e., it is an attempt to discover some set of entities upon which all reference ultimately depends. But the great achievements in analysis have not been of this kind. The task of analysis is not to break down content but to exhibit form. Though still disputed, Russell's theory of definite descriptions performed this service, as did Wittgenstein's truth-functional analysis of sentential connectives. We might, then, distinguish analysis with ontological motives from analysis with logical motives, even though the two can easily become involved with one another. The main target of Wittgenstein's criticism is the drive toward an ultimate ontological analysis. At times, his impatience toward this activity carried over to attempts at logical analysis. This tendency in Wittgenstein became—for a while at least—a defining characteristic of many of his followers and produced two decades of exchanges with logicians that were grandly at cross-purposes.

9
Family resemblance

"You take the easy way out." These words introduce one of the most discussed features of his later philosophy: the notion of family resemblance. He imagines someone complaining that he has gone on and on about language-games but has never said what a language-game is. He has, therefore, yet to explain the essence of language. Wittgenstein acknowledges this:

> Instead of producing something common to all that we call language, I am saying that these phenomena have no one thing in common which makes us use the same word for all,—but that they are *related* to one another in many different ways. And it is because of this relationship or these relationships, that we call them all "language." (PI, #65)

Wittgenstein's first illustration concerns games themselves. Now instead of deciding in advance that there *must* be something common to all games in virtue of which they are games, Wittgenstein recommends that you look and see. If you do:

> [Y]ou will not see something that is common to *all*, but similarities, relationships, and a whole series of them at that. To repeat: don't think, but look! (PI, #66)

Here Wittgenstein makes a straightforward statement of fact: if we examine those things we call games, we will not find any single property in virtue of which they are called games; instead we find that they are grouped together by a whole series of overlapping similarities. We can give a crude representation of this idea using the following diagram:

O_1	O_2	O_3	O_4	O_5	O_6
A	B	C	D	E	F
B	C	D	E	F	A
C	D	E	F	A	B
D	E	F	A	B	C

O_1 through O_6 represent a set of objects; the letters represent properties they possess. Here each object shares three features with two others in the group, but there is no single feature that runs through the lot. This is a tame representation of what Wittgenstein has in mind when he says that our examination of games will show "a complicated network of similarities overlapping and crisscrossing: sometimes overall similarities, sometimes similarities of detail" (PI, #66). Wittgenstein characterizes these similarities as "family resemblances" (PI, #67).

A more interesting example of such a family is the number system.

And for instance the kinds of number form a family. . . . Why do we call something a "number"? Well, perhaps because it has a—direct—relationship with several things that have hitherto been called number; and this can be said to give it an indirect relationship to other things we call the same name. (PI, #67)[14]

We can imagine someone admitting that the notion of a game is vague and ambiguous in the ways that Wittgenstein indicates, but not see any reason to make a fuss over it. Here, however, vagueness is not at issue. The cardinal numbers, the rational numbers, the real numbers, etc., are each well defined—that is, each extension of the number system is carried out with rigor. What is not well defined, or better, what is not the subject of definition at all, is the extension of the concept that might take place in the future. Wittgenstein makes the point this way in the *Philosophische Grammatik*:

Compare the concept of a number on one hand and the concept of a cardinal number on the other with the concept of a proposition. We consider the cardinal numbers, the rational numbers, the irrational numbers, and complex numbers as numbers; whether we call still other constructions numbers because of their similarity with these, or wish to draw a definitive boundary here or elsewhere, is up to us. In this way, the concept of a number is analogous to the concept of a proposition. In contrast, we call the concept of a cardinal number $[1, \xi, \xi +1]$ rigorously well defined, that means it is a concept in a different sense of the word. (PG, 70)[15]

This allusion to the Tractarian definition of a cardinal number brings out the differences between Wittgenstein's early and later views in a striking way. During the Tractarian period, Wittgenstein modeled his account of language, that is, his account of the general propositional form, on the definition of a cardinal number—indeed, the format of his definition of the general propositional form mimics the format of the definition of the cardinal numbers. In his later writings it is the non-technical notion of a number which is open-ended and not sharply defined that becomes a model of how most of our language functions.

Wittgenstein hammers away at this preconception that for a concept to be usable, it must be precisely determined by a system of rules. For Wittgenstein, even proper names can lack determinate meaning.

We may say, following Russell: the name "Moses" can be defined by means of various descriptions. For example, as "the man who led the Israelites through the wilderness", "the man who lived at that time and place and was then called 'Moses' ", "the man who as a child was taken out of the Nile by Pharaoh's daughter" and so on. (PI, #79)[16]

So, if someone asks me who I mean by "Moses," I will give him such a description. But research might show that any one of these facts concerning Moses did not obtain. Would I then say that Moses did not, after all, exist? The answer to this, of course, is no; I will simply say that one of the things that I previously believed about Moses is not true. But wasn't "Moses" defined, at least in part, as a person possessing this trait that I am no longer willing to attribute to him? Well perhaps he was, but now the burden of definition has shifted to other traits that I am still willing to attribute to him. We can say that the individual concept associated with the name "Moses" is both overdetermined and underspecified. It is overdetermined in the sense that there is a super-abundance of descriptive information available for a definition, but underdetermined since no one set of these characteristics has been actually specified as definitive. Furthermore, what we *would* offer as a definition might change from one circumstance to another:

> And this can be expressed like this: I use the name "N" without a *fixed* meaning. (But that detracts as little from its usefulness, as it detracts from that of a table that stands on four legs instead of three and so sometimes wobbles.) (PI, #79)[17]

In #80 Wittgenstein offers an example of a quite different way that the application of a concept need not be bounded by sharply defined rules. Suppose I call something a chair, but when I go to fetch it, it disappears. With this I decide that my original judgment was in error, only to find that the chair now reappears and I am able to sit in it, etc. We can imagine such strange events continuing indefinitely. Here I am not trying to decide whether I am dealing with a chair rather than, say, a stool; I am trying to decide whether I am dealing with a *real* chair rather than an *illusory* chair.

> Have you rules ready for such cases—rules saying whether one may use the word "chair" to include this kind of thing? But do we miss them when we use the word "chair"; and are we to say that we do not really attach any meaning to this word, because we are not equipped with rules for every possible application of it? (PI, #80)

Wittgenstein expects a negative answer to these rhetorical questions.

Finally, the feeling can persist—and it certainly dominated Wittgenstein's thought when writing the *Tractatus*—that an indefinite sense would not be a sense *at all*. This would be like locking a man in a room but leaving one of the doors unlocked—again we seem to have done nothing at all. "An enclosure with a hole in it is as good as *none*" (PI, #99). "But," Wittgenstein asks, "is this true?" (PI, #99). Of course it is not true, for we can imagine locking just those doors that the person will try first and thereby discouraging him, etc. (There is a way for the fly to get out of the flybottle, but it rarely does.) In the same way, our concepts are not secured against every possible contingency (if it makes sense to speak of *every* possible contingency). Nor do we have settled rules to deal with those cases which we can easily imagine (Wittgenstein's chair disappearing). It is just a brute fact that the application of most of our concepts is not sharply bounded by rules. They are no less concepts for this fact. Nor are they, by this fact alone, any less serviceable. Sometimes a loosely defined concept is just what we need; sometimes it is not. These questions are settled within the context in which concepts find employment.

Here we can give a further characterization of the difference between Wittgenstein's early and later views about language. Throughout his philosophical career Wittgenstein recognized that our actual language seems wholly lacking in the purity and rigor the logician demands. In the Tractarian period he discounted this vagueness, ambiguity, indeterminacy, etc., and argued that this logically pure structure must somehow underlie our everyday language. Language, that is our everyday language, disguises thought. It takes a man of great insight, a logician, to tell us what we really mean. In the *Investigations*, Wittgenstein takes this vagueness, indeterminacy and ambiguity as revealing the structure of thought itself.

> The more narrowly we examine actual language, the sharper becomes the conflict between it and our requirement. (For the crystalline purity of logic was, of course, not a *result of investigation:* it was a requirement.) (PI, #107)
> We see that what we call "sentence" and "language" has not the formal unity that I imagined, but is the family of structures more or less related to one another. (PI, #108)

10
Comments on family resemblance

I do not think it is possible to offer an *a priori* critique of Wittgenstein's notion of family resemblance for, after all, the question is essentially factual: Do many of the concepts of our everyday language function as Wittgenstein says they do? This question gains philosophical significance when we ask whether such notions as game, number, statement, deriving, etc., each encompasses a family of cases with no common feature running through each family. Here we can only look and see, and in general, I seem to see what Wittgenstein says he sees.

Even so, I think that the notion of family resemblance is peculiarly susceptible to abuse and therefore should be used circumspectly. Let me illustrate this with a case where, to my mind, Wittgenstein himself goes badly wrong. In #77 he discusses the possibility of drawing sharp rectangles corresponding to vague ones. He remarks, quite correctly, that "several such sharply defined rectangles can be drawn to correspond to the indefinite one." He continues in these words:

> But if the colours in the original merge without a hint of any outline won't it become a hopeless task to draw a sharp picture corresponding. to the blurred one? Won't you then have to say: "Here I might just as well draw a circle or heart as a rectangle, for all the colours merge. Anything—and nothing—is right."—And this is the position you are in if you look for definitions corresponding to our concepts in aesthetics or ethics. (PI, #77)

Here I am interested in the (almost casual) application of these ideas to the "concepts in aesthetics and ethics." We can first notice an assumption embodied in the closing sentence of this passage: concepts of aesthetics and ethics function descriptively just as the concept of being red functions descriptively. A distinctive feature of these concepts, however, is that they are radically polytypic, i.e., they specify classes containing subclasses of wildly divergent kinds with no clear relationships between them. Over against Moore, Wittgenstein is saying that it is the hyper-complexity—rather than the utter simplicity—of these notions that makes them incapable of definition.

In contrast with this position it has been argued that evaluative expressions do not function descriptively. Suppose that the *Oxford English Dictionary* is right in saying that the term "good" is our "most general adjective of commendation." Now if the *Oxford English Dictionary* has correctly explained the use of this term then, for Wittgenstein, it has, *eo ipso*, explained its meaning. We do, of course, commend things for all sorts of *reasons*, and these reasons themselves probably constitute a family as diverse in its membership and as indistinct in its structure as the analogy in #77 suggests. Yet this does not show that the term "good" is itself vague or ambiguous. Indeed, if the *Oxford English Dictionary* is correct, its meaning is *relatively* clear-cut as opposed, for example, to the meanings of such words as "game" and "furniture."

Above I have used the phrase "if the *Oxford English Dictionary* is correct," but the point I am making does not depend upon the authority of that venerable work. The point is systematic. The notion of family resemblance has its most natural application to descriptive terms. The troublesome feature of the notion of family resemblance is that if we make a mistake in treating an expression as descriptive when it is not, a commitment to the doctrine of family resemblance will help to conceal and thus perpetuate this mistake. One can adopt a very naive referential view about the way such words as "good," "real," "know," "true," etc.

function and then protect the position by invoking a sophisticated theory of family resemblance. Wittgenstein, it seems, was not immune to this error. Admittedly, I am leaning very hard on a single passage in the *Investigations*, and it was Wittgenstein himself who called attention to the dangers of misunderstanding the role of the "odd job words" in our language (*Blue Book*, pp. 43–4). Still, misused, the doctrine of family resemblance can help to perpetuate the misunderstanding of these "odd job words."

In the end, I think that the notion of family resemblance has two chief virtues. (i) It helps dispel the commitment to definiteness of sense by exhibiting a set of concepts that violate this standard but are still perfectly serviceable. We have seen in studying the *Tractatus* that this demand for definiteness of sense was a driving force that led away from everyday language as it actually appears to the postulation of a sublime structure that underlies it. Wittgenstein was hardly alone in accepting this demand. (ii) Somewhat differently, recognizing the existence of family resemblance classes will lead us to abandon the idea that definitions, of the standard kind, are always possible and, if we are doing things right, actually necessary for the systematic development of a subject matter. Sometimes such a quest is out of place, and when it is pursued in these cases, it can seem that we are dealing with issues of the greatest profundity, instead of not dealing with an issue at all. At the same time, the doctrine of family resemblance does not leave us with nothing to do; instead it invites us to trace out relationships, and this should be done with whatever degree of rigor the subject matter allows.

11
Wittgenstein's treatment of proper names

Early in the *Investigations* Wittgenstein attacks the view that the meaning of a term is the object it stands for. This, he says, is to confuse the meaning of a word with its bearer (#40). Earlier I remarked that the position under attack should not be confused with another that has a wholly different tendency. This other view, which is associated with J. S. Mill, is that the function of a proper name is to refer to (pick out) an object and, as such, it has no meaning or no meaning beyond this. I do not think that Wittgenstein ever examines this position explicitly and there seems to be no reason—given his general orientation—why he could not adopt it. In fact, however, he seems to adopt a position incompatible with it. This comes out in the passage already cited where he is discussing the meaning of the proper name "Moses:"

> We may say, following Russell: the name "Moses" can be defined by means of various descriptions. (PI, #79)

Thus when I assert something about Moses, I am, in effect, saying that such-and-such a person having such-and-such features did such-and-such. But this view presents problems. For example, whatever facts we might cite in explaining whom we mean by "Moses," we could absorb the discovery that one of these facts did not obtain without, for that reason, being forced to say that Moses did not exist. As we saw, Wittgenstein's solution to this problem is to treat the defining traits of Moses as a loose family where many clusters of traits can take over the role of defining characteristics as the occasion demands. In recent years, John Searle has been the chief proponent of this view and for his troubles has been the main target of the attacks by philosophers who wish to reject it.[17]

What exactly is wrong with the idea that a proper name can be defined by means of a set of descriptions (either loosely or strictly specified)? I think that the core of the matter, as expressed by Saul Kripke, is that when I speak, say, about Nixon, I am speaking about *Nixon* and I am not presenting an abbreviated description under which (I hope) a certain thing falls. There really isn't much of an argument here, but rather an assumption, to use David Kaplan's word, that there is something transparently "fishy" about treating proper names as disguised descriptions. That is, no one would be inclined to hold such a view unless it seemed the *only* plausible way of giving an account of how proper names function. The most obvious question about names is how a particular name is related to the thing it names. Under the disguised description account, the thing named is just that thing (if any) that uniquely satisfies the description corresponding to the name. Recently, as an alternative to this, it has been suggested that the relationship between a name and the thing named is actually *causal or historical*. Very roughly, a name becomes the name of a thing through a historical act of dubbing. The use of the name to name just this object is then preserved as it is passed along from language user to language user. We thus get the result that a person who now speaks about Moses may do so even though he may be very hesitant about attributing a single trait to him. His use of the word "Moses" is connected to the man Moses through the historical transmission going back to an act of dubbing. Of course, the person who uses the name "Moses" to refer to Moses need not know anything about these historical facts of transmission. It is as a member of a historical tradition—not as a historian of that tradition—that the words we use inherit their reference.[18]

Here two questions naturally present themselves: (i) who is right, Wittgenstein-Searle on one side or Donnellan-Geach-Kripke, etc., on the other; and (ii) for the purposes of investigating the fundamental features of Wittgenstein's later philosophy, how much does it matter who is right? With respect to the first question, I confess that I am not sure what I wish to say,[19] but regarding the second question, it seems to me clear that it will not matter much—with respect to the fundamental features of Wittgenstein's later philosophy—how this first question is answered. Let me explain.

Here we must attend to the main thrust of Wittgenstein's remarks about proper names. Adopting the Russellian standpoint, he treats proper names as definable by a set of descriptions. His main point is that these descriptions do not form a fixed and well-defined set. Could he have made the same point in the causal-historical frameworks sketched above? The point that Wittgenstein is insisting upon is that we do not always (or even usually) use words under the governance of strict rules. Now according to the causal-historical theory, we can use proper names to refer to individuals because we are inheritors of a referring tradition. But suppose we look at that tradition itself, say, with respect to the name "Moses." How clear-cut are the rules governing the employment of this name? Is it even always clear whether a reference is historical rather than story-relative? The answer is surely no. Wittgenstein's discussion of proper names occurs in a context where he is attacking the idea that our everyday use of language is modeled (or should be modeled) after the strict rules of a logical calculus. He chose to preach this sermon within the context of a Russellian account of proper names (I suppose because he found it compelling); it could have been presented as easily within the context of this alternative account of proper names.

Perhaps I have spent too much time on this particular issue, for if I am right, it does not take us very deeply into Wittgenstein's later thought. Yet recent developments in this area are often viewed as decisive steps against speech act theory, ordinary language philosophy, and in back of this all, Wittgenstein. To ignore these developments might give the impression, however faulty, of having dodged basic issues.

12
Some remarks on philosophy

The critique of the *Tractatus* is capped—and I think brought to a close—by a series of aphorisms concerning philosophy. Wittgenstein has shown, in a variety of ways, that our language is not everywhere bound by strict rules, senses need not be definite, concepts need not have essences associated with them, etc. All this goes deeply against the Tractarian standpoint which he portrays in these words:

> The strict and clear rules of the logical structure of propositions
> appear to us as something in the background—hidden in the
> medium of the understanding. I already see them (even though

through a medium): for I understand that propositional sign, I use it to say something. (PI, #102)

This ideal of strict and clear rules of logical structure was not something discovered—*a result of investigation*—instead it was one of the requirements of investigation (PI, #107). This ideal becomes unshakeable. "It is like a pair of glasses on our nose through which we see whatever we look at. It never occurs to us to take them off" (PI, #103).

Why does a philosopher adopt this *particular* standpoint—put on this *particular* pair of glasses? I don't think Wittgenstein answers this question, but he does speak in general of the way philosophizing can arise and maintain itself. Impressed by a certain feature of language, we elevate it to the status of a model for the description of all language. We become absorbed in certain similes and distort phenomena to fit under them. The grammar of our language is of little help because it lacks the kind of *perspicuity* needed to expose and block the assimilation of diverse cases (PI, #122). Nor do the constraints of the everyday employment of these notions come to our aid, for "the confusions which occupy us arise when language is like an engine idling, not when it is doing work" (PI, #132). This echoes an earlier remark that "philosophical problems arise when language goes on holiday" (PI, #38). But if this is how philosophical problems arise, their solution must reverse this direction:

> When philosophers use a word—"knowledge", "being", "object", "I", "proposition", "name"—and try to grasp the *essence* of the thing, one must always ask oneself: is the word ever actually used in this way in the language-game which is its original home?
>
> What *we* do is to bring words back from their metaphysical to their everyday use. (PI, #116)

Here the following question naturally arises: "Suppose the philosopher's use does not agree with the everyday use of a term, why should that make any difference? Why should the everyday use of a word be made legislative for all uses? Everyday language has not proved adequate for the sciences; why should things be different for philosophy?" These questions are, in fact, misconceived. Wittgenstein recognizes that the advance of science often demands the regimentation of everyday language and, beyond this, the development of a technical vocabulary. These developments within the language are the results of demands at a given stage of inquiry. But the philosopher's departures from everyday discourse are different, and this difference is, for Wittgenstein, definitive of the philosophical enterprise. The philosopher's departure from everyday language does not extend a practice; it is a flight from practice. When the philosopher abandons the everyday practice that gives a word its meaning, he puts no other practice in its place.

But why shouldn't the philosopher's departure from everyday language constitute a distinctively philosophical use of a word which is itself embedded in a philosophical practice or philosophical language-game? The answer to this, I think, is that Wittgenstein believes that the distinctively philosophical use of a word just is its employment detached from any particular practice. Of course, putting matters this way merely begs the question. It also gets Wittgenstein's enterprise out of focus. It is important to see that Wittgenstein's aim in the *Investigations* is not to establish some such general thesis as that philosophical problems arise when language goes on holiday. Wittgenstein is not writing a natural history of philosophy even if some of his remarks contribute to such a project. The investigation is focused on particular philosophical problems, and it is these problems which have come down in the tradition that give Wittgenstein's remarks their significance.

> It was true to say that our considerations could not be scientific ones. . . . And we may not advance any kind of theory. There must not be anything hypothetical in our considerations. We must do away with all *explanation*, and description alone must take its place. And this description gets its light, that is to say its purpose, from the philosophical problems. . . . The problems are solved, not by giving new information, but by arranging what we have always known. (PI, #109)

Of course, someone might wish to establish a general thesis about the nature of philosophizing that exhibits Wittgenstein's remarks about philosophy as *empirical* truths. This would involve the formulation of hypotheses about particular philosophers and gathering data to test these hypotheses. To repeat, there is no reason why this could not be done, but this is not the form that Wittgenstein's inquiries take. Wittgenstein's remarks are given their focus and their significance from the philosophical problems that call them forth. I think, therefore, it best to treat the general pronouncements on philosophy as *regulative ideas* for the treatment of these problems.

Once we recognize that Wittgenstein's problems are philosophical rather than *meta*-philosophical we can understand why he finds the search for explanation out of place. For Wittgenstein, philosophical problems are not genuine problems: they present nothing to be solved, nothing upon which an explanatory hypothesis can be brought to bear. A philosophical investigation should respond directly to a philosophical problem by exposing its roots and removing it:

> For the clarity that we are aiming at is indeed *complete* clarity. But this simply means that the philosophical problems should *completely* disappear.

The real discovery is the one that makes me capable of stopping doing philosophy when I want to. (PI, #133)

When Wittgenstein says that the real discovery allows us to stop doing philosophy when we want to, he doesn't simply mean that it allows us to stop doing traditional philosophy; he means that it allows us to stop doing philosophy altogether. If his philosophical investigations gain their significance from the traditional philosophical problems that call them forth, then they lose their significance when these problems "completely disappear."

Wittgenstein's approach, then, is not only destructive but self-destructive. This is reminiscent of the *Tractatus* which concludes with the image—drawn from Sextus Empiricus—that his work is like a ladder which must be thrown away after one has climbed up it (TLP, 6.54). There is a better image—also found in Sextus Empiricus—characterizing the method of the *Philosophical Investigations:*

[A]perient drugs do not merely eliminate the humours from the body, but also expel themselves along with the humours.[20]

I shall return to this comparison between Wittgenstein's later philosophy and traditional scepticism in the final chapter of this work, but here it is enough to say that, if I am right in suggesting that Wittgenstein's primary concern was first-order philosophical problems and their elimination, then his general pronouncements on philosophy should be taken as regulative ideas and, perhaps, only after-the-fact musings. In any case, Wittgenstein offers no explicit defense of these statements, so there are no arguments here to evaluate. Their worth will only emerge in their application, and that means we must return to the detailed discussions in the text.

X

Understanding

1
Introduction

In #138 Wittgenstein turns from his attack upon Tractarian themes to consider a criticism of his own identification (or near identification) of meaning with use:

> But we *understand* the meaning of a word when we hear or say it; we grasp it in a flash, and what we grasp in this way is surely different from the "use" which is extended in time! (PI, #138)

It is important to see that Wittgenstein here recognizes a genuine phenomenon: we do sometimes grasp the meaning of a word in a flash or, all at once, recognize how a series can be continued. This quite naturally suggests that understanding the meaning of a word (or understanding in general) is a mental state that can be attained at a given time and, furthermore, we can recognize ourselves (at that time) as attaining it.

To take a simple example, what comes before my mind when I understand the meaning of the word "cube"? Perhaps an image appears—in particular, an image of a cube. But what makes this image an image of a cube? This may seem an idle question until we remind ourselves that it is possible (and usually easy) to think of alternative methods of projection for a given figure. In this way, the picture of a cube might also be taken as a picture of a triangular prism (PI, #139). So the occurrence of a particular image does not settle the question of meaning.

> What is essential is to see that the same thing can come before our minds when we hear the word and the application still be different. Has it the *same* meaning both times? I think we shall say not. (PI, #130)

Wittgenstein will ring endless changes on this simple argument, showing time and again that a change in the context of application can yield a change in meaning, and therefore meaning cannot be identified with anything independent of the context of application.

2
"Now I can go on!"

We can next consider a richer case of understanding. A teacher is instructing a student in the decimal notation. We can imagine how this instruction proceeds. First the teacher helps the student write out the numbers 0 through 9. The student is then expected to repeat this on his own. How the instruction will continue will depend upon the student's responses. The normal student will make some mistakes which the instructor corrects. We can also imagine a student whose replies are so utterly random that they give the instructor no purchase for the further shaping of responses. If this persists, the instruction will be terminated and the student declared a mathematical incompetent. We can also imagine the instruction continuing in the normal way until the student masters the number system completely and can count on indefinitely.

Now what has happened as the student passes from not understanding the number system to understanding it? I think Wittgenstein's answer is that *we have just told you:* a training of a given sort takes place, etc., etc. But there is a feeling that there must be more to understanding than this; actual counting is merely a *manifestation* of this understanding. This is right in one way: a person can count correctly and still not understand counting, and people who do understand counting sometimes miscount. We can imagine a person learning the first 637 numbers by rote. This would be a remarkable achievement, but still, the person would not know how to count. On the other side, a person who does know how to count can make a great many mistakes, especially in a distracting setting.

So there is more to counting than doing something in conformity with a rule, or mere conformity to a rule seems too external to amount to *understanding* how to count. This much is a platitude; the issue here is what construction to put on this platitude. Since we see a need for something *more*, one temptation is to posit a mental state and then say that the person genuinely knows how to count when his performance proceeds from this mental state. But simply positing such a mental state is no help; Wittgenstein puts the criticism this way:

> But there is an objection to speaking of a state of mind here, inasmuch as there ought to be two different criteria for such a state: a

knowledge of the construction of the apparatus, quite apart from what it does. (PI, #149)

But isn't this unfair? The person who explains understanding by saying that it is a consequence of being in a particular mental state is not *positing* anything, he is reporting a plain matter of fact. To move to another example, I am shown a sequence of numbers and asked which number comes next. After a moment I grasp the principle of the series and announce, "Now I can go on!" Here it seems that understanding has occurred at a particular moment in time, and my remark reports this.

Wittgenstein's response to this example moves through two stages. (i) He will first argue that nothing that occurs at the time of this report can guarantee understanding, and therefore understanding is not some state that the utterance "Now I can go on!" reports. (ii) What, then, does such an utterance report? Wittgenstein answers that this first-person utterance is not a report at all. As we shall see, this approach is characteristic of Wittgenstein's treatment of first-person psychological utterances.

Let us imagine some of the things that might take place when the student suddenly feels he can go on. Perhaps a formula occurs to him; or he notices that the numbers increase by a simple principle (e.g., 2, 4, 6, etc.); or the sequence is one with which he is familiar (the sequence of primes or Fibonacci sequence); or he just gets a feel for the sequence. The point that Wittgenstein makes—and it is utterly simple—is that any of these things could occur and, for all that, the person might still not understand the sequence.

> But are the processes which I have described here *understanding?*
>
> "B understands the principle of the series" surely doesn't mean simply: the formula "$a_n = \ldots$" occurs to B. For it is perfectly imaginable that the formula should occur to him and that he should nevertheless not understand. "He understands" must have more in it than: the formula occurs to him. And equally, more than any of those more or less characteristic *accompaniments* or manifestations of understanding. (PI, #152)

We have no trouble imagining any one of these things happening and yet, when the test is made, the person cannot continue the sequence of numbers correctly. In most cases, though not all, this would lead us to say that the person did not know how to continue the sequence. A qualification is needed here to cover bizarre cases of the following kind: a mathematician looks at a sequence of numbers and sees at once that it is the sequence of Fibonacci numbers. "I know that one," he declares, but before he has a chance to show this he becomes deranged and proceeds to write down numbers randomly. If we know that the derangement set in after he made his declaration, we would probably acknowledge that he did know how to go on, only he lost the ability before he had a chance to exhibit it. I take it that it is obvious why we would say this. The point, then, that Wittgenstein is making is that nothing occurring at the time of a performance shows that it is done with understanding; instead, we must appeal to the circumstances that surround the action to settle this question.

Here it is important to distinguish Wittgenstein's considerations from sceptical doubts of a wholly general kind. No matter how far the student continues the sequence correctly, we can imagine developments that will convince us that he did not really understand what he was doing. But just because we can imagine ourselves doubting, this does not mean that we are now in doubt or even that we *should* be in doubt.[1] Given the normal background of training and the exhibition of a quality performance, we say that a person understands (or knows) how to count. There are, of course, no fixed boundaries to the concept of a "normal background of training" nor any fixed standards for the quality of a performance. (And we will encounter cases where we are at a loss to say whether we are dealing with a case of understanding or not.) Wittgenstein, of course, finds nothing surprising—and nothing objectionable—about this. So Wittgenstein is not arguing that appeals to mental states are of no use because they fail to rule out the abstract possibility that conformity to a rule is merely accidental, for *nothing* can rule out that abstract possibility. It is always a mistake to try to secure a special advantage by appealing to sceptical arguments of this general kind. I do not think that Wittgenstein makes this mistake—at least in this argument. Instead, he uses a perfectly familiar pattern of argument: we cannot identify x with y, for the criteria for identifying y are quite independent of the occurrence of x. We cannot identify understanding with being in any particular mental state, for the criteria establishing understanding (which concern success in application) are quite independent of being in any particular mental state.

3

Deriving

A feeling can persist that Wittgenstein's criticisms are unfair. The person who cites the occurrence of a formula in explaining how she understands isn't suggesting that it consists of nothing more than having a formula flit through her mind. She claims to understand because she uses the formula as the basis for the steps she takes; she *derives* these steps from the formula. So it is this mental act of deriving that is crucial to a correct account of understanding.

Wittgenstein explores this topic by examining the process of deriving spoken words from a printed text. To simplify the example, he ignores the sense of these spoken words: the envisioned person acts as a kind of reading machine. Replaying the familiar argument, Wittgenstein first notices that we cannot distinguish reading from non-reading (say from pretending to read) by an appeal to any state of consciousness:

> [W]e have to admit that—as far as concerns uttering any *one* of the printed words—the same thing may take place in the consciousness of the pupil who is "pretending" to read, as in that of the practiced reader who is "reading" it. (PI, #156)

Wittgenstein gives the argument a nice turn by imagining someone reading from a page, but under the influence of a drug that generates all the characteristic feelings of pretending to read (PI, #160). Even though the person himself might not agree, he would, nonetheless, be reading.

But to turn to the matter of *deriving*, isn't it obvious that the difference between the person who reads and a person who only pretends to read is that the former derives what he says from the text, whereas the latter does not? I do not think that Wittgenstein wishes to deny that in reading we must derive the spoken words from the text whereas in pretending to read we need not do this. The issue here is whether deriving supplies the wanted key to understanding.

To make our example simpler, suppose we give someone a table showing which cursive letters correspond to printed letters. He then copies printed texts in cursive letters using the table to guide him. Here, surely, he derives the one sort of letter from the other. We can, however, imagine various things happening:

1 He makes the transcription in the way expected—reading the table straight across.
2 He reads the table at an angle, putting down a cursive B for a printed A, etc.
3 He uses a variety of rules, changing them (perhaps systematically, perhaps unsystematically) as he goes along. At some point we will say that he is no longer deriving the cursive letters from the printed letters, but, of course, there is no particular point where this change occurs.

Here Wittgenstein asks rhetorically whether this shows that the word "to derive" has no meaning (PI, #163). Of course it does not show this. What it does show is that the word "to derive"—and similarly the word "to read"—apply to a family of cases (PI, #164).

What is this entire discussion intended to establish? We look at particular cases of deriving and find them unproblematic, but too particular—too special—for our theoretical purposes. Surely it cannot be essential to deriving that I run my finger across a table in a certain way. So I look at other instances of deriving in the hope of finding the common element essential to deriving. These hopes are not fulfilled. In a particular case:

> [T]he meaning of the word "to derive" stood out clearly. But we told ourselves that this was only a quite special case of deriving; deriving in a quite special garb, which had to be stripped from it if we wanted to see the essence of deriving. So we stripped those particular coverings off; but then deriving itself disappeared. (PI, #164)

I think that this is an important passage in revealing the deep philosophical significance that Wittgenstein attached to the notion of family resemblance. We feel that deriving cannot just be a matter of undergoing a certain training, running our fingers across a chart, and then writing things down, for it is easy to think of cases of deriving where all of these specific activities are lacking. But if we are dealing with one special case out of a group of others, then we want to say there must be some underlying general characterization which each of these special cases exemplifies. This, of course, is precisely what Wittgenstein wishes to deny. We think that our description has missed the essential element of deriving when we discover that every item in our description is non-essential for deriving. We thus think that a further (and deeper) description is necessary. But if we acknowledge that instances of deriving form a family of cases, then we realize that the more that is needed is not a further (and deeper) description of individual cases, but rather a comparison of cases that all lie at the same level.

4
Experiencing the because

Like Hume, Wittgenstein turns the example of reading on *every side* looking for the supposed essential element that runs through all its instances. Don't words come in a special way when I am reading, in a way that is different from the way that they come when I am making them up? When I am reading, the words come automatically (PI, #165). But this will hardly do as the characterization of the essential element in reading. Wittgenstein suggests that we look at an arbitrary scribble and let a sound occur to us; this sound may also occur automatically.

But haven't we ignored the most obvious feature of reading? When we read, the word shapes somehow *cause* our utterance. Wittgenstein's response to this suggestion (and the discussion that follows) reveals one of the fundamental aspects of his later philosophy:

> Causation is surely something established by experiments, by observing a regular concomitance of events for example. So how

149

could I say that I *felt* something which is established by experiment? (PI, #169)

Here Wittgenstein confidently invokes some conception of causality, but it is not clear what that conception is or why he should be so confident about it. Presumably he has something of the following sort in mind: when I make a singular causal judgment (e.g., *these* word shapes caused me to say such and such a word), I am invoking a general law that covers like cases. This general law can only be established through tests covering a number of cases. How these tests come out is not something that can be felt in a particular case. This does not mean that Wittgenstein accepts a regularity theory of causal statements—although he may hold such a view. We need only attribute to him the view that a singular causal statement has implications for other like cases, and, this being so, a singular causal statement cannot be established solely through reference to an individual case.[2] Although none of this is worked out in detail, the views expressed here seem an echo of the views earlier expressed in the *Tractatus:*

> 5.1361 We *cannot* infer the events of the future from those of the present.
>   Belief in the causal nexus is *superstition.*

A person who claims to be aware of (or able to feel) a causal relation, apparently accepts some version of the causal nexus theory. It is not clear what Wittgenstein holds affirmatively about causal relations, but it does seem clear that on this issue at least, Wittgenstein did not depart from the view expressed in the *Tractatus.*

The idea that the word shapes are the cause of my utterances can be expressed in different ways. For example, I can say (quite correctly!) that in reading I am *guided* by the words. This leads Wittgenstein to consider the phenomenon of being guided, and, once more, he discovers only a family of interrelated cases.

> "But being guided is surely a particular experience!"—The answer to this is: you are now *thinking* of a particular experience of being guided. (PI, #173)

But the descriptions we give of particular instances of being guided seem to us unsatisfactory. Wittgenstein suggests that we make an arbitrary doodle and then make a copy of it. Let us suppose that we have done this; we would hardly hesitate in saying that we used the one figure as a guide for drawing the other.

> But now notice this: *while* I am being guided everything is quite simple, I notice nothing *special;* but afterwards, when I ask myself what it was that happened, it seems to have been something

indescribable. *Afterwards* no description satisfies me. It's as if I couldn't believe that I merely looked, made such-and-such a face, and drew a line. (PI, #175)

What I find hard to believe is that my being guided consisted in *nothing more* than my doing various things in a given context, for the things I notice seem accidental—things that are often absent in other cases of being guided:

> When I look back upon the experience I have the feeling that what is essential about it is an "experience of being influenced," of a connexion—as opposed to any mere simultaneity of phenomena . . . I should like to say that I had experienced the *"because"* and yet I do not want to call any phenomenon the "experience of the because." (PI, #176)

Wilfrid Sellars once remarked to me that the final sentence in this passage goes to the heart of Wittgenstein's later thought. What I am seeking is the "experience of the because" but nothing, it seems, will count as such an experience. I think that Sellars was right in giving prominence to this passage, but Wittgenstein's precise intentions are hardly clear. The dominating theme that leads up to this claim is that cases of being influenced (or being guided, etc.) form only a family of cases where no characteristic of a given case is essential to being influenced, etc. This might suggest that "experiencing the because" also forms only a family of cases with no essential property running through all the cases. But this is not what Wittgenstein says: we are not embarrassed by a superabundance of ways we experience the because; we do not want to count *anything* as an instance of experiencing the because.

It is time to drop the curious phrase "experiencing the because" and attempt to replace it with a more idiomatic expression. Suppose someone asks why I am writing a series of Fs across a piece of paper. I tell him that I am learning italic script and practicing the letter F. I look at the instruction manual and attempt to imitate the model for the letter F. I write the letter F in the way that I do *because* it is presented in a certain way in the manual. Here various things can take place. I examine the letter in the manual—perhaps tracing over it with my pen; I then do my best to imitate this letter in my own hand. Various experiences take place: I examine the letter in the manual; I examine the letters I have written; I notice various similarities and disparities between them. There is no question that here I am being *guided* by the letter in the manual. I form the letters the way I do *because* the letter in the manual is formed the way it is. All kinds of experiences take place during this activity, but the question at issue is whether any experience corresponds to writing-the-letter-in-a-certain-way-because-it-is-presented-in-a-certain-way-in-the-manual. Wittgenstein says that the answer to this question is no. If we tell a story of being guided, there seems to be no item in that story that we are willing to identify specifically as *the* event of being guided.

Now *why* does Wittgenstein take this line? Is he appealing to experience? Is he saying that he has examined various cases of being guided but has never found an experience corresponding to doing something because of something else? His phrasing sometimes suggests such an appeal, but arguing in this way is not characteristic of his usual style. In fact, I think that *no* argument is to be found that supports this fundamental commitment. At every stage of his career, Wittgenstein was committed to the radical contingency of the world as it is presented to us. In the Tractarian period, the distribution of atomic facts in logical space was wholly brute and inexplicable. Yet the logical space in which these atomic facts were embedded formed a coherent and internally related system. With the loss of this underlying crystaline structure, we are left with only the brute and inexplicable system of facts in the world. We arrive at the doctrine of radical contingency by subtracting the necessary underlying structure from the Tractarian world view. This, I think, is the general standpoint of Wittgenstein's later philosophy. I don't think Wittgenstein ever defends this standpoint; instead, he attempts to think through its consequences. Wittgenstein's later philosophy was, I think, two sides: first a thoroughgoing critique of efforts to impose necessary structures upon the world, and second an attempt to think through the consequences of this rejection for logic (broadly conceived) and for the philosophy of mathematics.

I shall return to these topics (and try to treat them with more care) in Chapter XI, but first we must tie up some loose ends. Going all the way back to #138, Wittgenstein was worried about cases where a person seemed to understand the meaning of a word in a flash. Such cases suggest that meaning is given in immediate experience and this, of course, is contrary to Wittgenstein's own view that the meaning of a word is its use in the language. Starting from the case of understanding the meaning of a word, Wittgenstein broadened his inquiry to include understanding of various kinds, i.e., doing things for a *reason*—doing one thing *because* of something else. Wittgenstein's general point is that none of these things can be identified with a particular occurrent mental state: not a *particular* mental state because an examination of instances reveals only a family of loosely interrelated cases—not an *occurrent* mental state because understanding involves an ability to do various things which, whatever mental state we may happen to be in, we may not be able to perform when called upon to do so.

Yet sometimes we speak as if understanding were a particular mental state occurring at a specific time. We say such things as "Now I understand!" or "Now I can go on!" (PI, #151). What are we to make of such remarks? Wittgenstein returns to this topic in ##179–81. Here he introduces a line of thought that will become important later in the *Investigations*. A variety of things might occur when someone understands how a series continues—perhaps a formula does occur to him, a formula, that is, that he has been trained to use.

> And now one might think that the sentence "I can go on" meant "I have an experience which I know empirically to lead to the continuation of the series." But does B mean that when he says he can go on? . . .
>
> No. The words "Now I can go on" were correctly used when he thought of the formula: that is, given such circumstances as that he had learnt algebra, had used such formulae before. But that does not mean that his statement is only short for a description of all the circumstances which constitute the scene for our language-game. (PI, #179)

At another time, there may be no mental activity to report on at all: the person simply feels that he can continue the series and does so—saying, before he begins, "Now I know how to go on."

> It would be quite misleading, in this last case, for instance, to call the words a "description of a mental state".—One might rather call them a "signal"; and we judge whether it was rightly employed by what he goes on to do. (PI, #180)

Later in the *Investigations* Wittgenstein returns to this theme and remarks:

> "Now I know how to go on!" is an exclamation; it corresponds to an instinctive sound, a glad start. (PI, #323)

These last passages introduce a new theme in the *Investigations*, a theme that will have central importance in Wittgenstein's treatment of psychological concepts. The main idea is simple enough: an expression that seems to be a report of a current mental state is not a report of a current mental state because *it is not a report at all*. First Wittgenstein suggests that the expression "Now I know how to go on," is not a report of my mental condition, but rather a *signal*. Whether the signal is correctly or incorrectly employed is borne out by what the person goes on to do. Setting aside exceptional circumstances, a person has employed this signal incorrectly if he is not, in fact, able to continue the series correctly when he makes the attempt.

Here it is surprising how little Wittgenstein says either as explanation or defense of the claim that "Now I know how to go on" functions as a signal. What sort of signal is it; to whom is it directed and for what purpose? Isn't it entirely natural to say that the person has spoken *falsely* if he announces that he knows how to go on but then fails in the attempt?[3] To put the same point differently, don't I flatly *contradict* this person if I say to him "No, you do not know how to go on" (perhaps I am convinced he has been fooled)? In speaking about him, *I* certainly have made an assertion, but if my assertion contradicts what he has said, then it seems that he must have made an assertion as well. Furthermore, how does the notion that this remark formulates a signal (PI, #180) relate to the idea that it "corresponds to an exclamation" (PI, #323)? Now I think that we will waste our time trying to find answers to questions of this kind in the present context. We simply must postpone this discussion until we reach a point in the text where Wittgenstein discusses these matters in closer detail.

XI

Sceptical Doubts and a Sceptical Solution to These Doubts

1
The same again

Elaborating upon an example used in the previous chapter, suppose the student has mastered the series of natural numbers and we now set him the task of constructing various numerical series; for example, starting with 0, we train him to produce a series by progressively adding 2 to each result. After a while we are satisfied that the student has mastered this procedure. Later, however, we ask him to pick up the series at 1000 and he continues in the following way:

1000, 1004, 1008, 1012

We tell the student that he has made a mistake, that he is no longer going on in the same way. He, however, is adamant and insists that he has been going on as before and in order to illustrate this he runs through an earlier portion of the series and says, "See, I am still doing the same thing." When we tell the student that he is no longer doing the same thing—increasing the numbers by 2—he replies that increasing the numbers by 2 means constructing a series of the following kind: 0, 2, 4, 6, etc., and that, he says, is just what he has been doing from 1000 on.

Here it is tempting to dismiss this example as showing nothing more than the possibility of mathematical dimwits, but it will be useful to articulate the basis of this judgment. We might put the criticism in the following way: "When I gave the order to construct a series by successively adding 2 to each result, it was already settled that 1000 should be followed by 1002. Thus the student went off the track when he wrote down 1004 instead." In a way this remark (including the track metaphor) is perfectly correct and innocent. At the time that I gave the order I would have said, straight off, that 1000 should be followed by 1002. Nothing special happens at 1000—there is nothing new to think about—I

155

just go on as before (PI, #187). Yet this way of speaking easily lends itself to a misleading representation which Wittgenstein explains in the following way:

> [Y]our idea was that that act of meaning the order had in its own way already traversed all those steps: that when you meant it your mind as it were flew ahead and took all the steps before you physically arrived at this or that one.
>
> Thus you were inclined to use such expressions as: "The steps are *really* already taken, even before I take them in writing or orally or in thought." And it seemed as if they were in some *unique* way predetermined, anticipated—as only the act of meaning can anticipate reality. (PI, #188)

When I gave the order I certainly *meant* that 1000 should be followed by 1002, but it is simply wrong to explain this by saying that *in some sense* these steps had already been taken. When I make the step from 1036 to 1038, I am not *repeating* anything that was already performed, perhaps in a more subtle way. The idea that the series already (in some sense) exists is an illusion. This raises two questions: (1) What is the source of this illusion? and (2) What are the consequences of rejecting it completely? These will be the topics of sections 2 and 3.

2
The machine as symbol for itself

In perhaps the most remarkable analogy in the *Investigations*, Wittgenstein considers the following example that parallels our tendency to believe that all the steps in a mathematical progression must (somehow) already exist. I examine a particular machine, say, a rather complex gear mechanism. As I study the mechanism I see that if I move one gear in a certain way, then another moves that way as well. That is, as I study the structure of the mechanism, I see how the relationships between the gears determine how they move. The way these gears will move in relation to one another is, we are inclined to say, built into the machine from the start:

> [T]he action of a machine—I might say at first—seems to be there in it from the start. What does this mean?—If we know the machine, everything else, that is its movement, seems to be already completely determined. (PI, #193)

Now suppose that we actually turn one of the gears in order to check our predictions. Here a number of things might happen: (1) the other gears move as I expected; (2) much to my surprise they do not move in this way; (3) the whole mechanism jams and, perhaps, one of the gears falls off its axle. In the first case I am content, in the second I look for my mistake, but in the third case I criticize the mechanism. It is this third case that is most interesting. When I decided that this gear had to move in a clockwise direction when this other was moved in a clockwise direction, did I forget that gears sometimes jam or fall off their axles? (How could I forget such a thing?) No, I didn't forget this, but I did set it aside when I tried to figure out how the gears *had* to work. This shows that I am treating the machine in a special way: I am treating the gears as *symbols* in a calculus used to compute gear motions. Let me explain. I can use diagrams to work out how a wheel will drive a set of other wheels, as shown in Figure XI.1:

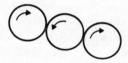

Figure XI.1

Here questions of slippage, deformation, friction, etc., do not come up. There is no slippage, deformation, or friction in diagrams—although diagrams can be used to represent such things too. But I can treat an actual machine in the same way; that is, I can treat its components as symbols used in calculation. Here Wittgenstein speaks of the "machine-as-symbol." Using the machine as a symbol, we can calculate how the gears will move in the same way that we might make this calculation on paper:

> But when we reflect that the machine could also have moved differently it may look as if the way it moves must be contained in the machine-as-symbol far more determinately than in the actual machine. As if it were not enough for the movements in question to be empirically determined in advance, but they had to be really—in a mysterious sense—already *present*. And it is true: the movement of the machine-as-symbol is predetermined in a different sense from that in which the movement of any given actual machine is predetermined. (PI, #193)

Here we make contact with our previous example. The steps in a numerical series seem somehow present from the start in the same way that the possible motions of a machine are somehow present from the start. And they are present in a way that is more determinate than anything revealed in the actual course of events. A particular exemplification of a machine may be faulty and a person's attempt to work out the mathematical series can contain an error, but the machine (*per se*) and the series (*an sich*) remain totally determinate in their structures.

The idea that the possibilities of motion are already (somehow) present in the machine or that the series of numbers is already (somehow) developed arises, Wittgenstein suggests, through our "crossing of different pictures." I can treat the machine as a symbol, that is, use its components representationally in order to make calculations. Here my results will have all the determinacy of a calculation, but, of course, they will not apply, with that determinacy, to any actual mechanism—including the one that I am using as a symbol. When I use the components of the machine representationally their movements are no more relevant than the movement of a diagram caused by shifting the paper upon which it is drawn. I can also treat the machine as a physical mechanism, that is, give the gears a whirl to see what happens. It is through crossing these two pictures that I arrive at the idea of an ideal movement or the movement of an ideal mechanism. I derive the ideal from the machine-as-symbol and the motion from the machine as physical object, but, of course, that which moves is not ideal and that which is ideal (the calculation) is not something that moves (even if the calculation concerns movement, and for example, has relevance to the prediction of movements). Through crossing pictures in this way, we get a ghost of a machine in a machine.

Let's go back to the development of the numerical series. Again, we can view a particular segment of such a series in two ways: either 1 as the result of some person's actual computation, or 2 as a specimen of how the series should be constructed. In the latter case it is taken as a rule (or part of a rule) for the construction of a series; in the former case we view it as the result of applying a rule. Again a confusion occurs (or, we might better say, an illusion arises) when we conflate these two ways of viewing a segment of the series. When we take a segment of a series as the standard for continuing the series then, as long as it is accorded this status, it is beyond criticism. It is set up as an ideal.[1] Now if we cross the idea of the series actually carried out (where a mistake is possible) with the notion of part of the sequence as a standard (where the question of mistake cannot come up), we get precisely that picture of the ideal sequence already carried out.

The notion of a completed sequence that no one has actually completed is mysterious, and demands a special kind of apprehension: an *intuition*. Here an intuition is some kind of non-empirical apprehension. The person comes to understand the series, it is said, through gaining an intuition of the ideal structure of that series. Training is an attempt to occasion this insight, that is, set the stage for having it. But if we follow Wittgenstein, we see that there is no pre-existing structure that can be the object of intuition.

I would almost be more correct to say, not that an intuition was needed at every stage, but that a new decision was needed at every stage. (PI, #186)

Of course, it is also wrong to say that a new *decision* is made at every stage: I'm supposed to follow the rule or develop the series in accordance with a model; I'm not supposed to make things up as I go along. Yet an exaggeration in this direction helps break the spell of the idea that in developing a series I am actually following a pre-existing path. But still, it is misleading to suggest that a decision is taken at every stage and Wittgenstein attempts to counterbalance this suggestion with another:

When I obey a rule, I do not choose.
I obey the rule *blindly*. (PI, #219)

This, however, is not right either, for the metaphor of acting blindly suggests that the person is acting wholly without a guide. It would be a miracle for someone acting blindly to continue the series correctly. The metaphor of acting blindly is, to my mind, an inelegant way of pointing to the fact that when we follow a rule—*as opposed to interpreting a rule*—our actions come without reflection, as a matter of course.

To summarize this much of the discussion: when we follow a rule there is a temptation to suppose that we are simply tracing out a necessary structure already given in the rule. Wittgenstein has argued that this is an illusion, and he has attempted to explain the source of this illusion. But if we are deprived of this illusion, what does justify our developing a series one way rather than any other? This is the question to be discussed next.

3
A "paradox" and its solution

I can introduce what Wittgenstein calls a *paradox* using the following considerations. Suppose we start with the sequence:

2 4 6 8 10

It is known that however we continue this sequence there will be a function (indeed endlessly many functions) that will yield this continuation. So the sequence of numbers taken this far (or however far) does not, by itself, settle what comes next. But it would seem that the situation is altogether different if the sequence is generated using some particular function, say $n + 2$, as a guide. Here, however, we cannot forget that in order to develop this series, we must know how to *use* the expression "$n + 2$," that is, we must know how to *apply* this formula (or some other formula which expresses, as we say, the same function). This, however, merely generates the original problem in a new form, for whatever way we continue the series, there will be some *interpretation* (indeed, endlessly many interpretations) of the formula I am using that will warrant this extension. This is given by the fact that there are endlessly many functions that warrant any extension and we need only interpret our formula as expressing one of these functions. This leads to what Wittgenstein calls a paradox:

> This [is] our paradox: no course of action could be determined by a rule, because every course of action can be made out to accord with the rule. The answer [is]: if everything can be made out to accord with the rule, then it can also be made out to conflict with it. And so there would be neither accord nor conflict here. (PI, #201)

The inferences that Wittgenstein draws are precisely correct: if everything can be made out to accord with a rule, then the notion of being in accord with a rule has lost its significance. The same point can be made in a different way: just as there are endlessly many interpretations available to show that whatever we do accords with the rule, there are, equally, endlessly many interpretations available to show that whatever we do is not in accord with the rule. This result, though not self-contradictory, is plainly paradoxical.

The answer to this paradox may seem obvious. Given the formula "n + 2," we are not permitted to interpret it as we please, say as expressing the function n^2 or even:

$$\frac{6 \, (n^3 - \pi)}{n}$$

If we allow such anarchy in interpretation, it is hardly surprising that we get odd and paradoxical results. We use the formula "n + 2" to express what we've all been taught to express by it, namely the function *n + 2*. Wittgenstein does not reject this answer; on the contrary, he argues that this gives the *whole* answer. Here is how this comes out in the text:

> What this shews is that there is a way of grasping a rule which is *not* an *interpretation*, but which is exhibited in what we call "obeying the rule" and "going against it" in actual cases. (PI, #201)

More forcefully:

> [A]ny interpretation still hangs in the air along with what it interprets, and cannot give any support. Interpretations by themselves do not determine meaning. (PI, #198)

When I interpret an expression, I present commentary on it, and perhaps try to replace one mode of expression with another.[2] It is plain, however, that understanding the interpretation depends upon a command of the concepts used in the interpretation, so if every interpretation is merely backed by another interpretation, meaning is never fixed.

The next question is how, if interpretations *by themselves* cannot determine meaning, meaning is fixed at all. Here is Wittgenstein's answer:

> Let me ask this: what has the expression of a rule—say a signpost—got to do with my actions? What sort of connection is there here?—Well perhaps this one: I have been trained to react to this sign in a particular way, and now I do so react to it. (PI, #198)

I don't know why Wittgenstein qualifies this remark with the word "perhaps," for he nowhere abandons the basic idea he here enunciates. He does, however, elaborate it in an important way. Wittgenstein is not saying that following a rule consists in nothing more than there being a causal relationship between a sign and my actions. I may be uniformly puzzled by a sign, but my being puzzled would not be *my* way of going by the sign. My response to the sign must conform to a customary way of responding to the sign:

> [A] person goes by a sign-post only in so far as there exists a regular use of sign-posts, a custom. (PI, #198)

Here then are two elements in Wittgenstein's account of following a rule: (1) a causal element, which gives Wittgenstein's solution to his paradox more than a passing similarity to Hume's "sceptical solution" to his own "sceptical doubts,"[3] and (2) a social element, which explains this causal relationship within the context of institutions, practices and customs.

> To obey a rule, to make a report, to give an order, to play a game of chess, are *customs* (uses, institutions). (PI, #199)

These reflections lead Wittgenstein to the remark which, if true, settles all the issues of the so-called private language argument, which is the subject of Chapter XII:

> "[O]beying a rule" is a practice. And to *think* one is obeying a rule is not to obey a rule. Hence it is not possible to obey a rule "privately": otherwise thinking one was obeying a rule would be the same thing as obeying it. (PI, #202)

But instead of getting ahead of the story, as Wittgenstein himself does, we can take things slowly. It seems that Wittgenstein's main contentions come to this. It is a fact of human nature that given a similar training people react in similar ways. For example, those who are trained in mathematics on the whole agree on their results. Those who cannot learn are excluded from further training and therefore do not have the opportunity to disagree later on at the constructive frontiers of mathematics where genuine disputes can arise.

> Disputes do not break out (among mathematicians, say) over the question whether a rule has been obeyed or not. People don't come to blows over it, for example. That is part of the framework on which the working of our language is based (for example, in giving descriptions). (PI, #240)

To learn to follow a rule is to become the master of a technique—a technique that is part of a social practice, institution or custom. *I* know how to do something when I do it the way *it's* done, but the way *it's* done amounts to nothing more than the way in which those people who are members of the institution (or who participate in the custom) do it.

All this may seem implausible (even subversive), for it suggests that truth is nothing more than a matter of convention. Wittgenstein notices this objection and replies to it in the following way:

> "So you are saying that human agreement decides what is true and what is false?"—It is what human beings *say* that is true and false; and they agree in the *language* they use. That is not agreement in opinions but in form of life. (PI, #241)

> If language is to be a means of communication there must be agreement not only in definitions but also (queer as this may sound) in judgments. This seems to abolish logic, but does not do so.—It is one thing to describe methods of measurement, and another to obtain and state results of measurement. But what we call "measuring" is partly determined by a certain constancy in results of measurement. (PI, #242)

One idea here is that the existence of an institution depends upon a background of facts that yield general *agreement*. Some of these facts concern the world we encounter:

> The procedure of putting a lump of cheese on a balance and fixing the price by the turn of the scale would lose its point if it frequently happened for such lumps to suddenly grow or shrink for no obvious reason. (PI, #142)

Other facts concern human nature. Consider the following example: it seems to me a fact about human beings that we can recognize the same shape through great variations in area. That is, we can recognize small triangles and large triangles as triangles. But we do not have the same ability to recognize equal areas independently of shape. That is, it is hard for us to tell, just by looking, whether a star and a circle have the

162

same area. Now suppose the situation were reversed; that is, suppose that we found it easy to recognize the same area, but hard to recognize the same shape; it seems obvious that the development of geometry would have been very different. It is in this way—and like ways—that our institutions are grounded in general facts of nature, including general facts of human nature. In virtue of such general facts agreement arises—the agreement necessary for the existence of institutions, practices and customs.

There is a standard objection to this whole way of thinking that might be expressed in the following way: "We can imagine a race of creatures so defective in memory that they are unable to learn how to count and so defective in the ability to abstract that they cannot command such concepts as double, triple, etc. It would seem that such creatures could not be taught that $7 \times 7 = 49$, but for all that, 7×7 *does* $= 49$. The situation would not alter if the envisaged creatures happened to be ourselves. To suppose otherwise is to confuse the *mathematical* conditions that guarantee the truth of this equation with the empirical conditions that make it possible for a human being to learn, understand or come to know this truth."[4]

This is a natural and important criticism and Wittgenstein returns to it a number of times, but perhaps his best discussion occurs in Part II of the *Investigations*.

"But mathematical truth is independent of whether human beings know it or not!"—Certainly, the propositions "Human beings believe that twice two is four" and "Twice two is four" do not mean the same. The latter is a mathematical proposition; the other, if it makes sense at all, may perhaps mean: human beings have *arrived* at the mathematical proposition. The two propositions have entirely different *uses*. (PI, p. 226)

So even if the existence of mathematics depends upon certain general facts about the world and about human nature, it does not follow that the propositions of mathematics are *about* these general facts. Mathematical propositions are not *reduced* to propositions of natural science. To use a dangerous metaphor, a mathematical proposition is expressed from *within* the institution of mathematics. The justification of a mathematical proposition is mathematical: mathematics must take care of itself. At the same time, we must realize that the *whole* institution of doing mathematics might have been different, and this can be brought home to us by reflecting upon the consequences for mathematical activity of changes in certain fundamental features of the world.

[Our] interest does not fall back upon these possible causes of the formation of concepts; we are not doing natural science; nor yet natural history—since we can also invent fictitious natural history for our purposes.

I am not saying: if such-and-such facts of nature were different people would have different concepts (in the sense of a hypothesis). But, if anyone believes that certain concepts are absolutely the correct ones, and that having different ones would mean *not realizing something that we realize*—then let him imagine certain very general facts of nature to be different from what we are used to, and the formation of concepts different from the usual ones will become intelligible to him. (my italics, PI, p. 230)

So a person who commands a set of concepts (made possible by certain general facts of nature) will naturally think that others who lack these concepts do not realize something he realizes. He will think that such a person is missing something. Wittgenstein suggests that we can shake this notion that our concepts give peculiar access to the world by reflecting upon the possibility that, with changes in the general features of the world, some of these concepts and the institutions that embody them might not arise at all.

How persuasive is this? We can imagine an opponent recasting his criticism in the following way: "Very well, Wittgenstein has not, as suggested earlier, confused the mathematical conditions that guarantee the truth of an equation with the empirical conditions that make it possible for a human being to learn, understand or come to know such a truth. He is suggesting instead that, with a change in certain general facts, we can imagine certain concepts not arising and therefore the truth of propositions involving these concepts would not be an issue. So he claims that there is no question of *our* realizing things that people in this other world would miss out on, for in the imagined world there is no corresponding question to ask. Well, if this is Wittgenstein's position, there is an obvious alternative to it. Why not simply say that given certain facts about human nature and given certain facts about the world, it has proved possible for human beings to form particular concepts and thereby get to know certain *other* facts about the world. Let us call the first batch of facts—those that concern human nature and the world that sustain our ability to form concepts—*enabling* facts. We can grant that with a change in these enabling facts there could be a radical change in our intellectual institutions, but why should this lead us to *give up* the idea that people using a different conceptual scheme do not realize something that we realize? Indeed, isn't this just what we would want to say in a number of cases? Suppose, for example, that our species had been born without eyes or any corresponding organ of sight, then, presumably, color concepts and the practice of colour-predication would not have arisen amongst us. Haven't we imagined a situation where we wouldn't realize many things that we do now realize, for example, that roses are sometimes red and violets almost always blue? Of course our truncated counterparts would not themselves realize that they did not realize something of this kind, but this would only show they were doubly ignorant."

I confess to a deep sympathy to a criticism of this kind, but Wittgenstein would answer it—and at the same time explain my feeling of sympathy—in the following way. Our conviction that our sightless counterparts in the imagined world would be missing something arises because we are speaking from within a certain practice. We as color predicators are imagining a world like our own except for the fact that people lack the organs necessary to learn how to predicate colors. Of course, it will seem that *they* are missing something. But suppose that we attempt a more sympathetic standpoint; judge the case from the perspective of our sightless counterparts, and thereby call the entire practice of attributing colors to things into question. Once the entire practice is called into question, is there any way of defending it? Wittgenstein's answer to this question, and all questions like it, is no! I can defend a claim that an object has a certain color, that is, I can defend it up to a point. I can explain that I have extensive training in identifying colors; I can get a color sample, etc.[5] But if the critic is challenging *the whole enterprise* of attributing colors to things, he will naturally find responses of this kind question-begging. He may even claim that we are obviously suffering from illusions that he, at least, is free of. When the argument reaches this level, we have probably run out of resources to continue it, and we are left only with our *confidence* that we are right.

XII

The Private Language Argument

Its occurrence in the text

More, it seems, has been written about Wittgenstein's private language argument than any other aspect of his philosophy. The reason for this, I think, is that the private language argument gets us back to the familiar ground on which modern philosophy has fought many of its battles. It has been a recurrent theme, at least since Descartes, that the foundation of knowledge is given in subjective self-certainty. There is ample room for disagreement within this tradition concerning the elements of this subjective certainty; they might be evident truths (e.g., "I think") or particular non-propositional items in consciousness (e.g., sense data), but, whatever these immediate contents of consciousness are, the task is to construct the edifice of knowledge on their foundation. (Conversely, one of the chief sources of scepticism has been the failure of all attempts to complete this task.) Perhaps the main reason, then, that the private language argument has attracted so much attention is that it seems to show that this whole approach (i.e., the approach of modern philosophy) is fundamentally misguided. Now I think that it is entirely possible that the private language argument, if correct, will have such far-reaching consequences, but the argument, as it develops in the text, has no such *immediate* focus. The first task is to see how the argument actually emerges in the text; the second is to assess its merits. Then we can speculate on its implications for the development of western philosophy.

As we saw, the first explicit reference to privacy occurs at #202:

"[O]beying a rule" is a practice. And to *think* one is obeying a rule is not to obey a rule. Hence it is not possible to obey a rule "privately": otherwise thinking one was obeying a rule would be the same thing as obeying it. (PI, #202)

Thus Wittgenstein's reasons for saying that obeying a rule is a practice provide the framework for examining the possibility of a private language. Let us recall, then, why Wittgenstein thought this. His reasoning really has two steps. First, he was interested in solving what he calls a paradox. If following a rule always involves an act of interpretation, then anything can be made out to be in accord with a rule and anything can equally be made out to be contrary to it. This, he says, shows "that there is a way of obeying a rule which is *not* an *interpretation*, but which is exhibited in what we call 'obeying a rule' and 'going against it' in actual cases" (PI, #201). If we look at actual cases, we discover that a person who follows a rule has been "trained to react to a sign in a particular way" (PI, #198). Training accomplishes what no amount of interpretation can: it determines that we proceed in a particular way out of all the possible ways that could be made out to be in conformity with the rule. I shall argue that this reference to training constitutes Wittgenstein's Humean (sceptical) solution to the sceptical paradox he has produced. It is a sceptical solution in Hume's sense because it grounds an otherwise unjustified (indeed, unjustifiable) belief in a brute fact of human nature. Under certain circumstances humans form beliefs and act in given ways regardless of their lack of justification. One argument against the possibility of a private language is that a similar sceptical solution to the paradox of alternative interpretations is not available. I shall call this the *training-argument*.

The second stage of Wittgenstein's reasoning is to move from the idea of *training* to that of a *practice*. A person might be trained to react to a sign in a particular way without thereby being taught to go by a rule. When we are taught to go by a rule, we are taught to react in a conventional or instituted way. That is, the kind of training that interests us here is that which introduces us into a practice (custom, institution, form of life), for using a language belongs in this category. It thus follows definitionally that a private language is impossible. But if that is all that Wittgenstein is saying, then his argument will have little interest. If there were a private activity that was like following a public rule in every respect save one, namely it had no public aspect, then we might want to deny that the person is following a rule, as we normally understand this notion. We might even want to say that such a person is not speaking a language since, in common parlance, a language is a public institution. Yet it would be hard to see what philosophical significance any of this would have, since it would be easy enough to adjust our language to avoid speaking in ways that violate such definitional constraints.

Wittgenstein's argument is not, however, definitional in this trivial way. What he says is that in the private case there would be no way of distinguishing *thinking* one was obeying a rule from *actually* obeying it. Everyone will agree that there *is* a difference between following a rule and just thinking that one is following a rule and any account that cannot provide for this distinction is therefore wrong. Now if we hold that following a rule is to be involved in a practice, then there is a way of distinguishing between following a rule and merely thinking one is. To follow a rule is to conform to a practice, that is, to act in the *generally* accepted way. What is generally accepted serves as the independent standpoint for assessing whether a person's actions conform to a rule (whatever *he* thinks). This, I think, is Wittgenstein's second main argument against the possibility of a private language. I shall call it the *public-check argument.*

So, for Wittgenstein, agreement between people "is part of the framework on which the working of our language is based" (PI, #240). But this emphasis upon the public use of language seems to ignore its private employment where the person's position is absolutely privileged and no one else is in a position to correct a mistake if, in fact, any is made. I sometimes talk to myself: I remind myself of things, encourage myself, note things for the future, etc. I might even keep a diary of my innermost feelings and moods for my own purposes, perhaps putting it into a cipher so that others cannot read it. Beyond this, I might even keep a diary that is essentially private:

> The individual words of this language are to refer to what can only
> be known to the person speaking; to his immediate private
> sensations. So another person cannot understand the language. (PI,
> #243)

Of course, if Wittgenstein's arguments leading up to #202 are correct, then no such private language is possible. Why then does he pick up the subject again at #243 and spend so much time on it? The answer, I think, is that Wittgenstein recognizes a primitive appeal in the notion of a private language. Part of the reason for this is that our language actually seems to *have* a component that is essentially private. When I speak about my after-images, I seem to be referring to something that only I can know directly. The actual existence of a private language, we might say, is the best evidence for its possibility. This, then, is one thing that Wittgenstein attempts after #243: he tries to show that reports of sensations are not descriptions of private episodes, but function in an entirely different way. Another thing that encourages belief in a private language is the assumption that it is easy to assign a meaning to a word: one merely allocates the word an object and that is the end of the matter. If I have a particular kind of twinge, I can assign it a name, then undertake to call twinges of that kind by the same name in the future. This, however, runs counter to another theme found earlier in the *Investigations:* the impossibility of fixing the meaning of a word through the use of an ostensive definition *all by itself.* A misunderstanding of our everyday sensation talk combined with a misunderstanding of how meanings are fixed conspires to generate the image of a private language. Much of the discussion following #243 is not, then, a direct attack upon the possibility of a private language, but rather an attack upon those misunderstandings that make a private language seem, not only a conceptual possibility, but also an actual fact.

Here, then, is how I shall proceed in this chapter. First (in Section 2) I shall examine Wittgenstein's attacks upon the misunderstandings that generate the illusion that our everyday sensation talk is somehow peculiarly *private*. Next (in Section 3) I shall examine Wittgenstein's attack upon the possibility of fixing the meaning of a private term simply through an act of ostension. In Section 4 I consider what I call the Humean sceptical solution to the paradox of alternative interpretations, and try to show that it establishes the contingent impossibility of a private language. In Section 5 I expound and then criticize what I have called the public-check argument. I claim that this argument fails. Finally (in Section 6) I offer a general assessment of Wittgenstein's claims.

2
Privacy and certainty

It seems natural to treat sensation talk as reports of happenings or events. That is, a person's assertion that she has a pain in her elbow is not different in grammatical form from the assertion that coal is found in Pennsylvania. There are, of course, important differences between these two claims, but this is explained, on the traditional approach, by pointing to a difference in *subject matter*. Given this start, there is an almost inevitable march to the conclusion that a person's claims to be in pain (etc.) are reports of utterly private occurrences. Why this drive in the direction of privacy? Wittgenstein explains this by showing that there *is* a sense in which privacy attaches to first-person reports of a sensation—but it is a sense, as we shall see, that is innocent of any commitment to private *entities*.

Right off the bat Wittgenstein gives *his* account of the character of first-person reports of sensations:

> Here is one possibility: words are connected with primitive, the natural, expressions of the sensation and used in their place. A child has hurt himself and he cries; and then adults talk to him and teach him exclamations and, later, sentences. They teach the child new pain-behaviour. (PI, #244)

This does not mean that the word "pain" refers to crying, for the "verbal expression of pain replaces crying and does not describe it" (PI, #244). Here Wittgenstein speaks of "one possibility" for the explanation of sensation talk, but nowhere offers any other, and the things he says next presuppose that something *very like* this account must be correct.

Let us suppose, then, that first-person reports of pain are a kind of "articulated crying." By this I mean that the child's natural tendency to moan and rub an injured arm can be made, with training, into the articulate expression "I have a pain in my arm." Perhaps crying originally served as a distress signal that called forth supporting responses in fellow human beings. As this distress signal becomes articulated, it can call forth help of a more specific kind. Something like this could well serve as the background for Wittgenstein's discussion of reports of pain, but his own approach does not rely on any single theory of this kind.

The main point, of course, is that this articulated expression which grows out of (and sometimes replaces) the natural expression of pain is not generically different from this natural expression. Crying is not a report about our feelings of pain, but an expression of them; it is not a bit of commentary on our pain behavior, but one of the items *in* our pain behavior. The word "ouch" is not a "laconic comment on the passing show." With suitable reservations,[1] the same can be said for the remark "I have a pain in my arm." Saying this is also part of our pain behavior, not a comment upon it. It is for this reason that a kind of privacy attaches to first-person reports of pain. To put matters simply, another person cannot express my pains, cannot cry my cries, or do my moaning for me. It is in this altogether trivial way that privacy attaches to my first-person reports of pain.

> The proposition "Sensations are private" is comparable to "One plays patience by oneself." (PI, #248)

Another person cannot renounce my rights either, but this is not because my grip is so strong that no exertion on his part can break it. We might make Wittgenstein's point this way: if you want to understand the *privacy* of first-person reports of pain, do not use descriptions of objects that are contingently private as your model (the room that only Jones can enter); instead compare these reports with performatives, exclamations, greetings, etc., and the mysterious and problematic quality of this privacy will retreat from them.

The notion that sensations are private is usually associated with another thesis: although others cannot know, for example, that I am in pain, this is something that *I* know and know with certainty. Wittgenstein denies this:

> It can't be said of me at all (except perhaps as a joke) that I *know* I am in pain. What is it supposed to mean—except perhaps that I *am* in pain? (PI, #246)

Here it makes some difference where we place the emphasis. It would seem to be very odd to wonder whether it is *I* who is in pain rather than someone else; it seems less odd (though far from usual) to wonder whether something is *painful* rather than, say, merely unpleasant. Yet we can think of cases of the following kind. I say to the director "I know that I am in pain, but Nureyev is worse off and the show must go on." In a similar way, a patient with religious scruples against the use of novocaine might say to his dentist "I know that this is *painful*," etc. In these cases "I know" has something of the force of "I have taken it into consideration;" but this does not detract from Wittgenstein's main point: in the majority of cases, questions whether a person knows *he's* in pain or knows he's in *pain* are out of place.

There are two ways in which we might explain the inappropriateness of these questions. (i) In general we do not ask questions when the answer is altogether obvious. Just as I do not ask a person if he knows what his name is (unless, perhaps, he is suffering from amnesia), I do not ask a person if he knows if he is in pain. These are things that people are always expected to know, and therefore there is no *point* in asking about them. We can call this the *pragmatic* approach to this issue.[2] (ii) Wittgenstein's answer is that this question is inappropriate because the "expression of doubt has no place in the language-game" (PI, #288). If there were such a word, we might say that it is easy to confuse the adubitable with the indubitable.

Here performatives provide a natural analogy for illustrating Wittgenstein's point. Of course, to say "I am in pain" is not to utter an explicit performative: if I say I am in pain, I am not thereby in pain. Yet the comparison with performatives is illuminating in this way: if we work under the assumption that the explicit performative "I promise to do such and such" is a report of a personal happening, we will be driven almost inexorably to the conclusion that it is a private happening that only the promisor can know with certainty. Here a strange image arises because two features of promising are seen out of focus. First, there is a sense in which privacy attaches to the claim that I promise something: only I can make my own promises.[3] Second, since promising is not making a report, neither the question of knowledge nor of doubt comes up. When these facts are seen under the spell of that particular picture of human language that holds that words stand for things and sentences are combinations of such words, this privacy is attributed to those objects which we hold to be the referents of these words. Next, the *irrelevance* of knowledge claims (*that* sense in which doubt does not arise) is converted into an indubitable grasp of the nature of these entities. Under the spell of a certain conception of the nature of human language, we naturally think that talk about our pains, intentions, etc., concerns private events that can be known only to those in whom they occur. To use one of Wittgenstein's favorite phrases, this is something that we find ourselves *inclined to say*, but if we give way to this inclination, we then find ourselves involved in paradoxes and hopeless muddles. These paradoxes will disappear

> . . . Only if we make a radical break with the idea that language always functions in one way, always serves the same purpose: to convey thoughts—which may be about houses, pains, good and evil, or anything else you please. (PI, #304)

What does all this establish? In one way, not a great deal; for example, it does not show the impossibility of a language where the words refer to what can only be known to the person speaking—to his immediate private sensations. What the discussion does instead is to diagnose the influences that make it seem natural to hold such a view about portions of our actual language.

3
The idle ceremony

Let us suppose for a moment that Wittgenstein is right in saying that our everyday utterances concerning pain (intentions, etc.) are not reports of private events or states accessible only to the person who suffers the pain (or forms the intention, etc.). Granting this does, of course, remove one support for a belief in the possibility of a private language: for what could be a better proof of the possibility of a private language than showing the very existence of a private language? But we can waive this point and raise the question directly: setting aside all questions concerning how our present language functions, is there any reason why a person could not construct a language for himself that would be private in the way that Wittgenstein intends this notion?

Wittgenstein considers an attempt at doing this which, with some embellishments, goes as follows: I decide to keep a record of a certain sensation S, which, as it seems to me, I often have. I find this sensation uncanny—even ineffable—for every attempt I have to "put this sensation into words" utterly fails. If this sensation occurs in certain contexts rather than others, I have yet to discover this. I thus find it quite impossible to explain this sensation to others, but I still undertake to record faithfully its occurrence in the diary I keep.

In this case, the meaning of a symbol is supposedly fixed through a private act of ostension or through a private ostensive definition: I concentrate my attention on the particular sensation and undertake in the future to refer to sensations of this kind by the letter "S." It is in this way that the letter "S" is assigned a meaning. Part of Wittgenstein's criticism of an attempt to fix a meaning in this way goes back to an earlier discussion in the *Investigations* where he argued in detail that an ostensive definition—by itself—does not fix the meaning of a term. Associating a word with an object can be a preliminary activity in learning how to use a word, but this activity alone leaves it entirely open how this word will be used in connection with that thing.[4] In the paragraph just before the question of a private diary is raised, Wittgenstein reminds the reader of this previous discussion:

> [O]ne forgets that a great deal of stage-setting in the language is presupposed if the mere act of naming is to make sense. (PI, #257)

Wittgenstein's first reaction to the person who is putting the letter "S" into his diary is to ask ". . . what is this ceremony for: for that is all it seems to be" (PI, #258). A little later he makes the same point using one of the striking analogies of the *Investigations*. "Why can't my right hand give my left hand money?" (PI, #268). We can imagine the right hand putting the money in the left hand, the left hand writing a receipt, etc. Again, we would be dealing with an idle ceremony. Since the surroundings needed for the exchange of a gift are missing, we are tempted to say "What of it?" This is also the proper attitude to take toward the keeper of the private diary, for she has yet to assign a *use* to the symbol she employs.[5] The mistake here is to assume that "once you know *what* the word stands for, you understand it, you know its whole use" (PI, #264).

The force of this criticism will not be apparent if we take it for granted that the letter "S" will just take its place alongside other sensation words. "Sensation," as Wittgenstein notices, "is a word of our common language, not of one intelligible to me alone" (PI, #261). So we have no right to assume that the letter "S" is just the name of another sensation until we spell out the connection between the letter "S" and the word "sensation" (and spell out its connection with other words *for* sensations). Nor will it help to retreat to more neutral words like *something* or *this*, saying that we can forget the word "sensation" and just claim that the letter "S" stands for a *something* or for a *this*! These words are also part of the public vocabulary, and we have no right to assume that the conditions for their employment are satisfied in the setting of the diarist's program.

> So in the end when one is doing philosophy one gets to the point where one would like just to emit an inarticulate sound.—But such a sound is an expression only as it occurs in a particular language-game, which should now be described. (PI, #261)

Next let us try to imagine a *use* for this letter "S." Here Wittgenstein produces a striking but curious example:

> I discover that whenever I have a particular sensation a manometer

173

shews that my blood-pressure rises. So I shall be able to say that my blood-pressure is rising without using any apparatus. This is a useful result. And now it seems quite indifferent whether I have recognized the sensation *right* or not. Let us suppose I regularly identify it wrong, it does not matter in the least. And that alone shews that the hypothesis that I make a mistake is mere show. (PI, #270)

I think that it is possible to interpret this passage in a variety of ways, but the most plausible reading is this. On various occasions I am inclined to put the entry "S" in my diary because I think that the appropriate sensation has occurred. I now discover that whenever I make such an entry a manometer indicates an increase in my blood pressure. I have now found an objective correlate for my private sensation and so a use for the letter "S." It can now be used in a language-game for the prediction of my blood pressure. But where has this correlation been made? Is it between the occurrence of a private sensation and the rising of my blood pressure or between my inclination to write down the letter "S" and the rising of my blood pressure? To see that it is the latter—not the former—we need only imagine the case where I make a great many "errors" in reporting on S, but the correlation between my reports and the rising of my blood pressure remains constant. We would have no independent way of distinguishing these two cases: the correlation holds between my having the sensation and the rising of my blood pressure as opposed to the correlation holding between my *thinking* the sensation has occurred and the rising of my blood pressure. Thus, just as the letter "S" gains a use in the language-game of predicting my blood pressure level, it loses all essential connection with a private sensation. This, in general, will be the problem in finding a use for the letter "S" by appealing to some public practice: whenever we find some public use for the symbol, the supposed private reference will drop out as inessential, since error in identifying this private reference need have no effect in playing the public language game. The reference to a particular sensation is like a wheel that turns nothing—"a mere ornament, not connected with the machine at all" (PI, #270).

Wittgenstein's reflections here are searching, but again, we must be careful in deciding what they establish. I think that they show at least two things, both important: (i) the construction of a private language may seem unproblematic only because we illicitly help ourselves to the logical features of expressions that occur in everyday language. This happens, for example, if we glibly assume that we shall use the letter "S" as the *name* of a private *sensation*. But that the letter functions either as a *name* or as a *sensation* word is something that must be established. We enter the world of a private language semantically naked. (ii) Furthermore, if we do give a symbol a public employment sufficient to fix its sense, then it is already up to the mark as far as significance goes, and there is no point in saying it also has a private reference.

None of this, however, shows that a private language is impossible; it only shows a number of illicit ways of introducing a private language for what they are. At the same time, it does exhibit how difficult it will be to construct a private language. We cannot simply borrow logical features from the public language, for we must show that the conditions underlying the public employment of a symbol are present in the private case as well. This will involve showing things that it never normally crosses our minds to show, for example, that a term functions as a name. Even so, the possibility remains that the "S" of the private language gains its sense through an equally private employment in a private language game, a private practice, or a private form of life. It is to this possibility that we turn next.

4
The training argument

We saw that at #202 Wittgenstein declares that it is impossible to obey a rule privately. I have suggested that the text here provides two distinct, though related, reasons for rejecting the possibility of a private language. The first turns upon Wittgenstein's *sceptical solution* to his sceptical doubts concerning rule following. I call this the training argument. The second turns upon the demand that we must have some way to distinguish following a rule from merely thinking we are following a rule. I call this the public-check argument. I think that the training argument establishes the contingent impossibility of a private language. I think that the public-check argument fails.

Perhaps we can gain some insight into these issues by looking back through #202 to the reasoning that preceded it. Wittgenstein was led to say that following a rule is a practice as a result of reflecting upon his *paradox* that anything can be made out to be in conformity with a rule under one interpretation or another. The moral he drew from this was that there must be a way of grasping a rule that is not a matter of interpretation, "but which is exhibited in what we call 'obeying the rule' and 'going against it' in actual cases" (PI, #201). What we find when we examine these actual cases is that the person who follows a rule has been *trained* to react in a given way. Through this training the person learns to respond in conventional ways and thus enters into a *practice*. Here, however, it is the matter of training that is crucial to the "sceptical" solution of Wittgenstein's "paradox." A solution is sceptical in Hume's sense when an unjustified (indeed, unjustifiable) belief is grounded in nothing more than a brute fact of human nature. Under certain circumstances we just do believe certain things, and that is the end of the matter. This is a persistent theme in Wittgenstein's writings and appears again, for example, in these comments from the *Remarks on the Foundations of Mathematics:*

> For it is a peculiar procedure: I go *through* the proof and then accept its result.—I mean: this is simply what we *do*. This is use and custom among us, or a fact of our natural history. (RFM, I, 63)

Or again:

> The danger here, I believe, is one of giving a justification of our procedure where there is no such thing as a justification and we ought simply to have said: *that's how we do it*. (RFM, II, 74)

Returning to the case of the private diarist, how will Wittgenstein's "paradox" be solved there? Whatever a person writes down, there will be interpretations of her privately given rule that show that she has acted in accord with it and, equally, other interpretations that show that she has not. To solve this "paradox" there must be a way, within the private language, of following a rule that is not a matter of interpretation. In the public case, this involves reacting to a sign in a conventional manner—something that is brought about through being trained by *others*. The private language has, however, been defined as one that only its user can understand, so *ex hypothesis*, at the start there is no trainer available who, understanding the language, can initiate someone into it. Thus in order to resolve Wittgenstein's paradox within a private language, we must entertain possibilities of the following kind:

(a) There is a way of grasping a rule that is grounded neither in training nor in interpretation. (Being created in the image of God or having a fully developed language programmed into our nervous systems at birth would be examples of this.)

(b) There is no paradox involved in the notion of an untrained trainer: that is, a person might train another to do something he cannot do or, starting from scratch, a person might train *himself* to do something. (People who cannot swim have taught others to swim, and people have taught themselves to swim. More to the point, there was a time, not many million years ago, when no languages existed. However it happened, the paradox of the untrained trainer did not prevent the emergence of human languages.)

I think that any of these possibilities could be filled out in more detail, but I shall consider just one example that Wittgenstein himself gives:

> William James . . . quotes the recollection of a deaf mute, Mr Ballard, who wrote that in his early youth, even before he could speak, he had thoughts about God and the world.—What can he

have meant? Ballard writes. "It was during those delightful rides, some two or three years before my initiation into the rudiments of written language, that I began to ask myself the question: how came the world into being?" (PI, #342)

There is something suspicious about Ballard's thoughts turning to God and the world during his delightful rides. Would his tale be more or less convincing if he had thought, during those delightful rides, about how much better smoked salmon tastes than pickled herring? In any case, I think that Wittgenstein's comment upon this case is correct:

These recollections are a queer memory phenomenon,—and I do not know what conclusions one can draw from them about the past of the man who recounts them. (PI, #342)

The event is so singular, and the surrounding information so spare, that we are not in a position to decide how to describe the case. But if we fill in further details, our hesitancy in deciding upon a correct description will melt away. Suppose Mr Ballard not only had these thoughts about God and the world during his delightful rides but also recalled details from his early life that are subject to independent verification, e.g., that one fall morning there was an eclipse of the sun that was about two-thirds total. Of course we would be right in suspecting a fraud in this case, but if such issues were resolved, I think that we would have no doubt that we were dealing with a case of recollection. To continue the fantasy, suppose that we discovered that Ballard had actually kept a record of these early experiences using a script that he had invented for this purpose. We examine his notebooks and see that it develops from rudimentary scratches into a highly articulated structure. Ballard refers to these notebooks to report complex and independently verifiable facts that no one could be expected to remember (e.g., "On my fourth birthday all my cousins but two were in attendance; they sent regrets"). A discovery of these facts would be revolutionary in its implications, but, nonetheless, I think that no one would deny that Ballard had somehow acquired a language of his own invention.

What does this fantasy have to do with the possibility of a language that is private in the strong sense given in #243? Ballard, as we imagine him, has not produced a private language, but privately produced a public language. That is correct, but the present question is whether a person might produce a language all on his own without the aid of another person who already possesses a language. The extended Ballard example shows that this is not something very hard to imagine. However Ballard came by his language, let us now imagine the keeper of the *essentially* private diary doing so in the same way.

This brings us to the decisive point: as we trace out various ways in which a private language might be developed, we do not encounter insuperable conceptual difficulties. What we do encounter is certain general facts about human nature. We can imagine creatures much like ourselves who somehow command a language without being introduced to this language by others who already command it. Such linguistic self-starters might also construct a private language in the strong sense of #243. In fact, however, human beings are not like this; there are no linguistic self-starters. We thus arrive at the factual conclusion that a necessary private language is contingently impossible.

Here someone might say that we cannot draw such a sharp distinction between conceptual issues and general facts about human nature, since the two are intimately related: we have the concepts we do because we are the kinds of creatures we are. I have no objection to stating matters in this way except that it cloaks the discussion in a haze of profundity. (It is always a sign that we have gone wrong if we feel that the direct way of saying something is not open to us.) In the end I think it is better to keep things simple—stay with the language we already possess—and put matters this way:

> Given the kind of creatures that human beings are, they can only acquire a language through training. Furthermore, they cannot train themselves in a language but must acquire it from others who already possess it.

> Therefore an essentially private language as defined in #243 is not possible for human beings as we understand them.

But do Wittgenstein's reflections show even the *contingent* impossibility of an essentially private language? The main idea is that it is only from others who possess a language that human beings, as we know them, can acquire a language. It then follows at once that no one could acquire a language that only he can understand. To return to a point touched on briefly before, this argument may seem too strong—rather than too weak—since it seems to rule out something that is generally supposed to have happened: in the evolution of man, language emerged. But the argument has no such strong consequence, for it says that human beings, as we know them, acquire their language from others who already possess a language. A variety of tales might be told how human beings came to have a language in the first place: presumably it arose through interactions with the world around them and interactions with one another. Of course, this is vague—and intentionally so—but we can notice that no explanation of this kind will open the way for the acquisition of an essentially private language. An interaction that one creature enters into with the world or with his fellow creatures is open to others as well. So if language arose through such interactions, it cannot be essentially private. So we can say something a *bit* stronger:

Human beings as we know them and as we plausibly speculate about
how they have been, are not capable of acquiring a language that
is essentially private.

I realize that many followers of Wittgenstein find a stronger argument
in the text, but this, it seems to me, is the strongest conclusion that
Wittgenstein's reasons will support. I have labelled this (apparently)
stronger argument the public-check argument, and I shall turn to it next.

5
The public-check argument

In #202 Wittgenstein declares that it is impossible to obey a rule privately
because in such a case there would be no way to distinguish following
a rule from merely thinking that one is following a rule. Wittgenstein
returns to this theme when he considers the case of the private diary
used to record the occurrences of the sensation S. Here I, as diarist, am
the sole judge of what is right or wrong in recording occurrences of this
sensation.

> One would like to say: whatever is going to seem right to me is
> right. And that only means that here we can't talk about "right".
> (PI, #258)

There is no way to justify claims that one report is right, another wrong,
because "Justification consists in appealing to something independent"
(PI, #261), and here no independent standpoint exists. A natural
response is that there is an independent standpoint for judging whether
the ascription of the letter "S" is correct or not. What I do is remember
the previous sensations I have called by the name "S" and then I am
careful to use this letter for the same thing again. In the same way I
recall the page of a timetable when I am trying to remember when a
train leaves. Wittgenstein rejects this comparison:

> If the mental image of the time-table could not itself be *tested* for
> correctness, how could it confirm the correctness of the first memory?
> (PI, #265)

Appeal to memory is of no use since it raises precisely the same question
anew: how are we to distinguish memory reports that are actually correct
from those that only seem to be correct, for, in the case of the private
diary, no independent standpoint exists for drawing this distinction.

If I have read Wittgenstein correctly here, I think that he has simply
gone wrong. Earlier I remarked that it is never correct to use *general*
sceptical arguments to secure a *special* advantage.[6] Let me spell this out.
By a general sceptical argument, I mean one that is independent of any

particular subject matter. For example, I might insist that anything asserted as known must be backed by evidence or grounds. Then when such grounds are presented, I produce the same challenge again, and so on *ad infinitum*. We know how Wittgenstein replies to sceptical challenges of this kind: he simply points out that in certain cases we *do not doubt*,[7] and our language games go forward on this basis. But to come to the point: since Wittgenstein constantly makes such an appeal in developing his own views, why can't I, as private diarist, do the same? How do I know that my appeal to memory is actually correct? Well, *this* is what it is like to remember something—here my reasons give out. If some further justification is demanded, then I must admit that I have none, but as Wittgenstein says, "to use a word without justification does not mean to use it without right" (PI, #289). To press matters further, we can examine Wittgenstein's own method for checking memory reports. Supposedly, in the timetable example, I can check my recollection by looking at a genuine timetable. To pick one sceptical doubt out of any number available, what is my criterion for saying they match? Is it that they *seem* to match? That doesn't help, for things may seem to match without matching, so we appear to need yet another standpoint for deciding whether my recollection really matches or only appears to match the real timetable. I hope that it is understood that I am not advancing these sceptical doubts in their own right; I only want to know the basis for applying them against the possibility of a private language while passing them by as idle when applied to a public language. How can we justify applying a general pattern of argument in this selective way? Unless Wittgenstein can answer these questions, his public-check argument, as I have called it, fails.

In general, the sceptic exploits the distinction between seeming and being and argues that we are not in a position to decide in particular cases whether something has a characteristic or only seems to. (This is just how Wittgenstein argues against the possibility of a private language.) In everyday life this challenge does not bother us because we accept a principle of the following kind:

If something seems to be *p*, then (defeasibly) it is *p*.

It doesn't take a philosopher to tell the plain man that things are not always as they seem, yet all of us start with this assumption and only abandon it under the pressure of countervailing reasons. If there seems to be a tree in front of me, I straightway think there is a tree in front of me,[8] and retreat from this belief only for good reasons. The wile of the sceptic is to reverse this presumption and demand that we anticipate and eliminate every possible circumstance that might arise and thereby defeat my presumption. Of course, this cannot be done. The mistake that plays into the hands of the sceptic is the attempt to meet his challenge head-on by producing indefeasible knowledge claims, that is, claims where there is no way of opening a gap between how things seem and how they are. In traditional language, we need a *given* as the indubitable ground of our knowledge. Without this, the sceptical engine cannot be employed selectively, but will destroy everything in its path.

Returning to Wittgenstein, we saw that he seemed to employ a general sceptical argument against the possibility of an essentially private language. The question now arises whether Wittgenstein can legitimize its use by showing that there is some area where it does apply. In different words, is there a doctrine of the *given* in Wittgenstein's later philosophy? I think that this is a difficult *textual* question, but the answer, I think, is yes.

To go back to the beginning, the problem with a person following a rule privately is that there is no objective (i.e., independent) standpoint to settle whether she is following a rule or only seems to be. For Wittgenstein, this objective standpoint is supplied by the practice that the person enters into when she is trained to follow the rule. But can't we also insist that there is a difference between *all* the members of a practice thinking that they are conforming to their rules and, in fact, actually conforming to them? If we can draw this distinction, doesn't this show that there is some standpoint outside the practice that is the source of objectivity? Wittgenstein's answer seems to be that there is no distinction between all the members of a practice *thinking* that they are participating in it and their *really* participating in it. To become a participant in a practice is to enter a form of life, and there is no recourse beyond forms of life:

> What has to be accepted, the given, is—so one could say—forms of life. (PI, p. 226)

Here, then, we have something like a doctrine of a *given*, but it is not yet clear what Wittgenstein intends by this. He continues this remark in the following way:

> Does it make sense to say that people generally agree in their judgments of color? What would it be like for them not to?—One man would say a flower is red which another called blue, and so on.—But what right should we have to call these people's words "red" and "blue" *our* "colour words"? (PI, p. 226)

More pointedly:

> But what would *this* mean: "Even though everybody believed that twice two was five it would still be four"?—For what would it be like for everybody to believe that?—Well, I could imagine, for instance, that people had a different calculus, or a technique which

181

we should not call "calculating". But would it be *wrong?* (Is a coronation *wrong?* To beings different from ourselves it might look extremely odd.) (PI, pp. 226–7)

So it seems that we cannot imagine that all of us in a practice are doing something *wrong*, for when we try this we only succeed in imagining a practice different from our own—one, perhaps, that strikes us as extremely odd.[9] We thus seem to have found a new form of immunity to a sceptical challenge: an attack upon the entire framework of, say, mathematics does not succeed since it results in undercutting the sense of the very question asked. "How do we know that we are not *all* continually making mistakes in mathematics?" The answer to this, it seems, is "If we were to entertain the idea that we are all continuously making mistakes in mathematics, then it would no longer be clear what is to count as mathematics."

The sceptic, however, need not retreat in embarrassment at this point. He could acknowledge that the thought that our mathematical reasoning might, on the whole, be erroneous, carries with it the consequence that our mathematical reasoning, as a whole, makes no sense. But why not pitch the sceptical question at this level: by what right do we suppose that our mathematical discourse even makes sense? We can, of course, ask the same question about every domain of discourse. Wittgenstein responds to this question directly in the *Tractatus:*

> 3.328 (If everything behaves as if a sign had meaning, then it does have meaning.)

This parenthetical comment is noteworthy in its logical form, for it contains just the pattern of inference from the *seems to be* to the *is* that blocks the sceptic's challenge—it closes the gap where the wedge goes in. We can make mistakes about the meaningfulness of a given proposition (philosophers apparently do this often), "but if *everything* behaves as if a sign had meaning, then it does have meaning." This view, though started in the *Tractatus*, is also fundamental to the *Investigations*. It explains what Wittgenstein means when he says that what has to be accepted as the given are forms of life.

So in general form, the argument goes as follows: we cannot ask whether *everyone* involved in a practice might always be mistaken in what he does, for such an assumption would destroy the practice itself, thereby depriving the concepts employed in this practice of their sense, and undercutting the very notion of a mistake. If we shift grounds and ask what guarantees that the concepts in a practice even make sense, then the answer is that nothing guarantees this except the functioning of the practice itself.

The question next arises how these considerations bear upon the possibility of a private language. If we grant that sceptical arguments do not hold against a public language (or a public practice), is there any reason to deny that the same defense might be made for a private language (or private practice)? As we look at the arguments, it is hard to see how the difference between privacy and publicity will make any difference here. The reasoning begins: "We cannot ask whether *everyone* involved in a practice might, on the whole, be mistaken. . . ." It doesn't seem to change anything in the argument if the *everyone* is reduced to the limiting case of just one person pursuing his private practice. Furthermore, if we challenge the claimant of a private language to show that the terms in her language have a sense, she is free to say that just the fact that everyone using them finds them meaningful is enough to show that they are meaningful. Again, it seems to make no logical difference that there is only a single person involved in the practice. Furthermore, I cannot insist that the claimant to a private language convince *me* (an outsider) that the words in her language have a sense, for it is only within an institution or form of life that words have an employment, and hence a sense. To insist that a word will make sense to one person only if she (or someone) can show that it makes sense to another merely begs the question by assuming that every language must be potentially public. Wittgenstein's argument seems to come to this: for an individual's use of a language to be significant, it must be possible to check it against a public use, but no similar demand can significantly be made of the public use itself. I do not think that Wittgenstein has provided adequate reasons for this differential treatment.

In sum, I have said that the public-check argument relies on what I have called a general sceptical argument. If this general sceptical argument shows the impossibility of all language, then its specific application to a private language is arbitrary. It is essential, therefore, to find a defense against this sceptical argument that protects a public language without at the same time being serviceable for the protection of a private language. It does not seem that this demand has been met, for when we construct what seems to be Wittgenstein's defense against a sceptical attack upon a public language, it yields a defense of a private language as a special case. A selective use of this argument is therefore question-begging. I conclude, therefore, that the text contains no acceptable argument against the possibility of an essentially private language that is stronger than the argument for its contingent impossibility discussed in Section 4.

6
The subject concluded

The last section ended on a negative note, suggesting that the public-check argument fails. I suspect that it is this argument (or some variation on it) that people have in mind when they speak of "the private-language argument." It is important to see, however, that when this argument is rejected the text does not become uninteresting, for there are at least three other themes interwoven in the *Investigations* of deep philosophical significance. I shall end this discussion of a private language by summarizing them.

(a) The illusion of private certainty

The assumption that we do possess knowledge of items in our consciousness that are essentially private seems perfectly natural—at least to the philosophers of the past few centuries. Wittgenstein attempts to explain this belief in the following way. First he sketches a theory of the way our first-person sensation talk functions: it is a modification of our natural expression of a sensation; it is an articulated replacement of the original inarticulate expression. Each of us (trivially) expresses his own sensation, and, since this is not a matter of reporting anything, (trivially) this is not an area where errors arise. These two trivialities become distorted however if we impose upon sensation talk a certain picture of the way language functions: words stand for things, and sentences are combinations of such words. Seen through the spectacles of this commitment, our sensation talk takes on the appearance of *reports* of private entities that are known (and known with certainty) only to the person who makes the first-person report.

(b) The critique of private ostensive definitions

This second theme is keyed upon the remark that "one forgets that a great deal of stagesetting in the language is presupposed if the mere act of naming is to make sense" (PI, #257). The central idea is not limited to *private* ostensive definitions, but has general application to all ostensive definitions. A definition is intended to give a meaning to a word, but this is not accomplished merely through correlating a word with an object. This is, at most, a step preparatory to assigning a meaning to a word, for even after the word-object correlation has been fixed, it still remains to be established how the word will be used relative to the object. The ostensive definitions that we employ successfully in everyday life succeed by exploiting the previously existing framework—a framework that it is easy to take for granted. It is also easy to assume that this framework stands ready at hand for the construction of a novel language such as a private language (in Wittgenstein's sense) or a phenomenalist language. This, however, is a mistake, and, once we realize that a private language must be constructed completely from scratch, we then recognize the magnitude of the project. We see, for example, that it is not merely a matter of undertaking to use a word as the name for a particular sensation, for we have no right to the notion of a *name* (not to mention a *sensation*) just like that.

(c) The training argument

Wittgenstein has argued that there must be a way of grasping a rule that is not a matter of interpretation, for there is always some interpretation available that will sanction whatever we do. To follow a rule without interpretation involves following it as a matter of course or, as Wittgenstein puts it a bit too strongly, it involves following the rule *blindly*. When we turn to actual examples of people following rules uninterpretatively, we discover that they act this way as the result of training. It is through training that human beings enter into linguistic practices—and this seems to be the only way that we can enter into a linguistic practice. Turning to an essentially private language, we have asked how a person who constructs such a language for himself could come to react to its rules uninterpretatively. We can imagine ways that this might happen—by the will and act of God, for example—but as a matter of fact, human beings come to follow rules uninterpretively only through being trained by others who already grasp these rules. But an essentially private language is one which, by definition, no other person could understand; therefore one person could not train another in a private language. We thus arrive at the result that an essentially private language is not open to human beings as we know them. This claim is put forward as a contingency, but is, I believe, the strongest claim that can be established in this area.[10]

XIII

Topics in Philosophical Psychology

1
Introduction

In the Preface to the *Investigations* Wittgenstein describes the text this way:

> I have written down all these thoughts as *remarks*, short paragraphs, of which there is sometimes a fairly long chain about the same subject, while I sometimes make a sudden change, jumping from one topic to another. (PI, p. v)

As the *Investigations* continues, the connected chains of remarks become shorter and the asides, interruptions and changes of subject more frequent. I don't point this out as a criticism, nor do I think that this is what Wittgenstein had in mind when he says, "I should have liked to produce a good book" (PI, p. vi). Wittgenstein's method of exposition is motivated by his conception of philosophy. A philosophical problem arises from confusions, misunderstandings, but not usually in a simple way. A particular philosophical problem can be the intersection of a number of misunderstandings, and as one is removed the center of gravity of the problem can shift to another. A philosophical perplexity, like a neurosis, can be *overdetermined* in its causes,[1] and because of this Wittgenstein's digressions, anticipations, flashbacks, sudden shifts of subject matter, etc., are not signs of the weakness of his method; on the contrary, they exhibit his understanding of the character of philosophical perplexities and the methods needed for resolving them.

We can say all this with suitable piety without suppressing the fact that Wittgenstein's method is continually frustrating to anyone trying to understand a particular aspect of his position. So far I have tried to follow the order of the text quite closely—taking things as they come—for by avoiding a wholesale reorganization, we also avoid imposing a heavy interpretation on the text from the start. Yet as we come to the second half of Part I of the *Investigations*, taking things as they come no longer provides a natural way of organizing a critical study. I shall therefore do in this chapter what I have not done in earlier chapters: take the text apart and put it together again to serve my purposes.

2
Plan for the treatment of psychological concepts

Under the above heading, the following prospectus for the analysis of psychological concepts appears in *Zettel:*

> Psychological verbs characterized by the fact that third-person of the present is to be verified by observation, the first-person not.
> Sentences in the third-person of the present: information. In the first-person present: expression.⌐((Not quite right.))
> The first-person of the present akin to an expression.
> Sensations: their inner connexions and analogies.
> All have genuine duration. Possibility of giving the beginning and the end. Possibility of their being synchronized, or simultaneous occurrences.
> All have degrees and qualitative mixtures. Degree: scarcely perceptible—unendurable.
> In this sense there is not a sensation of position or movement. Place of feeling in the body: differentiates seeing and hearing from sense of pressure, temperature, taste and pain. (Z, #472)

Then later:

> Continuation of classification of psychological concepts.
> Emotions. Common to them: genuine duration, a course.
> (Rage flares up, abates, vanishes, and likewise joy, depression, fear.)
> Distinction from sensations: they are not localized (nor yet diffuse!)
> Common: they have characteristic expression-behaviour.
> (Facial expression.) And this itself implies characteristic sensations too. Thus sorrow often goes with weeping, and characteristic sensations with the latter. (The voice heavy with tears.) But these sensations are not the emotions. (In the sense in which the numeral 2 is not the number 2.)
> Among emotions the directed might be distinguished from the undirected. Fear *at* something, joy *over* something.
> The something is the object, not the cause of the emotion. (Z, #488)

Along with sensations and emotions, Wittgenstein treats the following psychological concepts within this same general framework: thinking, remembering, imagining, being conscious, wishing, wanting, expecting, understanding, hoping, longing, recognizing, intending, and dreaming. He also examines such apparently internal phenomena as reading to oneself and calculating in one's head.

Although individual concepts demand special treatment, there are a number of themes that recur throughout the discussion. On the negative side, Wittgenstein continually attacks the idea that these concepts are used to formulate reports of private mental states or private mental processes. (It is for this reason that the phenomena of reading to oneself and calculating in one's head fit naturally into the investigation.) It is also characteristic of the discussion that it centers upon the *first-person present* uses of these concepts. Wittgenstein rather takes it for granted that the third-person employments of these concepts simply give information that can be verified by observation. Finally, the key for the treatment of all first-person employments of these concepts involves the notion of *expression (Äusserung)*. We have seen that this was the central idea in Wittgenstein's analysis of first-person utterances of pain. We can now examine how he tries to adapt and extend this strategy to cover a whole range of psychological concepts which, as he realizes, exhibit a great diversity among themselves.

3
Expression

Wittgenstein has two ways of formulating his basic idea about the first-person employment of psychological concepts: he sometimes says that these utterances *express* a given emotion; at other times he suggests that they are *part* of a kind of behavior. A good example of these two ways of speaking is found in *Zettel:*

> The statement "I am expecting a bang at any moment" is an *expression* of expectation. The verbal reaction is the movement of the pointer, which shows the object of expectation. (Z, #53)

Then a bit later:

> If I say "I am expecting . . . ",—am I remarking that the situations, my actions, thoughts, etc. are those of expectancy of this event; or are the words: "I am expecting . . . " *part* of the process of expecting? (Z, #65, my italics)[2]

To give a feeling for Wittgenstein's position on these matters, here are a few more passages showing his tendency to speak in these two ways:

The words with which I express my memory are my memory-reaction. (PI, #343)

The memory-image and the memory-words stand on the *same* level. (Z, #650)

When someone says "I hope he'll come"—is that a *report* about his state of mind, or a *manifestation* of his hope? (PI, #585)[3]

By nature and by a particular training, a particular education, we are disposed to give spontaneous expression to wishes in certain circumstances. (PI, #441)

Wittgenstein's tendency to speak indifferently of the sentence "I am expecting . . . " as *expressing* an expectation and as being *part* of the process of expecting shows that he sees no important difference in these two ways of speaking. Starting from the side of expression, my expectation that a friend will come is expressed in a variety of ways: I pace nervously about the room, glance repeatedly out the window, check my appointment calendar, say such things as "Oh, he's late," etc. (see PI, #444). It is in this and other ways that my expectation is expressed through my behavior. Starting from the side of behavior, we can just as well hold that my saying "I am expecting . . . " is part of the expectation behavior. It is this claim—that my remark "I am expecting . . . " is a *part of* rather than a *report on* my expectation—that gives Wittgenstein's position its distinctive turn.

Let me comment upon a possible misunderstanding that would stand Wittgenstein's position on its head. When he says that behavior as well as certain utterances can *express* an emotion, he does not mean that the behavior and the utterance are the mere outward tokens of the real thing that lies within. This is precisely the picture that Wittgenstein is trying to overcome (see PI, #308). What is correct here is that we do not want to identify having an emotion (e.g., being angry) with any particular bit of behavior. Being angry is not just a matter of saying "I am angry," for, obviously, one can say this without being angry. Even if we extend the pattern of behavior to include the rich repertoire of angry behavior (anger-behavior), we can imagine this taking place on a stage and therefore not suppose that we are dealing with genuine anger. These facts reinforce the idea that the behavior of an angry person is merely the outward manifestation of his anger within, for, without an appeal to such an underlying cause, how can we distinguish between behavior that genuinely expresses anger from behavior that only seems to express anger?[4] Wittgenstein's answer to this question, and all questions of this kind, is that we do not draw such a distinction by going *behind* the phenomena, but instead, we place the phenomena in a broader setting. That the behavior takes place on a stage does not set a problem for drawing this distinction between real and feigned anger, for, as everyone knows, this is precisely the kind of fact we appeal to in deciding whether a person is angry or not.

To return to the main line of reasoning, Wittgenstein claims that in saying I am angry I express my anger—I do not report upon some inner happening. But speaking this way can invite a misunderstanding of a different kind: if I am not reporting an *inner* happening or state, then it may seem that I am reporting some *outer* happening or state. The point, however, is that the expression "I am angry" does not make a report at all. Wittgenstein makes this clear from the start when the position is first broached with respect to expression of pain:

> "So you are saying that the word 'pain' really means crying?"—On the contrary: the verbal expression of pain replaces crying and does not describe it. (PI, #244)

The same idea lies behind his somewhat cryptic response to the charge that he is a behaviorist:

> "Are you not really a behaviorist in disguise? Aren't you at bottom really saying that everything except human behavior is a fiction?"—If I do speak of a fiction, then it is of a *grammatical* fiction. (PI, #307)

It is through misunderstanding the grammar of the first-person employment of psychological concepts that the fiction of inner happenings and states emerges. It is a mistake to *deny* that such inner states exist, for this concedes that the notion of an inner state is perfectly in order, and anger, for example, just doesn't happen to be such an inner state. Wittgenstein makes this point explicitly, but in a curious way. At one point he actually does say that "thinking is not an incorporeal process," but then quickly corrects himself:

> But how "not an incorporeal process"? Am I acquainted with incorporeal processes, then, only thinking is not one of them? No; I called the expression "an incorporeal process" to my aid in my embarrassment when I was trying to explain the meaning of the word "thinking" in a primitive way. (PI, #339)

And this striking passage occurs in the *Remarks on the Foundations of Mathematics:*

> Finitism and behaviorism are quite similar trends. Both say, but surely, all we have here is. . . . Both deny the existence of something, both with a view to escaping from a confusion. (RFM, II, 18)

The mistake of finitism and behaviorism is to deny what their opponents say: we need more distance between ourselves and a conceptual confusion than is supplied by a negation sign. So we can conclude that in intention and content, Wittgenstein's treatment of the first-person employment of psychological concepts does not involve the behavioristic thesis that they are descriptive of overt behavior. This, however, is not the end of the matter, for Wittgenstein's treatment of *third*-person uses of psychological concepts seems straightforwardly behavioristic. This is suggested in the prospectus I have cited from *Zettel*, and it seems everywhere taken for granted in his other writings on psychological concepts. I shall return to this topic at the close of the chapter and argue that this is one of the fundamental weaknesses of Wittgenstein's position.

4
Linguistic expression

Saying "I expect . . . ", according to Wittgenstein, is "part of the process of expecting" (Z, #65). All the same, it is a very special part of this process, and the same can be said for all other first-person utterances involving psychological concepts. The verbal expression of an emotion, sensation, propositional attitude, etc., is not on the same level with the other *natural* modes of expression. For example, crying and saying "I am in pain" are not on the same level, since "the verbal expression of pain replaces crying" (PI, #244).

A fuller account of these matters is found in *Zettel:*

> Being sure that someone is in pain, doubting whether he is, and so on, are so many natural, instinctive, kinds of behaviour towards other human beings, and our language is merely an auxiliary to, and further extension of, this relation. Our language-game is an extension of primitive behaviour. (For our *language-game* is behaviour.) (Instinct). (Z, #545)

Earlier he explained what he means by "primitive" in these words:

> But what is the word "primitive" meant to say here? Presumably that this sort of behaviour is *pre-linguistic:* that a language-game is based *on it*, that it is a prototype of a way of thinking and not the result of thought. (Z, #541)

The emphasis in these passages is upon the dependency of the verbal expression upon natural and instinctive expression. The primitive expression provides the *prototype* for the verbal expression—this is an important idea for it suggests that the verbal expression does not depart in any fundamental way from the primitive response from which it sprang.

At the same time, Wittgenstein does not minimize the extent to which our primitive responses can be developed and made articulate through the use of language.

> A dog believes his master is at the door. But can he also believe his master will come the day after tomorrow? (PI, p. 174)

Could a dog hope that his master will come the day after tomorrow, or dread this? The answer to all of these questions is no, for it seems that the command of a language is a prerequisite for the formation of any of these attitudes. It is not clear where we would draw the line between those emotions (attitudes, etc.) that are open only to creatures that command a language and those that can be sensibly attributed to creatures with no language. Can an animal feel shame, guilt, rancor, envy, etc.? If Wittgenstein is correct, we should be able to find the ground for each of these feelings in some primitive (i.e., pre-linguistic) response to the world and other humans in it. We may share these primitive responses with animals. Yet it hardly seems plausible that we could differentiate these feelings (shame from guilt, envy from rancor, etc.) at this primitive level. These distinctions depend, in part at least, on subtle and complex distinctions in ideational content, and we attribute such subtle and complex ideas only to creatures that command a language.

> Can only those hope who can talk? Only those who have mastered the use of a language. That is to say, the phenomena of hope are modes of this complicated form of life. (PI, p. 174)

We can also add, although I do not think that Wittgenstein ever says this explicitly, that the words we use for describing feelings, emotions, etc., come in a system containing contrasts (guilt rather than shame), matters of degree (rambunctious rather than spirited), and so on. Thus when we ascribe a particular feeling or emotion to a person, we locate it in a field (a logical space) of concepts. It makes a difference whether I attribute *hope* or *confidence* to someone, but this difference only emerges within a complicated form of life open only to users of a rich and subtle language.

The idea that the verbal expression of an emotion is part of the behavior that constitutes having that emotion has another important consequence for Wittgenstein: it provides, he thinks, the solution for the problem of "intentional objects."

> A wish seems already to know what will or would satisfy it; a proposition, a thought, what makes it true—even when that thing is not there at all. Whence this determining of what is not yet there? This despotic demand? (PI, #437)

Again, if I expect an explosion, how is my current state of mind connected with the explosion? The explosion does not exist and it may, in fact, never exist, but I expect it nonetheless. Wittgenstein's first point is that we will never solve this problem if we cling to the picture that the remark "I expect . . . " is a report of an inner mental state that will be satisfied upon the occurrence of a particular event.

Let us imagine some ways that this picture might be filled out in detail. One idea is that the relationship between an expectation and the event that will fulfill it is entirely *contingent*. To expect an explosion is to be in a state of mind that will (or would) be fulfilled when an explosion occurs. The advantage of this approach is that it is not embarrassed by cases where the expected event does not occur. There is no problem here of working out the relationship between an existent mental state and its non-existent object, for the claim that someone expects something is treated as the conditional that something will happen if a given condition is realized. The person who expects an explosion is one who will have his expectation satisfied if (and only if) an explosion occurs. One curious feature of this account is that we can wildly misunderstand our own expectations. I might think that I am expecting an explosion, but then discover that the expectation is satisfied when a cool breeze blows across my face. Even though I thought that I was expecting an explosion, it has turned out that I was expecting a cool breeze to blow across my face. Only the most rigorous empiricist in the philosophy of mind could accept this result.

Still holding to the picture that expectation involves a relationship between an inner mental state and some event, we can try to avoid the above difficulty by making this relationship non-contingent or *internal*. It is a necessary truth that an explosion, and only an explosion, will satisfy my expectation of an explosion. But it seems that this relationship must exist between the expectation and the explosion whether it occurs or not. Now, instead of treating this as a problem, we can treat it as a solution: abstracting from existence, we posit the explosion-whether-it-exists-or-not. We no longer have to worry about a relationship failing through the non-existence of one of its terms, so we can now say that, in expectation, a relationship obtains between the mind and such an *intentional* entity. Since I have not given this position an adequate statement, it would be improper to criticize it. We can notice, however, that the introduction of intentional entities is an example of the general strategy of solving conceptual issues through expanding an ontology to include items that have as their defining features just the traits needed to solve a problem.

On the assumption that expectation involves a relationship between a mental state and some event that fulfills it, we seem to be faced with two unhappy choices: (i) the fulfilling event is an ordinary event, but the relationship between expectation and its fulfillment is contingent, or (ii) the relationship between an expectation and what fulfills it is necessary (or internal), but the fulfilling event cannot (always) be identified with an ordinary event. Each of these views gains most of its plausibility from the shortcomings of its competitor.

Obviously Wittgenstein will attempt to avoid these choices by denying that a statement of what one expects is a report of some inner episode. Saying "I expect . . . " is, on his view, part of the expecting behavior. How, exactly, does this help solve the problem we have been discussing? Here is what he says:

> [W]hat's it like for him to come?—The door opens, someone walks in, and so on.—What's it like for me to expect him to come?—I walk up and down the room, look at the clock now and then, and so on.—But the one set of events has not the smallest similarity to the other! But perhaps I say as I walk up and down: "I expect he'll come in"—Now there is a similarity somewhere. But of what kind?! (PI, #444)

We are expected to know the answer to this closing question. There is a similarity between the utterance "I expect he'll come in" and the utterance which we make upon his coming in: "He is coming in." Since the same concepts are used in each utterance, we have hit upon the kind of internal relationship we have been seeking. So Wittgenstein concludes that "it is in language that an expectation and its fulfillment make contact" (PI, #445).

Perhaps we can best show the point of this reasoning by considering a natural objection. "Wittgenstein has only shown that there is a (trivial) internal relationship between the *report* of an expectation and the *report* of a state of affairs that fulfills it. He hasn't shown how the expectation itself is related to the state of affairs that fulfills it. We hardly can close that gap by noticing that the same words are used in each of these reports." The heart of Wittgenstein's reply to this criticism is to deny the gulf between the expectation itself and the report of the expectation: the report, to say it again, is part of the process of expecting. I think that we now see why Wittgenstein puts such stress on this notion. It tells us how a wish can anticipate the object that fulfills it: the formulation of a wish is part of wishing and the formulation specifies what is wished for. Issuing orders provides a model for all these cases: in issuing an order I tell someone to do *such and such* and the formulation of the order—at least typically—specifies what will count as fulfilling it, namely, doing *such and such*.

Through a particular training our primitive responses are given a verbal articulation, and thereby in expressing these responses we are able to exploit the resources of the language at large. It is important that we use the common vocabulary—not some special vocabulary—in the expression, say, of a pain. If I say that I have a pain in my right foot, I am using the phrase "right foot" in the same sense as when I say that my right foot is slightly smaller than my left.

> One may have the feeling that in the sentence "I expect he is coming" one is using the words "he is coming" in a different sense from the one they have in the assertion "He is coming". But if it were so how could I say that my expectation had been fulfilled? If I wanted to explain the words "he" and "is coming", say by means of ostensive definitions, the same definitions of these words would go for both sentences. (PI, #444)[5]

Actually, Wittgenstein isn't forced to say that the verb "is coming" has the *same* sense in "I expect he is coming" and "He is coming," for it would be sufficient for his purposes to show a systematic connection between these two uses.[6] But the most straightforward way to have an expectation and its fulfillment make contact in language is to have the expression of the expectation and the statement of the fact that fulfills it employ the same concepts in the same way.

A consequence of explaining the relationship between an expectation and its fulfillment through an appeal to language is that we limit the application of this concept—and *all* others that are treated in the same way—to creatures that command a language. Yet it is a fact that these concepts are not so limited, for we often attribute pains, beliefs, expectation, desire, etc., to dumb animals. Here I think Wittgenstein would invoke the distinction between *primary* and *secondary* uses of a word (first mentioned in PI, p. 216). The home base for the application of psychological concepts is human behavior, but we naturally extend these concepts to non-human activity when we are struck by similarities between the two.

> [O]nly of a living human being and what resembles (behaves like) a living human being can one say: it has sensations; it sees; is blind; hears; is deaf; is conscious or unconscious. (PI, #281)

We can even extend these concepts to apply to inanimate objects. In a fairy tale we have no trouble with the idea that the pot can see and hear things, but in fairy tales pots also speak, walk about, etc. (PI, #282). Struck by certain similarities to human behavior, we have no hesitation in applying psychological concepts beyond this, their primary, domain of application.

This reply may not seem good enough. As we have spelled out the relationship between expectation and its fulfillment, we have seen that a recourse to language is *essential* for making it intelligible. So when we apply this concept (and, of course, many others) to animals, we have either dropped out that which is essential to these concepts or, spinning a little fantasy around them, we suppose that animals do command a language. Of course we do sometimes spin such fantasies around animals, especially our pets, but, more interestingly, we sometimes do extend concepts in ways that drop out features we originally thought essential to them. Consider the game of solitaire (patience). It seems definitionally true that solitaire is a game played by one person,[7] yet games exist called *double* solitaire which are, indeed, two-person games. In a simple version of double solitaire, each player deals out her own hand, but may play on the other's stacks. The player who gets rid of the greater number of cards wins. It is not hard to see why this game is still called solitaire: it *looks like* solitaire. It has, to use one of Wittgenstein's favorite phrases, the characteristic physiognomy of a game of solitaire.

Wittgenstein offers a curious example of the secondary use of a word:

> Given the two ideas "fat" and "lean", would you be rather inclined to say that Wednesday was fat and Tuesday lean, or *vice versa?*
> (PI, p. 216)

I find that I agree with Wittgenstein in thinking Wednesday fat and Tuesday lean, and most people I have asked agree as well. (That "Wednesday" is a longer word than "Tuesday" is not the explanation, for in the original the words are "Dienstag" and "Mittwoch.") Wittgenstein cites this strange example in discussing what he considers a secondary use of the word "calculate" when we say that someone is calculating in his head. But the example seems too exotic for the case at hand. I have no idea why I think that Wednesday is fatter than Tuesday—at least no idea that I am willing to venture in public—but I have respectable reasons for saying that a person has performed a calculation in his head. Usually enough of the standard surroundings of calculation are present to make this transition natural. I am dealing with a person who has had our regular school training; he is given a problem that falls within his normal competence; he does not produce an answer at once. Instead, he falls silent for a moment (or perhaps mumbles to himself) and comes up with an answer. If I ask him how he got the answer so quickly, he may say that he used the trick of dividing by eight and moving the decimal point instead of multiplying directly by one hundred and twenty-five. Of course, something is missing: he has not produced the characteristic pattern of symbols that we recognize as a calculation, and the production of such a pattern of symbols is essential to calculation in its original or primary form. In this way the extension of the concept of calculation to include calculating in one's head is like the extension of the concept of solitaire to include double solitaire. In each case something quite essential seems to drop out, but the new domain of application preserves so much of the characteristic *look* of the primary domain of application that the transition is made without difficulty.

The distinction between the primary and secondary uses of words gives Wittgenstein a way of dealing with cases where emotions, beliefs, etc., are ascribed to creatures that do not employ a language (infants and animals, for example). We find it easy to say that an animal or an infant feels pain, because the natural and primitive expression of pain is often manifest in the verbal expression of pain. Relatively speaking, pain and the verbal expression of pain are close together. We ascribe pain to a wriggling fly (#284), especially if it is wriggling after being swatted. We do not ascribe remorse or rancor to a fly, for its behavior does not provide a foothold for such emotions. Of course, this response may seem too pat. Whatever example we cite of the fulfillment of a desire, expectation, etc., where the fulfillment is not specified in a verbal expression of a desire, expectation, etc., can be written off as a *secondary* employment of the concepts in question. In this way the position seals itself off from any possible criticism. Even so, the argument doesn't have to be carried out in this way. The distinction between primary and secondary uses of terms could be given an independent specification and then used without prior prejudice to decide whether psychological concepts are ever used in their primary sense in speaking about creatures who lack a language. I am not suggesting that Wittgenstein has actually done this.

I think that the main objection to Wittgenstein's account of psychological concepts is that it seems prima facie implausible. "When I say that I have a pain in my foot, I am saying something about my foot, namely, that I have a pain in it. Of course this is different from saying that I have an artery in my foot or, even, that I have a wound in my foot. These are different kinds of assertions with different kinds of verification procedures, etc., but surely they are all assertions (reports, descriptions) about my foot!!" The first response to this outburst is that it involves a misunderstanding. In saying that first-person utterances of pain are not assertions that a given person has a pain, Wittgenstein is not *denying* that people have pains. Fair enough, but Wittgenstein himself formulates the complaint that common sense insists upon:

> "Yes, but there is *something* there all the same accompanying my cry of pain. And it is on account of that that I utter it. And this something is what is important—and frightful." (PI, #296)

Wittgenstein's reply is at once brilliant and deeply unsatisfying:

> Only who are we informing of this? And on what occasion? (PI, #296)

Of course, the critic's remark is not an ordinary statement, but one uttered with a philosophical intent: i.e., it is an attempt to point out something missing in Wittgenstein's account of the expression of sensation. Indeed, what seems to be missing is the pain itself. But what is meant here by the *pain itself*? Isn't this just another way of charging Wittgenstein with denying that people have pains (which is, of course, just wrong)? Thoroughly mesmerized by a certain picture of the way language functions, we treat attacks upon the picture as denials of plain matters of fact. (In the same way philosophers have attacked conventionalist and constructivist accounts of mathematics by insisting that two plus two *does* equal four.)

I think that we can say all of this and still feel that the complaint of common sense has not been fully answered. The difficulty, I think, is that Wittgenstein has said too little on the constructive side about the character of expressions of sensation. He has had a deep insight into the locus of a fundamental philosophical problem: we generate intractable philosophical problems by treating first-person expressions of sensation (emotion, intention, etc.) under the picture theory of meaning. He has also offered a general sketch for an alternative way of viewing this discourse: an expression of an emotion is part of the emotional behavior, not a report on it. This approach gains some support by suggesting how an expectation (hope, desire, etc.) is non-contingently connected to the state of affairs that would fulfill it.

What is surprising, however, is how much Wittgenstein does not discuss. For example, he says almost nothing about the *third*-person employment of psychological concepts. He seems content to believe—as he says in *Zettel*—that the third-person use of these concepts gives *information* and is *verified by observation* (Z, #472). Well, what information do I offer when I say that someone has a pain in his foot? Presumably I cannot do what the possessor of the pain himself cannot do: I cannot report the occurrence of a state private to the possessor of the pain. Am I then asserting that a particular pattern of behavior has occurred—rather like limping, but more complicated? This suggests that the ascribing of a sensation, emotion, intention, etc., to a person differs from describing his bodily motions only as a matter of degree. Wittgenstein actually makes a gesture in the direction of such a theory:

> Our attitude to what is alive and to what is dead, is not the same. All our reactions are different.—If anyone says: "That cannot simply come from the fact that a living thing moves about in such-and-such a way and a dead one not", then I want to intimate to him that this is a case of the transition "from quantity to quality". (PI, #284)

Another possible theory—and Wittgenstein seems to hint at this as well (see, for example PI, ## 286, 287)—is that my ascription of a pain to another expresses my feelings toward him: my pity or sympathy. Yet it is hard to see how this theory can be worked out to include the ascription of expectations and intentions to another.

The point is that Wittgenstein works none of these matters out in detail. Smith's remark that he intends to go to New York and my remark that Smith intends to go to New York must stand in some very close relationship to one another. According to Wittgenstein, Smith's remark is part of the process of intending to go to New York, but then what am I asserting if I say—perhaps to Smith himself—that he does *not* intend to go to New York? Do I use the word "intend" (and the other words in the sentence) in the same sense he does? If not, how do I manage to contradict what he has said? If I do use these words in the same sense that he does, then, going back to the beginning, how does my assertion that he intends to go to New York differ in meaning from his remark to the same effect? I don't think that the text contains answers to questions of this kind and, in sum, it leaves the relationship between the first-person and third-person uses of psychological concepts wholly unexplained.

Let me conclude with a speculation concerning Wittgenstein's tendency to ignore the third-person use of psychological concepts. I do not think that Wittgenstein was primarily interested in the correct analysis of psychological concepts: the focus of his attention was, instead, on such traditional problems as solipsism, the Cartesian *cogito*, etc. This comes out most clearly in the *Blue Book* where Wittgenstein speaks about two uses of the word "I:"

> There are two different cases in the use of the word "I" (or "my")
> which I might call "the use as object" and "the use as subject."
> Examples of the first kind of use are these: "My arm is broken," "I
> have grown six inches." . . . Examples of the second kind are "*I*
> see so-and-so," . . . "*I* have a toothache." (BB, pp. 66–7)

Misunderstandings of "I" used *as subject* lead to philosophical illusions:

> We feel then that in the cases in which "I" is used as subject, we
> don't use it because we recognize a particular person by his bodily
> characteristics: and this creates the illusion that we use this word to
> refer to something bodiless, which, however, has its seat in our body.
> In fact *this* seems to be the real ego, the one of which it was said,
> "Cogito, ergo sum". (BB, p. 69)

So it is the word "I" (in one of its uses) that is the center of confusion—the psychological terms that come further down the sentence are of relatively little importance. The same general approach, if not the terminology, is carried over to the *Investigations*, where it is the first-person present uses of psychological concepts that demand special treatment. The uses in other persons and tenses are allowed to take care of themselves—presumably in ordinary ways.

Actually, this is a very curious strategy. Of the two following sentences, the first is presumably problematic, the second not:

I have a toothache.
I have a bump on my forehead.

Wittgenstein seems to suggest that it is not the *different* elements that make one problematic, the other not, but the *common* element, the word "I," which is said to be used in two different ways: first *as subject*, then *as object*. Could we then reverse things, using the "I" in the first sentence *as object* and the "I" in the second sentence *as subject?* Or can the word "I" be used *as subject* only in special contexts? What are these contexts like?

For my own part I find it difficult to believe that there are two such uses of the word "I." What is true, I think, is that *first-person present* statements have peculiar features just because the person making the remark is identical with the person about whom the remark is made. To take one example, it would surely be odd for a person to say that he *believed* his name was N N. This is not something a person *merely* believes but presumably *knows*.[8] Yet this does not show that a person has special access to his own name. Nor do we need any special theory to distinguish the force of ascribing a name to oneself from the force of ascribing a name to another. (E.g., "When I say that my name is N N, I am not telling you that a certain person has that name, I am telling you *my* name.") First-person utterances in the present tense are particularly liable to interference between what is being said and the rules that govern the saying of it, just because the speaker, who is being governed by these rules, is the person spoken about. For example, there is nothing paradoxical about saying "The market will collapse before the end of the year, although most people do not believe it." It does sound paradoxical—it's called Moore's paradox—to say "The market will collapse before the end of the year, but I don't believe it." But such oddities do not force us to draw a distinction between two uses of the word "I" as in the *Blue Book*. Nor do they force us to give a special account of the first-person employment of psychological concepts—the heir to the *Blue Book* doctrine as it appears in the *Investigations*.[9]

It is also important to remember that certain psychological concepts, or apparent psychological concepts, such as *knowing*, *seeing*, and intending, are peculiar, or at least special in their employment. For example, by ascribing an intention to a person we often make his behavior intelligible through indicating how the items in the behavior fit together to achieve a given result. (A person can do the same thing when he states his *own* intentions.) Given a primitive theory of the way in which language works, it is easy to misunderstand these concepts and posit items in consciousness of the most extraordinary kind. But if we are both bamboozled by the oddities of the first-person present and misled by the surface grammar of psychological assertions, then we probably have all the confusions needed to generate what is called Modern Philosophy. Wittgenstein concentrates upon what he takes to be the misunderstandings of the first-person present. I do not think that he has given a very plausible account of the use of this construction,[10] but, more importantly, his one-sided interest in this issue leads him to neglect a close examination of psychological concepts themselves. It is as if he assumes that a correct analysis of first-person present utterances will at once solve the main problems concerning psychological concepts. That, however, is not true.

5
Seeing as

Part II of the *Investigations* contains a famous (and perplexing) discussion of the phenomenon of changing aspects. We look at a drawing of a double cross and first see it as a black figure on a white ground, then as a white figure on a black ground. More famously, we look at a drawing of a duck and then, to our surprise, it strikes us as a drawing of a rabbit.

Wittgenstein begins his discussion of these cases by distinguishing two uses of the word "see:"

> The one: "What do you see there?"—"I see *this*" (and then a description, a drawing, a copy). The other: "I see a likeness between these two faces"—let the man I tell this to be seeing the faces as clearly as I do myself. (PI, p. 193)

Thus if A and B are asked to sketch the faces they have seen, it could come out that they have seen the same thing through the striking similarities in the drawings they produce. Yet A may notice a likeness between the faces that B fails to recognize. This shows, according to Wittgenstein, a categorical difference ([ein] *kategorische Unterschied*) between these two "objects" of sight (PI, p. 195). Wittgenstein calls this later sort of seeing "noticing an aspect" (PI, p. 193). Noticing an aspect is a common phenomenon, but it appears in its most arresting form in the so-called ambiguous figures of the kind mentioned at the beginning of this section. Here we see something first under one aspect, then under another. For example, we first see the drawing as a flight of stairs falling away from us, then we see it as coming toward us, as if from underneath. In a case like this, we are inclined to say that we really *see* the drawing one way and then *see* it the other. This is not something we make up; it is, we might say, a part of our visual experience.

In an enigmatic passage, Wittgenstein makes the following remark about visual experience:

What is the criterion of the visual experience?—The criterion?
What do you suppose?
The representation of "what is seen". (PI, p. 198)

I'm not entirely sure what Wittgenstein means by this passage, but one plausible reading squares with the general development of his argument. Suppose that two people, A and B, are looking at a duck-rabbit drawing. A sees it as a duck drawing; B sees it as a rabbit drawing. There is a sense in which they are seeing the same thing and another sense in which they are not. This difference could be brought out by asking each to produce a set of drawings corresponding to what he sees. We might first ask each to produce an accurate *copy* of what he has seen, and then a series of drawings of other things that have the same look. Though too pat to occur in real life, we can imagine the result. The similarities between the attempted copies would reveal the sense in which they have seen the same thing. The sharp difference between the remaining drawings would reveal the sense in which they have seen something different (see PI, p. 197).

Wittgenstein's basic point is that we fall into confusion when we merge these categorially different uses of the word "see." An attempted assimilation can go in either direction: (i) all cases of seeing can be treated as cases of seeing-as, or (ii) seeing-as can be viewed as just another kind of seeing.

(i) The idea that seeing is always a matter of seeing-as has the ring of a profound discovery. Indeed, many people suppose that psychological investigation has put this contention beyond dispute. Wittgenstein treats it as a conceptual confusion:

One doesn't "take" what one knows as the cutlery at a meal *for* cutlery; any more than one ordinarily tries to move one's mouth as one eats, or aims at moving it. (PI, p. 195)

For example, if I say "Now I am seeing this as a knife," I will not be understood, unless, that is, the knife appears in a strange context where it is not easily recognized. Against this, someone might argue that when I recognize a knife I am recognizing a similarity between this item and other items that are called knives. So every act of seeing involves noticing an aspect; cases only differ in their novelty or vividness. Wittgenstein would probably reply that this cannot be the fundamental account of perceptual recognition, for, in order for there to be perceptual recognition at all, there must be a form of recognition that is *not a matter of interpretation*. None of this commits Wittgenstein to naive realism in the theory of perception. He can easily acknowledge that perception is mediated by *causal* factors, that is, causal factors enter into what we can see and how we see it. But we do not get an account of these causal factors by the conceptual trick of reducing all cases of seeing to cases of seeing-as. Indeed, nothing is accomplished by this move since the notion of seeing-as presupposes the notion of seeing and gains its significance from the contrast it enjoys with it.

(ii) A different kind of confusion can arise if we treat seeing-as as just another sort of seeing. Here Wittgenstein maintains that it is a mistake to put the organization of the visual impression on the same level with colors and shapes (PI, p. 196). He associates this with the "idea that the visual impression is an inner object" which makes it, he suggests, "into a chimera; a queerly shifting construction" (PI, p. 196). One reason that we might invoke such an inner object is to explain where the change of organization takes place. Since the figure visibly does not alter, something *else* must alter. An inner image has often commended itself at this point. But how will an inner image help? Is it an image of the ambiguous duck-rabbit drawing? This will not do, for now we are confronted with an inner object that undergoes aspect-change and, although the seat of the mystery has been shifted, the mystery itself has not been solved. Then are the inner pictures a series of unambiguous duck-image followed by an unambiguous rabbit-image, etc.? We find nothing in experience corresponding to this, for part of our experience is that the thing we see, in an important sense, does not change. Our difficulty is that we want the inner picture to play *both* roles: we want it to be an exact copy since, in noticing an aspect-change, we notice, in some strong sense, that nothing changes at all. We also want the inner picture to be like those other pictures of ducks and rabbits that we invoke to explain what does seem to change. But now we are making incompatible demands upon the picture. This incompatibility is not relieved by making the picture an inner picture.

Wittgenstein's own remarks about aspect-change are broad and programmatic. He suggests that "the flashing of an aspect on us seems half visual experience, half thought" (PI, p. 197). It seems both "seeing and thinking" or even an "amalgam of the two" (PI, p. 197). How then are we to characterize this phenomenon? One thing we might do is simply describe how this phenomenon is related to others—both in relevant similarities and differences. We could simply stop with this description. This, I think, is Wittgenstein's suggestion, although he recognizes that the task of the description may be highly complicated:

Is being struck looking plus thinking? No. Many of our concepts cross here. (PI, p. 211)

Wittgenstein also ties the phenomenon of seeing-as to his central idea of mastering a technique:

"Now he is seeing it like *this*", "now like *that*" would only be said of someone *capable* of making certain applications of the figure quite freely.

The substratum of this experience is the mastery of a technique.
(PI, p. 208)

This suggests that an aspect-change seems natural to us because we are able to apply the figure freely (or as a matter of course) to represent a duck or to represent a rabbit. Our experience of the diagram is a reflection of our ability to employ the diagram smoothly in a given way. This, I think, provides the background for understanding the following startling remark:

[W]hat I perceive in the dawning of an aspect is not a property of the object, but an internal relation between it and other objects.
(PI, p. 212)

This is the only mention of *internal relations* in the *Investigations*, and it needs some explaining. I think that Wittgenstein's explanation of internal relations would follow his treatment of necessity. When things appear as if they *have to be* connected in a certain way, this shows that we are bringing them under a rule that we have mastered and apply routinely (blindly). Although Wittgenstein does not use the phrase in that context, this is how he explains the internal relations in the numerical sequence 2, 4, 6, 8. . . .

But isn't it really peculiar that an ability to apply a figure in a given way should be a *logical* condition for a certain kind of experience? We have, of course, seen a position somewhat similar to this with respect to the emotions. Since hoping is a manifestation of a complicated form of life involving complex propositional attitudes toward the future, it seems that only a creature who has mastered the use of language can hope (PI, p. 174). Yet the situation with respect to the duck-rabbit figure seems somehow different. Couldn't a child, perhaps, notice that the diagram undergoes a strange alteration without having a command of either the concept duck or the concept rabbit? Wittgenstein, in fact, acknowledges that this might happen with a simpler diagram—the double cross where figure and ground seem to alternate:

Those two aspects of the double cross (I shall call them the aspects A) might be reported simply by pointing to an isolated black cross.
One could quite well imagine this as a primitive reaction in a child even before it could talk. (PI, p. 207)

In speaking of a *primitive* reaction, Wittgenstein surely means a reaction that antedates a particular training or the particular mastering of a technique. So, at least in some cases, Wittgenstein freely acknowledges that the phenomenon of aspect-change cannot be explained by a previous mastery of concepts. Now for most philosophers an admission of this kind would seem completely fatal to the view being presented. Wittgenstein seems wholly undisturbed. That we cannot extend the application of aspect-change from one case to another merely shows, according to him, that they are less similar than we originally supposed:

> You only "see the duck and rabbit aspects" if you are already conversant with the shapes of those two animals. There is no analogous condition for seeing the aspect A. (PI, p. 207)

There is something deeply unsatisfying about a move of this kind, but, of course, we have met it before. It seems that those things which we will call aspect-changes form only a family, where certain features that are logically crucial in some cases simply drop out in others. We have no right to insist that there must be a single theory of aspect-change that covers both the duck-rabbit and the double cross. We can explain what we can explain, but very quickly Wittgenstein leaves explaining alone and falls back upon describing similarities and differences in various cases.[11]

6
Wittgenstein's know-nothing approach

Wittgenstein repeatedly insists that explanation has to come to an end somewhere, that at some point reasons give out, that interpretations cannot forever be backed by other interpretations, etc., etc.

> If I have exhausted the justification I have reached bedrock, and my spade is turned. Then I am inclined to say: "This is simply what I do." (PI, #217)

But it often seems that the spade is turned after barely scratching the surface. One of the best expressions of the attitude I have in mind occurs in a passage in *Zettel:*

> Here we come up against a remarkable and characteristic phenomenon in philosophical investigation: the difficulty—I might say—is not that of finding the solution but rather that of recognizing as the solution something that looks as if it were only a preliminary to it. "We have already said everything.—Not anything that follows from this, no *this* itself is the solution!"
> This is connected, I believe, with our wrongly expecting an explanation, whereas the solution of the difficulty is a description, if we give it the right place in our considerations. If we dwell upon it, and do not try to get beyond it. The difficulty here is: to stop. (Z, #314)

The attitude expressed in this passage is the source of one of the major difficulties (indeed, frustrations) in trying to evaluate Wittgenstein's philosophy, for he typically stops his investigations at the point where many philosophers think that the problems have only been stated. For example, the notion of a language-game plays an important role throughout Wittgenstein's later thought, but if we ask what a language-game is, we are told that language-games merely form a family of interrelated cases. Some general things can be said about language-games that hold, perhaps, for the most part, but the best way to introduce the notion of a language-game is through giving a series of examples, and Wittgenstein proceeds to do just this.

> One gives examples and intends them to be taken in a particular way.—I do not, however, mean by this that he is supposed to see in those examples that common thing which I—for some reason—was unable to express; but that he is now to *employ* those examples in a particular way. Here giving examples is not an *indirect* means of explaining—in default of a better. The point is that *this* is how we play the game. (I mean the language game with the word "game".) (PI, #71)

So in the end, and the end is encountered almost at once, we are told that a language-game is *this, this* and *this*. The italicized demonstrative is the *leitmotiv* of Wittgenstein's later philosophy:

> *This* is how we think. *This* is how we act. *This* is how we talk about it. (Z, #309)

During the last centuries philosophers have, of course, offered explanations of how concepts (general ideas) can be derived from particular instances, and psychologists have added to these stories. The abstractionist account is, I suppose, the oldest, but Wittgenstein rejects this because in many cases there seems to be no common element that runs through all the items in virtue of which they fall under a concept. Indeed, Wittgenstein seems to reject *all* mentalistic accounts of acquiring a command of a concept, for whatever mental state one considers, it always seems possible that one could be in that state and yet not command the concept, i.e., not understand how to employ an expression correctly.

An alternative to such mentalistic explanations is that examples serve as stimuli that establish physiological connections in the central nervous system. On this approach there would be no reason to assume that either the teacher or the learner is aware of the mechanisms that underlie the training. Indeed, this seems a reasonable view for Wittgenstein to take seriously, for it would provide another example of a fact of human nature underlying the possibility of a language-game. Wittgenstein, however, shows little sympathy for an approach of this kind. Returning to the example of reading discussed earlier,[12] he makes the following remark concerning the suggestion that the ability to read is grounded in certain connections established in the brain and the nervous system:

> That it is so is presumably a priori—or is it only probable? And how probable is it? Now ask yourself what do you know about these things?—But if it is a priori, that means that it is a form of account which is very convincing to us. (PI, #158)

Needless to say, we don't know very much about these things, and it is important to be skeptical of the advocates of artificial intelligence or computer simulation, who often confuse their research projects with results. But surely more than a prejudice lies behind the desire to find physiological explanations of psychological phenomena. In the first place, and this is most important, learning how to read and developing the command of a concept through training are the kinds of phenomena for which explanation seems appropriate. This is not because they are odd or unusual; they just seem to be of the wrong *order* to be simply brute and inexplicable. In the same way, it would seem inappropriate to treat rain as one of the inexplicabilia of our world. (Imagine someone saying, "It just rains, that's all; explanation has to come to an end somewhere.") These phenomena do not seem sufficiently fundamental to be accorded a primitive status. Second, the assumption that these explanations may ultimately refer to the mechanism of the central nervous system only shows that we tend to return to a well that gives no signs of drying up.

But Wittgenstein will have none of this, and at times his reservations concerning physiological explanation are almost strident. Here are some passages that occur late in *Zettel:*

> No supposition seems to me more natural than that there is no process in the brain correlated with associating or with thinking; so that it would be impossible to read off thought-processes from brain-processes. (Z, #608)

This is probably right, for it seems implausible that there is any simple isomorphism between reading and brain processes that would allow us to *read the one off* from the other. But Wittgenstein goes beyond this plausible criticism to something stronger:

> I saw this man years ago: now I have seen him again, I recognize him, I remember his name. And why does there have to be a cause of this remembering in my nervous system: Why must something or other, whatever it may be, be stored up there *in any form?* Why *must* a trace have been left behind? Why should there not be a psychological regularity to which *no* physiological regularity

207

corresponds? If this upsets our concept of causality then it is high time it was upset. (Z, #609)

But must there be a physiological explanation here? Why don't we just leave explaining alone? But you would never talk like that, if you were examining the behaviour of a machine! Well, who says that a living creature, an animal body, is a machine in this sense? (Z, #614)

There are, of course, straightforward answers to some of these questions. One reason for supposing that there must be a cause for remembering in the nervous system is the known fact that damage to the nervous system sometimes destroys the ability to remember. This, of course, has been known for centuries.

Here it seems possible to offer a criticism of Wittgenstein's later philosophy that parallels a criticism that I made earlier of the *Tractatus*. With respect to the *Tractatus*, I argued that Wittgenstein had no right to favor any one ethical or metaphysical pronouncement over any other. The doctrine of showing provides no opportunity for special pleading. Similarly, I do not think that methods of Wittgenstein's later philosophy give him grounds for favoring one empirical hypothesis (or one scientific research project) over any other. Wittgenstein's personal opinions about the possibility of producing a trace theory of memory are of no interest to us, for, after all, what does *he* know about such things?

At this point someone might object that Wittgenstein's criticisms only concern philosophical investigation and have nothing to do with empirical investigation.[13] Actually, Wittgenstein's attack upon explanation makes considerable sense when it is directed against philosophical explanations of the traditional kind. Such an attack would be of a piece with his rejection of philosophical questions and, hence, philosophical propositions. There are no philosophical explanations because there are no philosophical facts to explain. The difficulty, however, is that Wittgenstein seems to carry his prejudice against explanation beyond philosophy into empirical areas. The passages from *Zettel* give one example of this, but others can be found in the *Investigations* as well. Wittgenstein's discussion of learning through examples provides one instance of this. Here is another. In #23 Wittgenstein asks how many kinds of sentences there are and replies:

There are *countless* kinds: countless different kinds of use of what we call "symbols", "words", "sentences". (PI, #23)

What kind of assertion is this? Is it, for example, empirical? Has Wittgenstein set out to count the kinds of sentences and discovered that they never seem to run out? Actually, it is hard to know what to make of the question "How many kinds of sentences are there?" when it is asked just like that. If someone asks me how many kinds of leaves there are, I might reply two kinds: (i) those that are scaly or needle-like and (ii) those that are broad and flat. In another context I might say that there are as many kinds of leaves as there are species of leaf-bearing trees. In yet another context, I might want to distinguish the kinds of leaves that grow in different parts of a tree (if such a distinction exists). Perhaps we want to say that there are countlessly many ways that we *might* want to classify leaves, but, in general, given some method of classification, it doesn't turn out that there are endlessly many kinds within the classification.

Wittgenstein does, in fact, give an indication of the sort of classification he has in mind, for he speaks of *assertions, questions and commands* (PI, #23). Using this as our starting point, do we really find countlessly many different kinds of sentences? Could we even find eighteen kinds of sentences of this order? I doubt it. So again, what are we to make of Wittgenstein's claim that there are countlessly many different kinds of sentences? I don't think that it is an empirical proposition, and perhaps not a proposition at all. It seems rather to express a commitment to the brute multiplicity of the phenomena of the world—a commitment to the inexplicability of things. It sounds like a remark that could have bearing upon empirical linguistics, but, if that's its intent, Wittgenstein has provided few empirical grounds for accepting it.

This commitment to inexplicability reveals itself in a variety of ways. One reason we seek explanations is that we find things surprising. Wittgenstein gives this commonplace a remarkable turn:

> Don't take it as a matter of course, but as a remarkable fact, that pictures and fictitious narratives give us pleasure, occupy our minds.
> ("Don't take it as a matter of course" means: find it surprising, as you do some things which disturb you. *Then the puzzling aspect of the latter will disappear, by your accepting this fact as you do the other*.) (my italics, PI, #524)

If we take this parenthetical remark seriously—and I have no doubt that it is intended seriously—we get a procedure that is just the reverse of explanation. In an explanation we often try to remove the strangeness of something by showing how it is derived from (or fits in with) things that are not strange. Wittgenstein suggests that instead we should be struck with the strangeness of the familiar and in this way the original case will lose its exceptional character. Thus instead of eliminating the contrast between the strange and the obvious by making everything obvious, Wittgenstein would have us eliminate this contrast by recognizing that everything is strange.[14]

It is hard to know what to say about such a view beyond noticing that it exists in the text. Wittgenstein does not develop this view in detail, and, needless to say, he never defends it. Yet it has persistent influence throughout the text, for we are continually denied explanation just where we want it—told that the story is over before it gets interesting. With respect to philosophical questions, this attitude is well grounded in the main tenets of his philosophy. With respect to empirical inquiries, it is simply out of place.

XIV

Topics in the Philosophy of Mathematics

1
Introduction

As we examine Wittgenstein's later treatment of mathematics, it will become evident that much is carried over from the Tractarian period. He never goes back on the idea that there are no logical or mathematical objects. This is the advanced idea of the *Tractatus*—the part that breaks with the primitive idea that words stand for things. Indeed, one useful way of viewing Wittgenstein's philosophical development is as a progressive expansion of this insight he first had with respect to logical and mathematical terms: not all terms function as proxies for objects.

Even so, there is a residual Platonism in the *Tractatus* that cannot be overlooked: the necessary form of the world which is mirrored in a logic and mathematics adequate for the description of the world. We have already seen that Wittgenstein abandons this notion of a sublime substructure that provides the unaltering arena for the play of contingencies. With this, there is no objective correlate for mathematics—either to be described or mirrored. If Platonism is no longer available, either in a traditional or Tractarian form, aren't we left with one half of the Tractarian synthesis: a conventionalism or pure formalism? This, I think, sets Wittgenstein's problem: to find a way of rejecting Platonism in mathematics unequivocally without thereby falling back into conventionalism.

2
Anti-Platonism without conventionalism[1]

To see the force of Wittgenstein's position, we can reflect upon the following simple line of reasoning.

"5 x 5 = 25" expresses a proposition.

211

Furthermore, it expresses a true proposition, and therefore, it must be true *of* something. Finally, since the truth in question is a necessary truth, the objects it is true of must be *ideal* rather than empirical.

Empiricists in mathematics—and here we can take John Stuart Mill as the most plausible representative—attack the argument at its final step. What we take to be necessity is nothing more than an overwhelmingly high degree of probability. By this doctrine we avoid the demand for ideal objects. The Logical Empiricists, true to their Christian name, attack one step earlier. All necessary truths are analytic and, as such, possess only formal truth, telling us nothing about a set of objects. It remained for Wittgenstein to attack the citadel by calling into question the root notion that mathematical equations are propositional in character.[2]

> We are used to saying "2 times 2 is 4," and the verb "is" makes this into a proposition, and apparently establishes a close kinship with everything we call a "proposition" where it is a matter only of a superficial relationship. (RFM, I, Appendix I, 4)

If mathematical constructions are only superficially related to those other things that we call propositions, what, in fact, are they like? On this score, Wittgenstein says two things, that, at first glance, may seem unrelated. First, he says that mathematics is normative:

> The proposition proved by means of a proof serves as a rule—and so as a paradigm. For we *go by* the rule. (RFM, I, Appendix II, 4)
>
> What I am saying comes to this, that mathematics is *normative*. But "norm" does not mean the same thing as "ideal." (RFM, V, 40)

Paralleling these passages are others that speak of our mode of acknowledging a mathematical expression:

> We give an axiom a different kind of acknowledgement from any empirical proposition. . . . An axiom, I should like to say, is a different part of speech. (RFM, III, 5)

On one occasion he brings these two themes together:

> I am trying to say something like this: even if the proved proposition seems to point to a reality outside itself, still it is only the expression of acceptance of a new measure (of reality). (RFM, II, 28)

Thus, if we say straight out what we in fact acknowledge in our employment of mathematical equations, mathematical expressions undergo the following transformation: "5 x 5 = 25" (acknowledged as a law) becomes "It is a law that 5 x 5 = 25."[3] That Wittgenstein had something very like this in mind is brought out by the following central passage:

The opposite of "there exists a law that p" is not "there exists a law that ~p." But if one expresses the first by means of P, and the second by means of ~P, one will get into difficulties. (RFM, IV, 13)

Thus despite the grammatical appearance, the expression "5 x 5 = 25" formulates a rule rather than a proposition.

Wittgenstein's idea is not outrageous, for it is an undisputed fact that we do use the expression "5 x 5 = 25" as a rule in the process of computing a complex product. What we want to know is how Wittgenstein's position differs from formalism in mathematics. The answer to this question is given in the following passages, which are some of the most important in Wittgenstein's writings:

Concepts which occur in "necessary" propositions must also occur and have a meaning in non-necessary ones. (RFM, IV, 41)

And, less abstractly:

I want to say: it is essential to mathematics that its signs are also employed in mufti [*in Zivil*].
It is the use outside mathematics, and so the meaning of the signs that make the sign game into mathematics. (RFM, IV, 2)

For example, the numeral 2 is used in expressing the empirical proposition that Mars has two satellites, and it is also used in expressing the "necessary" proposition that 2 + 2 = 4. Wittgenstein here insists that without significant occurrences in expressions of the first sort the numeral 2 could not have significant occurrences in expressions of the second sort.

Wittgenstein's reflections on this point take a curious form: he carefully considers an empiricist view that calculating is an experimental procedure, i.e., in calculating we set out to discover what results from applying certain rules to, say, given numbers. This view, however unattractive in other respects, is at least hard-headed:

It looks like obscurantism to say that a calculation is not an experiment . . . people believe that one is asserting the existence of an intangible, i.e., a shadowy, object side by side with what we can all grasp. (RFM, II, 76)

An experimental analysis of calculation blocks the road to Platonism by treating mathematical propositions as propositions *about* human activity. But this will not do, according to Wittgenstein, just because mathematical propositions are not statements about people at all:

We say, not, "So *that's* how we go!," but "So *that's* how it goes!" (RFM, II, 69)

But if we reject the empirical interpretation of mathematical

213

expressions, how do we preserve their sense without falling back into Platonism? Wittgenstein has two main answers: (i) the vocabulary of mathematics provides us with *modes of description*, and (ii) the laws of arithmetic supply us with *rules for the identity of descriptions*.

(i) The following quotation illustrates the first point:

> "It is interesting to know *how many* vibrations this note has." But it took arithmetic to teach you this question. It taught you to see this kind of fact.
>
> Mathematics—I want to say—teaches you, not just the answer to a question, but a whole language-game with questions and answers. (RFM, V, 15)

This does not commit Wittgenstein to the position that the note did *not* have so many vibrations before people learned to count, for his claim places no restrictions on the past tense use of our vocabulary. Furthermore, Wittgenstein is not saying that this vocabulary *creates* these empirical facts; in his own words, we are taught to *see* this kind of fact. This is worth saying if only to block a superficial comparison between Wittgenstein and Benjamin Whorf. This, however, is not the occasion to pursue these matters in detail, for it is the second point noted above that is most important for our purposes.

(ii) The second idea, that the laws of arithmetic supply us with rules for the identity of descriptions, is suggested in the following passage:

> For arithmetic to equate . . . two expressions is, one might say, a grammatical trick.
>
> In this way arithmetic bars a particular kind of description and conducts descriptions into other channels. (RFM, V, 3)

Again, we can consider the simple identity statement that 5 x 5 = 25. This expression can play a double role in our mathematical activities. For one thing, it is an item we learn by heart as part of the multiplication table, and it is used, pretty much mechanically, when working out complex products. Here it is much like a rule for decoding—given these signs, we write down others under the governance of a rule. If we attend to just this use of the expression, we shall be led in the direction of a pure formalism, with the result that we will have no account of the *point* of having such expressions.

Beyond this, the expression relates two ways of describing a collection of things. The sense of the numeral "25" is grounded —or was originally grounded—in the practice of counting. The sense of the expression "5 x 5" is grounded in a more complex practice: roughly, through counting, we put things into equi-numerous batches of a certain number and then we count up the total number of items in the batches. The identity statement lays down the principle that where one mode of description is correct, so, too, is the other. Notice that the expression "5 x 5 = 25" is not used to formulate a proposition *about* these procedures, rather it *shows* this interconnection by providing a rule for passing from one expression to the other.

But how do we *know* when two modes of description are so related? Suppose I try to convince someone that five times five equals twenty-five by having him count out five batches containing five items each and then have him count up the total. Is it obvious that he will come up with the expected result? To vary one of Wittgenstein's examples, suppose that I try to convince him that five times five equals twenty-five by producing the following picture:

```
X X X X X  1.
X X X X X  2.
X X X X X  3.
X X X X X  4.
X X X X X  5.
```

Then to vary the example, I do the *same thing* again in a somewhat different form:

XXXXX XXXXX XXXXX XXXXX XXXXX

Each time I have him count up the total to convince himself that five batches of five comes to twenty-five. I now ask him to carry out the same procedure, and, not wishing to appear unoriginal, he produces the following display:

```
X X X X X  1.
X X X X X  2.
X X X X X  3.
X X X X X  4.
        X
        5.
```

Has he done what we told him to do? Well, what he has done meets my description perfectly, for he has totted up five batches each containing five things. Yet he has not done what we *wanted* him to do; he has yet to master the technique that underlies our use of the expression "5 x 5." Furthermore, since our use is part of the instituted practice, he has yet to grasp the role of the expression "5 x 5" in *mufti*.

Here we want to convince our student that, despite the superficial *differences*, we have done the same thing twice over in our performances, whereas he, despite the superficial *similarities* with our performance, has actually done something quite different. Of course, our student might remark that the only difference he can see is that counting the items in our pictures we get the total twenty-five, whereas when he counts the items in his array he gets twenty-one. But we can hardly invoke this fact to show him that he has not done what we have done, for the whole point of the exercise was to *prove* that five times five equals twenty-five.

We might try to get around these difficulties by making our instructions more specific; and it's a fact that sometimes making instructions more specific increases a student's chances of getting things right. And it is another fact—this time a conceptual fact that we examined in detail in Chapter XI—that no matter what he does, there will be some interpretation that will support the claim that he has done the same thing again. Of course, these interpretations will soon strike us as gratuitous—even mad—and we have no inclination to play at this game when engaged in the practical affairs of life. But still, from an abstract point of view, anything can be shown to be in conformity with the instructions we have given, and nothing as well. Yet people do, on the whole, follow such instructions correctly, so again we encounter a profoundly Humean theme: a complete conceptual indeterminacy overbalanced by nothing more than a brute fact of human nature.

> For it is a peculiar procedure: I go *through* the proof and then accept its result.—I mean: this is simply what we *do*. This is use and custom among us, or a fact of our natural history. (RFM, I, 63)

Returning to our story, the student, even after mastering the appropriate techniques, can still come up with the wrong answer. To say that a person knows how to count does not mean that he cannot miscount. Miscounting is not a skill, knack or achievement, but still presupposes skills, knacks and achievements. It is simply wrong, then, to say that mathematical identity statements predict the result that a person will reach if he carries out a certain computation. Yet we do insist that they predict what he will get if he carries out these activities *correctly*. We now want to know how inserting the word "correctly" can make this difference. Wittgenstein's answer runs something like this: although our training in mathematics consists—at least in part—of checking results, the outcome of this activity is not a generalization about what turns up when people count things, group things, etc., but instead, we are led to view the result of our exercise as a paradigm for carrying out future computations. Once we elevate a specific result to the status of a paradigm, the language of correct and incorrect computation finds its place. For the upshot of our instruction is not the conclusion: (i) *this time* the product of five times five is twenty-five; nor even, (ii) in general the product of five times five is twenty-five; but instead, (iii) it is a rule that the product of five times five is twenty-five. That it is acknowledged as a rule is brought out by its subsequent employment, where it is followed as a matter of course. In this way, "mathematics forms a network of norms." (RFM, V, 46)

216

3
Invention and discovery

Does the mathematician invent or discover truths of mathematics? To the extent that one is attracted to conventionalism, it seems that mathematical results are artifacts of the mathematician; if Platonic instincts dominate, these results will strike us as discoveries concerning an independent subject matter. Mathematical activity gives support to both these feelings. Here an example will help. Schopenhauer used the diagram shown in Figure XIV.1 to prove that the Pythagorean Theorem holds for isosceles right triangles.

Figure XIV.1

It is easy to see that the area of the square constructed (downward) from the hypotenuse of the shaded triangle is equal in area to the sum of the areas of the two squares constructed on its legs.[4]

Now in this proof, how much was invention, how much discovery? Constructing the diagram in this special way is something that *we* did and the same might be said about the interpretation we placed upon it. We not only constructed the diagram, we put it to work in a particular way. Yet if these actions were creative, they were not creative *ex nihilo*, for they took place against a background of established practice. When we said, for example, that it should be obvious that the square constructed upon the hypotenuse is equal in area to the sum of the squares constructed upon its sides, I was not stilting the discourse for a philosophical purpose. Looking back, it is perfectly natural to say that we *discovered* something in the diagram. We get the feeling that this mathematical relationship existed all along and our diagram only helped to make it evident.

What I have to say here strikes me as inadequate—both to the problem and Wittgenstein's treatment of it—but it may be a simplification on the side of the truth. From the outside (that is, without the adoption of paradigms), all mathematical procedures will seem "separate and loose" and every step will appear as a decision or creative act. It is only from the inside of mathematics (that is, only when we are operating within the dominion of rules) that the way seems prepared for us. In a proof *we* bring prior procedures into a new relationship with one another.

This is a genuinely creative act. What *they* do (if I may speak in this way) is bestow their paradigmatic character on the results of our activities. At least this is what happens when a proof is successful. Without the creative act of placing old procedures in novel and striking juxtaposition, there would be nothing new under the mathematical sun. Without the system of antecedent paradigms, everything in mathematics would be new and hence capricious. I want to say something like this: our feeling that mathematical proofs discover new truths about independent objects is a montage effect resulting from our doing something new with paradigms (putting them into a novel relationship) while at the same time operating under them.

4
Infinity

One of the embarrassments in the *Tractatus* (perhaps even a scandal) is its failure to offer a direct discussion of transfinite cardinals. In reflecting upon this omission, I suggested that it resulted from a commitment to a primitive constructivism in mathematics. If a "number is the exponent of an operation," then we can construct finite cardinals that are as large as we please, but, of course, we will not be able to construct a transfinite cardinal. In passages collected in the *Remarks on the Foundations of Mathematics* Wittgenstein comes to terms with this issue.

Since nothing here turns upon technical detail, I shall be very informal in explaining Cantor's arguments for transfinite cardinals. Starting with the finite case, we can discover that two sets contain the same number of objects (have the same cardinality) by counting them. But we can also discover that two sets have the same cardinality if the items in each can be paired (put into one-to-one correlation). To cite the standard example: I can establish that there are as many men as women in a room if I note that each man is dancing with one woman and, conversely, each woman is dancing with one man. We can thus use this notion of a one-to-one correlation as a criterion for sameness of cardinality.

For finite sets none of this is problematic or even very interesting, but surprising results emerge when this terminology is extended to infinite sets. First, we make a decision to speak about the integers and rational numbers as sets: the set of integers is just all the integers and the set of rational numbers is just all the rational numbers. Suppose we compare these two sets. At first blush it seems that there must be *more* rational numbers than integers, for there is a rational number corresponding to each integer (1/1 to 1, 2/1 to 2, etc.) but endlessly many rational numbers with no corresponding integer having the same value. It turns out, however, that there is a way of putting the rational numbers into one-to-one correlation with the integers. The following chart has the numerators across the top, the denominators down the side. We then put the rationals into one-to-one correlation with the integers using the indicated pattern (redundancies are deleted).

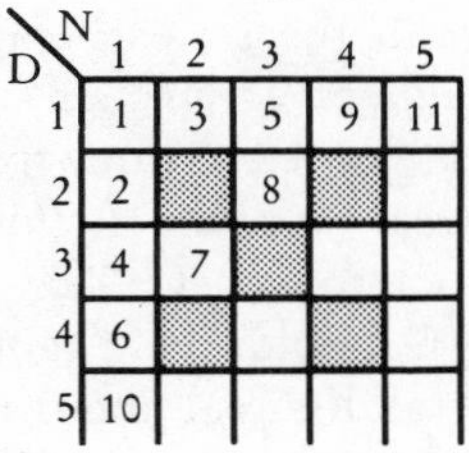

D \ N	1	2	3	4	5
1	1	3	5	9	11
2	2		8		
3	4	7			
4	6				
5	10				

Figure XIV.2

We are now in a position to say that there are as many integers as rational numbers, or that the set of integers and the set of rationals have the same cardinality. Given our vulgar instincts, we probably have mixed feelings about this result. It certainly seems that there should be more rationals than integers, for there are so many rationals between each integer. On the other side, since both sets seem infinite, maybe it is not *too* surprising that there are as many numbers in the one set as the other: after all, there are infinitely many numbers in each.

The next step in the argument removes even this solace. Cantor showed that two sets could both be infinite, yet still differ in the number of items they contain, i.e., there are infinite sets with different cardinalities. To see this, we need only consider real numbers between 0 and 1 (or, rather, between 0.0000 . . . and 1.0000 . . .). Of course there is no way of listing them in order of magnitude, for between any two of them, we can always find another. Yet the same situation exists for the rational numbers, and there Cantor was able to find a way of putting this set into one-to-one correlation with the integers. Can the same thing be done with the set of reals? Cantor produced an ingenious argument to show that this cannot be done. Suppose, *per impossibile*, that some such ordering has been proposed. It starts out like this:

```
0.1 2 4 5 9 7 6 5 . . . . . .
0.7 8 4 5 3 0 0 9 . . . . . .
0.2 0 0 0 0 0 0 0 . . . . . .
0.3 3 3 4 4 4 5 5 . . . . . .
0.5 7 8 4 3 9 9 6 . . . . . .
. . . . . . . . .
```

However this series is generated, we can provide a principle that produces a number that will not occur in the series. We take the sequence of numbers that forms the diagonal and construct a new number by altering each number in it by 1. (The diagonal number for the above array is 0.18043 . . . which we convert to: 0.29154. . . .) It is easy to see that this number will not occur in the series being generated, for the nth number in the series will be incorrect in its nth place.

What conclusions are we supposed to draw from this result? Certainly, there are at least as many real numbers as integers, for there is a real number corresponding to each integer (1.000 . . . to 1, 2.000 . . . to 2, etc.). But the converse does not hold; the diagonal procedure shows that there is no way of matching all the real numbers with integers. We thus come to the conclusion that there must be more real numbers than integers (and therefore more real numbers than rational numbers). The set of integers and the set of rationals have the same cardinality; that was the first, by now mild, shock. We now discover that behind this first transfinite cardinal there stands another, dwarfing it. At this point we feel that we have been introduced into the "mysteries of the mathematical world." "This," Wittgenstein says, "is the aspect against which I want to give a warning" (RFM, I, Appendix 2, #10).

It is not always conceded that Wittgenstein understands modern mathematics, but in this case, at least, he grasps the situation with perfect clarity. His position comes to this: we have a clear notion of a class with finitely many members and then we make the decision to extend the notion to classes with infinitely many members (e.g. all the integers). We also have a clear idea how the notion of a one-to-one correlation can be used to establish that two finite classes have the same cardinality. Once more, we make the decision to extend this criterion to classes with infinitely many members. With these commitments behind us, Cantor's argument shows that the cardinality of the class of real numbers must be greater than the cardinality of the class of integers (or rational numbers). But surely nothing forces us to extend our concepts in these ways, and thus the idea that Cantor has proved the existence of a hierarchy of transfinite cardinals is simply an exaggeration.

Does Cantor then prove nothing? Of course he proves something: there is a kind of ordering possible for the rational numbers that is not possible for the reals. That much is incontestable. The difficulty turns upon how this result is exploited:

> The dangerous and deceptive thing about the idea: "The real numbers cannot be arranged in a series" or again "the set . . . is not denumerable" resides in its making what is a determination, formation, of a concept, look like a fact of nature. (RFM, I, Appendix 2, #3)

That is, it is easy to think that Cantor's proof reveals the existence of hitherto unknown mathematical entities—a hierarchy of transfinite cardinals—but an austere formulation of his results carries no such implication.

> The following sentence sounds sober: "If something is called a series of real numbers, then the expansion given by the diagonal procedure is also called a 'real number', and moreover said to be different from all members of the series."

> Our suspicion ought always be aroused when a proof proves more than its means allow it. Something of this sort might be called "a puffed-up proof". (RFM, I, Appendix 2, #3)

Or again:

> If it were said: "Consideration of the diagonal procedure shews you that the *concept* 'real number' has much less analogy with the concept 'cardinal number' than we, being misled by certain analogies, are inclined to believe," that would make good and honest sense. But just the *opposite* happens: one pretends to compare the "set" of real numbers in magnitude with that of the cardinal numbers. The difference in kind between the two conceptions is represented, by a skew form of expression, as difference in extension. (RFM, I, Appendix 2, #3)

Perhaps Wittgenstein is unfair to Cantor, for the extension of sets to include infinite aggregates and the carrying over of one-to-one correlation to establish equal cardinality for such sets seems a natural development at a certain stage of mathematics. Yet Wittgenstein's basic point is sound: the non-flamboyant content of Cantor's proof is that an ordering is possible for the rationals that is not possible for the reals. This, in itself, has nothing to do with size. But doesn't the impossibility of establishing a one-to-one correlation between the reals and rationals prove that they have a different cardinality? Wittgenstein's answer is that we are not forced at this point, for even if we accept the possibility of infinite sets, we may decide that it makes no sense to retain the idea of one-to-one correspondence as the basis for assigning the same cardinality to different sets. (Remember, the home ground for that insight was finite sets.)

Of course, over time, the domain of numbers has been progressively expanded. Why not extend the same courtesy to the transfinite cardinals? Wittgenstein's answer, I think, is that such an extension is legitimate only if it is more than an empty formalism. Here the difficulty is not to be misled by certain striking pictures that a formalism might suggest. To understand the significance of a symbol, we must examine the role it actually plays in mathematical calculation:

> The result of a calculation expressed verbally is to be regarded with suspicion. The *calculation* illumines the meaning of the expression in words. It is the *finer* instrument for determining the meaning. If you want to know what the verbal expression means, look at the calculation; not the other way about. (RFM, I, Appendix 2, #1)

Wittgenstein views the talk about transfinite cardinals, non-denumerable sets, as so much verbal commentary recited over the actual mathematical operations. This commentary seems to give the diagonal procedure a profound significance, but if we start in the opposite direction by examining the argument itself, we then see that the imagery of transfinite cardinals is only so much puffing.

> "Ought the word 'infinite' to be avoided in mathematics?" Yes: where it appears to confer a meaning upon the calculus; instead of getting one from it. (RFM, I, Appendix 2, #17)

Couldn't an application for transfinite cardinals be found? Perhaps such an application has been found, for remember, this application need not be immediate. Yet these topics are a matter of dispute amongst mathematicians themselves. Abraham Robinson has spoken as follows on this subject:

> My position concerning the foundations of Mathematics is based on the two main points of principles:
> (i) Infinite totalities do not exist in any sense of the word (i.e., either really or ideally). More precisely, any mention, or purported mention, of infinite totalities is, literally, *meaningless*.
> (ii) Nevertheless, we should continue the business of Mathematics "as usual," i.e., we should act *as if* infinite totalities really existed.[5]

The second principle is more than an abstract plea for toleration, which, given the content of the first principle, might sound disingenuous. Robinson's point is systematic and concerns the way terms in a mathematical theory gain their significance:

> [T]he direct interpretability of the terms of a mathematical theory is not a necessary condition for its acceptability; a theory which includes infinitary terms is not thereby less acceptable or less rational than a theory that avoids them. To *understand* a theory means to be able to follow its logical development and not, necessarily, to interpret, or give a denotation for, its individual terms.[6]

I see no reason why Wittgenstein could not adopt a similar view, but, in fact, the tendency of his discussion has a different emphasis. When he raises the question "What can the concept 'non-denumerable' be used for?" he seems to expect a fairly direct answer. This reflects a tendency (I think no more than a tendency) to ask for the meaning of a *word* in the context of a proposition or in the context of a language-game rather than to ask for the significance of a *proposition* in the context of a theory. At the same time, if Wittgenstein is correct, those who introduce us into the mysteries of mathematics do so by assigning a role to an expression without attending *at all* to the actual application of the expression. A generous notion of application is needed to understand the role of symbols in complex and abstract theoretical structures. Yet Wittgenstein's basic point remains untouched: this application is not given by the pictorial imagery that the symbolism, via various analogies with other symbolism, suggests.

Finally, then, is Wittgenstein a finitist in mathematics? If a finitist is a person who denies the existence of infinite sets, then the answer to this question is no. Such a denial suggests that the idea of an infinite set makes perfectly good sense, but there do not happen to be any such sets. Wittgenstein's position is that the notion of an infinite set has yet to be given a sense. This brings us to a passage noticed earlier:[7]

> Finitism and behaviourism are quite similar trends. Both say, but surely all we have here is. . . . Both deny the existence of something, both with the view to escaping from a confusion. What I am doing is, not to shew that calculations are wrong, but to subject the *interest* of calculations to a test. (RFM, I, Appendix 2, #18)

5
Wittgenstein's anti-foundationalism

Wittgenstein was impatient with the idea that mathematics stands in need of a foundation. His attitude here is simply one instance of his general critique of foundational studies, for, in the sense that philosophers have used the term, Wittgenstein came to think that *nothing* stands in need of a foundation.

> What does mathematics need a foundation for? It no more needs one, I believe, than propositions about material objects—or about sense impressions, need an *analysis*. What mathematical propositions do stand in need of is a clarification of their grammar, just as do these other propositions. (RFM, V, 13)

Mathematics has its foundation in human practice and needs no other.

As for work that goes under the heading of studies in the foundations of mathematics, he flatly denies that this *portion* of mathematics is the underpinning for the rest of the mathematical edifice.

> The *mathematical* problems of what is called foundations are no
> more the foundations of mathematics than the painted rock is the
> support of the painted tower. (RFM, V, 13)

In back of this attitude is the doctrine that the proposed foundational
systems derive whatever sense they have from the systems they are
intended to support, and not the other way around. For example, in the
decimal notation we have a "short" calculation and corresponding to it
in the Russell notation we have an extraordinarily long calculation. Does
the long calculation either justify or elucidate the "short" calculation?
According to Wittgenstein, no![8]
In an even less charitable mood, Wittgenstein views foundational
research as an examplar of reasoning carried on with the connection to
application totally ignored.

> The question, "What was it useful for?" was a quite essential
> question. For the calculus was not invented for some practical
> purpose, but in order "to give arithmetic a foundation." But who
> says that arithmetic is logic, etc. (RFM, II, 85)

And problems within the foundations of mathematics can also arise
through this severance from application. We start out with principles
that are both intelligible and plausible through their connection with
ordinary discourse, then later we get into trouble by extending the system
in ways initially never dreamed of. We introduce a predicate such as
"heterological" and then a contradiction is found, but how is the notion
of a heterological predicate connected with the initial reasons for setting
up the calculus?

> What Russell's "-f(f)" lacks above all is application, and hence
> meaning. (RFM, V, 8)

Why not, following Wittgenstein's suggestion, just call the derived
contradiction a *true* contradiction and note, perhaps with satisfaction,
that it is part of our system (RFM, V, 21)?
The worry, of course, is that the presence of the contradiction will
render the system *useless*. Here, belatedly, a recognition of the importance of application reappears. We are now set the task of *sealing off* the
contradiction while at the same time preserving the features of the system
we want. If we cannot accomplish this, this merely shows that our
system is not transparent to us; we do not know our way about.

> But how is it possible not to know one's way about in a calculus:
> isn't it there, open to view? (RFM, II, 80)

Wittgenstein seems to suggest that this would not happen if we stayed
in touch with application at every stage in the development of the system:

I would like to say something like this: "Is it usefulness you are out for in your calculations?—In that case you do not get any contradiction. And if you aren't out for usefulness—then it doesn't matter if you get one." (RFM, II, 80)

This suggestion is not far-fetched. In effect, it amounts to the demand that every extension of a system be accompanied by a relative consistency proof within the domain of intended application. Anyway, these passages clarify Wittgenstein's supposedly *laissez-faire* attitude toward contradictions:

"Then you are in favour of contradiction?" Not at all; any more than of soft rulers. (RFM, IV, 12)

When *Remarks on the Foundations of Mathematics* first appeared, it was not greeted with a favorable response, especially by those working in the foundations of mathematics who, among other things, saw their livelihood challenged. Since that time, the winds of dogma have shifted, and finitism and constructivism in mathematics are no longer considered unrespectable. Wittgenstein—and this is a general complaint about his way of doing philosophy—did not work out these finitist-constructivist themes in detail. Yet he did give expression to the underlying motives that lie behind this approach to mathematics and logic. More significantly, his treatment of problems in the philosophy of mathematics is of a piece with his general approach to philosophical problems. More strongly, I think that the discussions in the philosophy of mathematics provide the clearest (and perhaps best) examples of Wittgenstein's philosophical methods.

XV

Wittgenstein and the History of Philosophy

In his biographical sketch, von Wright says "that Wittgenstein's new philosophy is, so far as I can see, entirely outside any philosophical tradition and without literary sources of influence. . . . The author of the *Philosophical Investigations* has no ancestors in philosophy."[1] I think that von Wright is substantially correct in this claim and most of what I shall say here is compatible with it. Setting aside questions of actual influence, I wish to ask another question: what philosophical movement does Wittgenstein's later philosophy most resemble? My answer is Pyrrhonian scepticism. I know that many will find this suggestion outrageous, for it is generally thought that one of Wittgenstein's contributions to philosophy was to have said something important against scepticism. Indeed, anti-scepticism seems to be a persistent theme from his earliest to his latest writings. Thus in the *Tractatus* he makes the following claim against scepticism:

> 6.51 Scepticism is *not* irrefutable, but obviously nonsensical, when it raises doubts where no question can be asked.

As we shall see, despite the profound changes in his philosophical position, Wittgenstein offers essentially the same response to scepticism in the very last things he wrote: the material collected by his executors under the title *On Certainty*. My claim, then, that Wittgenstein's philosophy bears a close resemblance to Pyrrhonism seems to run counter to a perennial aspect of his thought. I shall try to show that this is not so, both for his early and later writings.

Returning to 6.51 of the *Tractatus*, Wittgenstein relates the meaningfulness of a question to the meaningfulness of a counterpart statement.

> For a doubt can exist only where a question exists, a question only where an answer exists, and an answer only where something *can be said.*

This passage entails three important claims. (i) Doubt is not merely a mental state on a par, say, with a sensation. It is possible to say of a person who claims to doubt that he does not doubt since his doubt lacks content. (ii) The passage further indicates that there is an internal relationship between questions and answers: "a question exists only where an answer exists." Of course, Wittgenstein is not saying that a question exists only when its answer is known. Speaking more carefully in an earlier entry he puts it this way:

6.5 If a question can be framed at all, it is also *possible* to answer it.

At the moment, perhaps no one knows the number of hours remaining before the beginning of the twenty-first century, but we do know how to go about figuring this out. (iii) Finally, the passage concerning the sceptic's questions relates what can count as an answer to *what can be said*. If there is no *possible* answer to the sceptic's question, then nothing can be said either true or false in response to it. The question, then, is a pseudo-question and the doubt, whatever feelings might be associated with it, a pseudo-doubt.

To see if this is a just criticism of scepticism, let us reflect upon the character of sceptical questions. The sceptic, when he appears in plain clothes, often challenges commonly held beliefs on the grounds that they are not supported by adequate evidence. This is simply tough-mindedness, and Wittgenstein has no complaint against it. Philosophical scepticism (and here I shall take the Pyrrhonian scepticism of Sextus Empiricus as my model) moves at a different level and is not concerned with the *degree* of evidential backing for commonly held beliefs. As long as people remain content with modestly reporting how things strike them and offering reasons in the ordinary way, the sceptic has nothing to say against them. The object of the sceptic's attack is the philosopher, in particular, the philosopher of a dogmatic cast who maintains that his opinions enjoy a special status above those of others.

The Pyrrhonian sceptic had a practical goal and laid down specific procedures for attaining it.[2] The sceptic's goal was peace of mind. He thought that he could reach this goal by freeing himself of *philosophical* anxiety. This, as it turns out, can be attained by reaching a state of suspension of belief or non-commitment (*epoche*) concerning philosophical subjects. The Pyrrhonian sceptic used various techniques to attain suspension of belief. Sometimes he tried to reach a state of equipollence by pairing off competing dogmatic views, e.g., Plato's commitment to transcendent forms against Aristotle's rejection of them. But the Pyrrhonians also developed quite general procedures that were serviceable against any philosophical position whatsoever. I shall call these the procedures of *general scepticism*.[3]

The methods of general scepticism can be illustrated by the five modes leading to the suspension of belief attributed to Agrippa; they are: disagreement, relativity, hypothesis, circularity, and infinite regress.[4] If a dogmatist makes a philosophical claim, the sceptic can initiate an interrogation either on the basis of disagreement or relativity. He can point out that other dogmatists have disagreed with what is asserted and therefore *reasons* are needed to support this claim over its denial. He can also point out that the dogmatist makes his statement from a particular standpoint (say, with respect to perception), and the privileged status of that standpoint needs defense. Once the inquiry has begun, the remaining three modes, hypothesis, circularity, and infinite regress, are intended to prevent it from terminating. If the dogmatist refuses to give any reason for his assertion, then he has merely put forward a hypothesis that has no claim upon our assent. If, on the other hand, he does provide a reason, this reason itself can be challenged. Now the dogmatist is trapped, for inevitably he must either

(1) give no reason,
(2) repeat some reason previously given,

or

(3) give a new reason.

The mode of hypothesis blocks the first response, the mode of circularity the second, and the third, needless to say, leads to a bad infinite regress.

It seems to be part of our philosophical heritage to treat this kind of argument with contempt, for it is not very different from the sceptical arguments produced by undergraduates intent on making trouble. It is also boring, since it repeats the very same arguments no matter what subject matter is presented. All the same, it seems incumbent upon philosophy to say something decisive in reply in order to clear its pedigree.

Before examining Wittgenstein's response to general scepticism, we can look briefly at what might be called the standard response: the tables are turned on the sceptics (*peritrope*), by applying their arguments back upon themselves. A piece of reasoning, it is said, that shows that no reasoning is adequate shows itself to be inadequate and therefore may be rejected. Having produced this argument, the critic of scepticism rarely stays for an answer. But the ancient sceptics were familiar with this maneuver and gave, I believe, the right response. First they admitted that sceptical arguments *are* self-refuting, but they saw no embarrassment in this since they never claimed to establish anything by reasoning. More to the point, the dogmatists can take no comfort from this result, since the burden now falls upon them to find something wrong with a pattern of reasoning embodying principles that they themselves accept. They may notice the self-refuting quality of the sceptic's argument, but this merely puts them on a treadmill, for, with reason restored, they will be led back to the same sceptical argument. David Hume put it this way:

> If the sceptical reasonings be strong, say they, 'tis proof, that reason may have some force and authority; if weak, they can never be sufficient to invalidate all the conclusions of our understanding. This argument is not just; because the sceptical reasoning . . . would be successively both strong and weak according to the successive dispositions of the mind.[5]

Since the standard refutation of scepticism using *peritrope* is no good, scepticism remains unanswered. Now I think that one of the reasons that Wittgenstein's philosophy is attractive is that it seems to give an adequate response to the sceptic's challenge. It is not hard to see how this works out within the Tractarian system. Any question with a sense must have an answer which is, in principle at least, determinable by an appeal to the contingent combination of things in the world. By its very intention, however, the system of sceptical challenges is non-terminating, and thus, by the principles of the *Tractatus*, must lack sense. General scepticism is nonsensical, then, just because it is, in principle, invulnerable.

I think that this response represents an advance over the use of *peritrope*, but within the context of the *Tractatus* this "refutation" has an ambiguous status since, in being meaningless, the sceptic's questions are no worse off than Wittgenstein's own pronouncements. Wittgenstein saw that his own propositions were meaningless, telling his reader to "throw away the ladder after he has climbed up it." (6.54) The allusion is to Sextus Empiricus, indeed, to Sextus's own response to peritropic refutation. One acknowledges the charge. Furthermore, Wittgenstein agrees on the central point of ancient scepticism: philosophy is not possible as a theoretical, discursive, or rational discipline. On the other side, through the doctrine of showing, Wittgenstein seems to believe that the noumenal can make itself manifest. More consistently, Wittgenstein should have placed the sceptic's self-defeating claims side by side with his own misfiring attempts to say things that can only be shown. The truth of philosophical scepticism might make itself known by the fact that philosophical reflection, when carried to its limit, leads to paradox and self-refutation. In the *Tractatus*, Wittgenstein was half a sceptic, or, better, a philosopher half way to becoming a sceptic. In his late writing he completed the journey.

The work that his executors entitled *On Certainty* is a compilation of notes written by Wittgenstein during the last year of his life. Here Wittgenstein reflects upon G. E. Moore's attempt to invoke common sense to refute various sceptical arguments produced, usually, by idealists. Most famously, Moore argued that those who denied (or expressed doubts about) the existence of material objects could be refuted by displaying a right hand then a left hand, thus proving the existence of at least two material objects. Similarly, Moore claimed to know (and know with certainty) that the world had existed many years before he was born and this, he thought, showed that those who maintained that time is unreal must be mistaken.[6]

Wittgenstein thought that Moore's refutations were ineffective against the targets at which they are aimed. Of course, Wittgenstein did not side with the idealists, nor did he deny Moore's common sense propositions. Instead, he expressed his reservations this way:

> The statement "I know that here is a hand" may . . . be continued, "for it is *my* hand that I'm looking at". Then a reasonable man will not doubt that I know.—Nor will the idealist; rather he will say that he was not dealing with the practical doubt which is being dismissed, but there is a further doubt *behind* that one. That this is an *illusion* has to be shewn in a different way. (OC, #19)

This, I think, is a key passage for understanding one of the central themes of *On Certainty*. Moore, at least as Wittgenstein reads him, supposes that philosophers often maintain (or hold positions that imply) propositions that are contrary to plain matters of fact. Moore rejects such philosophical claims on the grounds that anything that implies a falsehood is false. Wittgenstein replies that the idealists will not disagree with Moore at the level of common sense, for he holds that their doubts or denials come at a different level. An idealist doubting that material objects exist is nothing like an ornithologist doubting whether the Ivory Billed Woodpecker still survives in the swamps of Louisiana. Moore's mistake is to suppose that they are on the same level. Wittgenstein wishes to reject the sceptical arguments of idealists as well but, unlike Moore, he sees that their doubts are second-order—and hyperbolic. Wittgenstein's claim is that these second-order (hyperbolic) doubts are illusions and that a proper refutation or dissolution of these doubts involves exposing them as illusions.

Despite the profound differences between Wittgenstein's early and late philosophy, the treatment of sceptical doubts is strikingly similar. In the *Tractatus* he said that "if a question can be framed at all, it is also *possible* to answer it." At the beginning of *On Certainty* he says:

> If, e.g., someone says "I don't know if there's a hand here" he might be told "Look closer". This possibility of satisfying oneself is part of the language-game. Is one of its essential features. (OC, #3)

Or again:

> The idealist's question would be something like: "What right have I

not to doubt the existence of my hands?" . . . But someone who asks such a question is overlooking the fact that a doubt about existence only works in a language-game. Hence, we should first have to ask: what would this doubt be like?, and we don't understand this straight off.

More specifically, we do not understand the character of the doubt until we understand the grounds for the doubt and understand what issues have to be settled in order to resolve the doubt.

The final sentence of the passage just cited contains one of Wittgenstein's important ideas. Traditionally, philosophers have tended to take the meaningfulness of questions for granted and then set directly about answering them. We know what it is to doubt and we know what it is to have hands, so surely there is no difficulty in understanding what it means to doubt that one has hands. This is Moore's standpoint, and for this reason he will attempt to refute the idealist by showing him his hands. Against this, Wittgenstein holds that the idealist's doubts cannot be answered because they make no sense. Beyond this, in a marvelous passage, Wittgenstein notes that Moore's own common sense statements go out of focus when directed against a meaningless doubt:

When one hears Moore say "I *know* that that's a tree" one suddenly understands those who think that *that* has by no means been settled.
The matter strikes one all at once as being unclear and blurred. It is as if Moore had put it in the wrong light. (OC, #481)

Of course, Wittgenstein is not siding with the idealist, saying that Moore, sitting in a park in broad daylight, does *not* know that there is a tree before him. He is saying that knowledge claims are context-bound and play quite a particular role within the language-games in which they are used.

We just do not see how very specialized the use of "I know" is. (OC, #11)

In a typical context where people claim to know things, they are responding to actual or potential doubts. One can always ask "How do you know?" and that is a call for reasons. The character of the reasons will vary with respect to the particular matters at issue. The difficulty with answering the sceptic's challenge, as formulated, for example, in the five modes attributed to Agrippa, is that the reasons I give will never be any better than the claim that I am trying to defend. It is part of the sceptic's tactics to raise just such questions. But where doubt is wholly unrestricted, nothing can be cited to resolve it. Here claims to know or doubt will be out of place, useless, and thus, according to Wittgenstein, without meaning. We thus arrive at the position that meaningful doubts can be raised, questions asked, answers given, etc., only within the context of a language-game that gives these activities substance. The guile of the sceptic is to ask questions and to force others to give answers to them outside the context of a particular language-game. This, I believe, is Wittgenstein's fundamental response to scepticism.

If all this is correct, where is the Pyrrhonism that I claim to find in Wittgenstein's philosophy? To answer this, we must, in Hume's words, "carry our sifting humours further," and ask the following question: if the activities of asking questions and answering them (raising doubts and settling them) are justified only in the context of a language-game, what justifies language-games themselves? We already know the answer to this: *nothing*. This is a persistent theme in Wittgenstein's late philosophy which, if anything, is given greater prominence in his last writings.

> The difficulty is to realize the groundlessness of our believing. (OC, #166)

> . . . the *questions* that we raise and our *doubts* depend on the fact that some propositions are exempted from doubt, are like hinges on which those turn. (OC, #341)

More famously:

> My *life* consists in my being content to accept many things. (OC, #344)

Three points are worth noting. (i) The demand that we accept many things is conceptual, not simply a sign of weakness. Without a background of accepted beliefs, we would have neither guideposts nor touchstones for thought. (ii) These things we accept are not first principles in the philosopher's sense; for the most part they are commonplaces. The bedrock of our thought is the thick sedimentary layer of the obvious. Of course, what is taken as a matter of course by one person need not be by another. Much will depend upon background and training, and some of our finer judgments (as in aesthetics) will depend upon a grasp of quite specific factors in their interrelations. There are, however, many things that we all accept straight off, and doubt and inquiry will arise concerning them only in the most extraordinary circumstances. Moore's propositions of common sense fall into this category. (iii) Most importantly, we typically learn fundamental background beliefs indirectly as part of other activities:

> Children do not learn that books exist, that armchairs exist, etc., etc.,—they learn to fetch books, sit in armchairs, etc., etc.
>
> Later questions about the existence of things do of course arise. "Is there such a thing as a unicorn?" and so on. But such a question

is possible only because as a rule no corresponding question presents itself. (OC, #476)

In trying to decide whether unicorns exist, I might consult certain books. I do not, however, raise the prior question of whether books exist. All this points to a fundamental tenet of Wittgenstein's later philosophy: our participation in language-games lies beyond justification; it is a brute fact of human nature:

> I want to regard man here as an animal; as a primitive being to which one grants instinct but not ratiocination. As a creature in a primitive state. Any logic good enough for a primitive means of communication needs no apology from us. Language did not emerge from some kind of ratiocination. (OC, #475)

I think that we can now see what Wittgenstein's later critique of scepticism comes to. The sceptic is pictured as a figure who constantly calls things into question, constantly asks for justification of even the most ordinary beliefs. If this is the sceptic's enterprise, then Wittgenstein has something to say against him. The very questions he asks depend *for their sense* upon a background of commonly shared beliefs. But the sceptic's doubts have a totalizing character—he will raise the same kinds of doubts concerning anything that is brought forward as evidence. But as the sceptic's doubts expand, their sense contracts, and, at the limit, become meaningless.

This, I think, is an interesting argument—a kind of transcendental refutation of vulgar scepticism—but how does it relate to classical (Pyrrhonian) scepticism? The answer is that these arguments do not bear upon Pyrrhonian scepticism at all. The Pyrrhonists (at least) had no interest in challenging common beliefs modestly held. It is simply wrong to say, as some have, that sceptics impose arbitrarily high standards on common belief and then gain an easy triumph when these standards cannot be met. Thompson Clark got it right when he said that the sceptic comes upon the scene "without an independent thought in his head concerning what knowledge requires."[7] The sceptic encounters philosophers who often disparage common belief and claim an authority for doctrines that transcends the brute acceptance of the plain man. The sceptic simply takes these philosophers at their word, meets them on their own grounds, and then shows that they cannot satisfy *their own* demands. Classical scepticism was not a call for the suspension of common belief, for it recognized that, for the most part, it is neither in our power to do so nor useful if it could be accomplished. Classical scepticism was a critique of philosophizing and the anxieties it generates. Once we have correctly identified the object of the Pyrrhonian attack, the similarity between their position and Wittgenstein's becomes evident. The following comes from the *Philosophical Investigations:*

> 133 The real discovery is the one that makes me capable of stopping doing philosophy when I want to.—The one that gives philosophy peace, so that it no longer is tormented by questions which bring *itself* in question.

Wittgenstein and the Pyrrhonians were concerned with the same object: philosophy as traditionally practiced. Their goal was the same: to eliminate it.

There is, however, a fundamental difference between Wittgenstein and the Pyrrhonists that supports von Wright's claim for Wittgenstein's originality. The methods of the ancient sceptics tended to be stereotyped, wooden, and external. Even if the various modes designed to induce the suspension of belief had this effect, they gave no indication of the sources of our drive to do philosophy nor did they give any explanation of why this drive should lead to deep anxieties. Of course, Wittgenstein gave philosophy a linguistic turn. Where the traditional sceptics, down to at least Hume, held that philosophical problems are, in principle, *unsolvable*, Wittgenstein claimed that they *lacked sense or meaning*. By seeing that a philosophical problem is meaningless we reach what might be called a suspension of concern, surely a more radical purge of our philosophical anxieties than the suspension of belief. But the appeal to language, by itself, does not explain the depth and originality of Wittgenstein's philosophy. The logical positivists also appealed to language in order to reject most traditional philosophy.

In contrast with the ancient sceptics and the modern logical positivists, Wittgenstein's techniques proceed from a profound understanding of the sources and character of philosophical perplexity. His critique of philosophical problems is always internal. To use one of his best metaphors, to untie a philosophical knot, one must repeat all the motions used in tying it, only in reverse order. I shall not speculate on how much Wittgenstein actually knew about ancient scepticism, for whether he revived it or rediscovered it on his own, his chief contribution is to force us to respond to the sceptical challenge by endowing it with seriousness and insight.

Notes

Chapter I *The Atomistic Ontology of the* Tractatus

1 Cf. "My whole task consists in explaining the nature of propositions" (NB, p. 39).
2 This begins at proposition 2.
3 See Russell's introduction to the *Tractatus*, p. xiii.
4 This is not to say that the Tractarian world cannot contain objects that *essentially* never enter into combinations—we might call them inveterate bachelors. I think that such objects are impossible as well, but for reasons to be discussed later on p. 26.
5 In fact, this line of reasoning is flawed in not considering the possibility of a *disjunctively* defined essence, i.e., it might be the defining characteristic of a thing that it *either* enters into states of affairs *or* exists entirely on its own. I do not know how Wittgenstein would reply to this criticism (he might consider it mere trifling).
6 Replaying the same reasoning used above, it is easy to see that the form of an object cannot be one of its contingent features.
7 The content of this parenthetical remark will be examined on pp. 33 ff.
8 See pp. 27 ff.
9 That is, we cannot conceive of an object except as being in some determinate combination with other objects (2.0121).
10 Later Wittgenstein speaks of the *infinite whole of logical space* (4.463).
11 See 6.3751.
12 See pp. 91 ff.

Chapter II *Picturing the World*

1 Here we might notice a terminological shift that has taken place in the text. Originally (at 2), facts were identified with *existing* states of affairs. At 2.06, however, Wittgenstein begins to speak of the existence of states of affairs as *positive* facts and their non-existence as *negative* facts. Thus, if we spell out 2.1 in the following way: "We picture both positive and negative facts to ourselves," then 2.11 falls into alignment with 2.1.

235

2 This matter is discussed in detail on p. 28.

3 Later the same claim is made about propositional signs (3.14).

4 This is reminiscent of Frege's practice of calling the sense of a proposition a thought. As with Frege, the notion of a thought should not be given a psychological interpretation.

5 An impossible situation cannot be pictured by a contradictory proposition since a contradiction does not express a thought or picture anything.

6 Pp. 45 ff. Wittgenstein's rejection of *non*-tautological *a priori* truths is examined in section 2 of Chapter VII.

Chapter III *Propositions*

1 This qualification has a point by hedging against a later discussion of propositions that do not express a sense, e.g. tautologies.

2 See the passage from the *Notebooks* cited on p. 15.

3 See G. Frege, *Translations from the Philosophical Writings of Gottlob Frege*, edited by Peter Geach and Max Black, Oxford, Basil Blackwell, 1952, pp. 56 ff.

4 G. Frege, *The Foundations of Arithmetic*, translated by J. L. Austin, 2nd edn, New York, Philosophical Library, 1953, p. x.

5 NB, p. 15e.

6 If we have a bent for the lunatic, we could use Harold Lloyd himself as a name for his name.

7 See pp. 11–13.

Chapter IV *The Logic of Propositions*

1 This ignores the possibility championed by Kripke that there can be necessary truths that are certified *a posteriori*. Wittgenstein does not consider this possibility explicitly, but it is surely part of his intention to construct a theory that excludes it.

2 4.442 I do not know why Wittgenstein first leaves a blank for the value F and then without any explanation puts in this value on the grounds of being more explicit.

3 Here the 2^n truth values in the left-hand parentheses correspond to the 2^n rows in a truth-table constructed for n variables.

4 Later Wittgenstein says explicitly that the propositions of logic "presuppose that names have meaning and elementary propositions have sense; and that is their connection with the world" (6.124).

5 Of course, this must be qualified so that tautologies and contradictions are not excluded from propositional status.

6 Max Black, *A Companion to Wittgenstein's Tractatus*, Ithaca, New York, Cornell University Press, 1964, p. 258.

Chapter V *Generality*

1 It seems, then, that one consequence of Wittgenstein's position is that, in its fully analyzed form, a proposition contains no *symbols* for functions. The

so-called truth-functional connectives are eliminated in favor of a format of Ts and Fs in the left-hand parentheses of the canonical notation. The right-hand parentheses contain only a list of name-combinations where each name stands for an object. These name-combinations are the elementary propositions. In them, the functional aspect is not expressed by any particular symbol, but instead by a set of symbols standing to each other in a determinate way. In the end, we seem to arrive at the disappearance of all functional expressions whatsoever. In this respect, the *Tractatus* is deeply nominalistic.

2 F. Ramsey, *The Foundations of Mathematics*, London, Routledge & Kegan Paul, 1931, p. 8.

3 For example, that objects can occur both in states of affairs and on their own, or that names can occur both in propositions and on their own. See p. 7 ff.

4 Which can be represented as "(N(N(N(Fx), NGx)))."

5 Some mind-boggling results appear if *n* is assigned a transfinite value, but such boggles are characteristic of transfinite regions.

6 4.128, 5.453, 5.553.

7 There is no point worrying over this particular proposition suggesting, perhaps, that the property of being self-identical is just that property that everything possesses. We might consider instead the following wholly general proposition: "There are at least three properties that exactly seventeen things possess."

8 F. Ramsey, op, cit., pp. 59–60.

9 G. E. M. Anscombe, *An Introduction to Wittgenstein's Tractatus*, London, Hutchison, 1959, p. 148.

10 The material in this section is discussed in more detail in the author's "Wittgenstein on Identity," *Synthese*, 56, 1983, pp. 141–54.

11 The symbol "=" does appear properly in equations (e.g. 2 + 2 = 7), but Wittgenstein does not (as Frege did) treat this as a sign for the identity of the individuals referred to on each side of the equation.

12 Max Black, *A Companion to Wittgenstein's Tractatus*, Ithaca, New York, Cornell University Press, 1964, p. 300.

13 Value judgments, as we shall see, are an exception to this rule.

Chapter VI   *The Naive Constructivism of the* Tractatus

1 See P. Geach, (1) "Wittgenstein's Operator *N*," *Analysis*, 41, no. 4, 1981, pp. 168–71, and also (2) "More on Wittgenstein's Operator *N*," *Analysis*, 42, no. 3, 1982, pp. 127–8. For Soames, see his "Generality, Truth Functions, and Expressive Capacity in the *Tractatus*," *The Philosophical Review*, XCII, no. 4, 1983, pp. 573–89. I responded to Geach's first note in my "Wittgenstein's Operator *N*," *Analysis*, 42, no. 3, 1982, pp. 124–7.

2 Geach (1), op. cit., p. 169.

3 Cf. Geach (2), op. cit., p. 128, where he accuses me of this very same confusion.

4 R. Fogelin, "Negative Elementary Propositions," *Philosophical Studies*, 25, 1974, pp. 189–97.

5 Soames, op, cit., p. 589n.

6 Soames, op. cit., p. 578.
7 Tautologies and contradictions fall under this principle in an empty way.
8 See R. Fogelin, "Wittgenstein and Intuitionism," *American Philosophical Quarterly*, 5, no. 4, October 1968.
9 There is a passing reference at 4.1272.

Chapter VII *Necessity*

1 This does not mean that everything necessary can be mirrored in and thus shown by propositions of logic (tautologies). Perhaps certain necessary structures can only be shown in other ways, say, by recognizing the meaninglessness of attempts to speak about them. I think that this is Wittgenstein's position, but this is difficult to document.
2 Wittgenstein's net analogy is fascinating in another way. It suggests that various physical theories present alternative conceptual schemes for the interpretation of nature. Picking up this analogy, as interpreters, we might view the Tractarian system as one net—one conceptual scheme—amidst others. It shows a complete misunderstanding of Wittgenstein's conception of logic to suggest that *he* held any such view.
3 Wittgenstein's reference to a place in the visual field is not essential to the discussion.
4 F. Ramsey, "Critical Notice of the Tractatus," *Mind*, 32, 1923, pp. 465–78.

Chapter VIII *My World, Its Value, and Silence*

1 Jaakko Hintikka, "On Wittgenstein's 'Solipsism,' " *Mind*, 67, 1958, pp. 88–91.
2 P. Engelmann, *Letters from Ludwig Wittgenstein*, Oxford, Basil Blackwell, 1968, p. 143.
3 Ibid., p. 110.
4 This is reported in John King's "Recollections of Wittgenstein," in *Ludwig Wittgenstein: Personal Recollections*, edited by Rush Rhees, Totowa, New Jersey, Rowan & Littlefield, 1981, p. 87.
5 This way of making the point was suggested by Lynne McFall.

Chapter IX *The Critique of the* Tractatus

1 Wittgenstein discusses his method in his preface to the *Investigations*.
2 See, for example, Russell's "Ludwig Wittgenstein," *Mind*, 60, no. 239, 1951, and "Philosophers and Idiots," *Listener*, 10 February 1955. Both are reprinted in Kuang-Ti Fann's *Ludwig Wittgenstein: The Man and His Philosophy*, New York, Dell, 1967.
3 "At the end of reasons comes persuasion. (Think what happens when missionaries convert natives.)" (OC, #612)
4 I don't know why Wittgenstein goes so far as to say that for this language-game the "description given by Augustine is right." He certainly cannot

mean that in this language-game the meaning of a word *is* its bearer. My assumption is that he just hasn't gotten around to challenging this point yet.

5 It is somewhat misleading to speak of *numerals* and *demonstratives* in this context, for the terms of this simple language-game lack the full development of the corresponding words in our language.

6 "But how many kinds of sentences are there? Say assertion, question, and command? There are *countless* kinds: countless kinds of use of what we call 'symbols,' 'words,' 'sentences' " (PI, #25).

7 Whether such an argument occurs in the discussion of a private language will be considered at pp. 179 ff.

8 *Of course*, reference failure can occur with the use of a demonstrative.

9 See pp. 138 ff.

10 This way of stating the issue is not exactly right since it doesn't seem plausible to say that the ascription of length to an object actually *refers* to the standard meter. That is, when I say that my desk is a meter wide, it seems implausible to say that I am talking about the standard meter as well as my desk. Although this is very intuitive, it seems better to say that the standard meter is involved in the institution I *invoke* (rather than talk about) when I ascribe a length to an object in the metric system. Yet even on this approach, it will be conceptually anomalous to say of the standard meter that it is a meter long.

11 Symbolically:

(i) $\Box\,(p \supset \Box\,p)$
(ii) $\Box\,(p \supset q)$
(iii) $\Box\,(p \supset \Box\,q)$

This argument is valid, for example, in S4.

12 G. E. Moore, *Principia Ethica*, Cambridge, Cambridge University Press, 1903, p. 8.

13 Nothing of the sort follows from the quite different view associated with Mill that a name has no meaning and merely functions to denote an object.

14 A passage with a strikingly similar intent is found in Russell's *Introduction to Mathematical Philosophy*, London, Allen & Unwin, 1919, pp. 63–4.

15 A shorter passage paralleling this occurs at PI, #135.

16 In section 10, I shall examine some recent criticisms of this account of the meaning of proper names.

17 See his *Speech Acts*, Cambridge, Cambridge University Press, 1969, Chapter 7, Section 2, and also his earlier essay "Proper Names," *Mind*, 68, 1958, pp. 166–73.

18 A discussion of this position in its various ramifications can be found in, for example: K. Donnellan, "Reference and Definite Description," *Philosophical Review*, LXXV, 1966, pp. 281–304; K. Donnellan, "Putting Humpty Dumpty Together Again," *Philosophical Review*, LXXVII, 1968, pp. 203–15; K. Donnellan, "Proper Names and Identifying Descriptions," *Synthese*, 1970, pp. 335–58; K. Donnellan, "Speaking of Nothing," *Philosophical Review*, LXXXIII, 1974, pp. 3–31; P. T. Geach, "The Perils of Pauline," *Review of Metaphysics*, 23, no. 2, pp. 287–300; S. Kripke, "Naming and Necessity," in *Semantics of Natural Language*, 2nd edn, edited by D. Davidson and G. Harman, Synthese Library, Dordrecht, D. Reidel, 1972.

19 It is still unclear whether the Donnellan-Geach-Kripke approach can be carried through to completion. In particular it is not easy to see how this account of proper names can yield a correct analysis of a negative existential proposition such as "Prester John did not exist." (Here see, in particular, Donnellan's article "Speaking of Nothing" cited above.)

20 Sextus Empiricus, *Outlines of Pyrrhonism*, translated by R. G. Bury, Cambridge, Mass., Harvard University Press, 1933, pp. 206–7.

Chapter X *Understanding*

1 See for example OC, #392.

2 Of course, with the proper background information, a causal relationship can be established through examining a single case, something even Hume acknowledged. But this is not to the present point.

3 That he speaks falsely does not necessarily mean that he speaks irresponsibly.

Chapter XI *Sceptical Doubts and a Sceptical Solution to These Doubts*

1 What is set up as an ideal can also be removed from that status. I might say "That's not the series I wanted, but this one." Here I write out another series of numbers for a starting point. There can also be a fluctuation between what counts as the standard and what counts as an item falling under the standard. (Here we can get the feeling that because nothing *has to* be held fixed, nothing *is* held fixed.)

2 Wittgenstein says that "we ought to restrict the term 'interpretation' to the substitution of one expression of the rule for another" (PI, #201), but this seems too narrow.

3 See Section 5 of Hume's *An Enquiry Concerning Human Understanding*.

4 Here the mathematical example is not necessary. The same point can be made about the truth that the sun is further from the earth than the moon. Again, in order to understand this claim, the person must be able to command such concepts as distance, etc.

5 But reasons of this kind soon give out.

Chapter XII *The Private Language Argument*

1 The expression "I am in pain" differs from a mere expression of pain in having an articulated structure that places it in systematic relationships with other expressions in our language.

2 H. P. Grice has made philosophers aware of the importance of such pragmatic interpretations, for example, in his important essay "Logic and Conversation," reprinted in *The Logic of Grammar*, edited by Donald Davidson and Gilbert Harman, Encino, California, Dickinson Publishing Company, 1975, pp. 64–153.

3 I shall not worry about such apparent exceptions as the mother promising for the child.

4 See the earlier discussion of this on pp. 115 ff.

5 "Don't consider it a matter of course that a person is making a note of something when he makes a mark—say in a calendar. For a note has a function, and this 'S' so far has none" (PI, #260).

6 P. 147.

7 This is not the same as saying we *cannot* doubt. As inquiry goes forward anything might become an object of doubt. In the same way, in certain very strange contexts I can come to doubt things that it never crosses my mind to doubt, for example, that I have a hand in front of me. Furthermore, it is often senseless to entertain a doubt about such a thing as that I have a hand in front of me, for having raised such a doubt I would be completely at sea concerning how to resolve it. This is one of the central themes of Wittgenstein's *On Certainty*. What is senseless to doubt is not thereby indubitable—a point that nicely parallels Wittgenstein's comments about the spurious indubitability of first person reports of pain.

8 Of course, I am not suggesting that a conscious (or, for that matter, unconscious) inference takes place.

9 For additional passages making this same point, see RFM, I, 134–5 and especially RFM, II, 81.

10 Recently an interpretation of the private language argument has been published by Saul Kripke that is strikingly similar to the one presented in the first edition of this work. Since Kripke does not acknowledge this similarity, and, since some might think that my work is dependent upon his, it might be useful to set the record straight. The page citations are to Kripke's *Wittgenstein: On Rules and Private Language*, Cambridge, Mass., Harvard University Press, 1982.

Kripke tells us that "most of the exposition which follows occurred to the present writer some time ago, in the academic year 1962–63" (p. 1). It seems that our illumination experiences came at about the same time, since the "sceptical paradox" interpretation of the private language argument was part of the graduate seminars I began to teach at the beginning of the 1960s. Kripke probably thought of himself as providing an alternative to the standard interpretations of the argument circulating at that time. I came upon this interpretation in rather a different way. Since I was not trained by anyone deeply influenced by Wittgenstein and since I was originally unaware of the standard (verificationist) interpretations, I approached the text naively. It seemed to me at the time that the central move in the private language argument occurred at #202 since that, after all, is just what Wittgenstein says.

Setting aside recollections, which can be selective and self-serving, my Wittgenstein manuscript was submitted to Routledge & Kegan Paul in 1974. After some delays, it was published in 1976, before Kripke presented his paper on the private language argument at a Wittgenstein conference in London, Ontario in that same year. Speaking about the impact of his interpretation on others, Kripke remarks that

Some of this discussion, especially that appearing after I gave my London, Ontario lecture, can be presumed to have been influenced by the present exposition, but some of it, in and out of print, can be presumed to be independent.

My own work is prior and falls into the second category.

How similar, then, are these two interpretations? They are not identical. For example, Kripke seems to miss the point of the machine as symbol metaphor in ##193–4 which, as I have argued, is one of the most important discussions in the *Philosophical Investigations*. I also emphasize the role of training in the solution of the sceptical paradox, whereas Kripke concentrates almost exclusively on what I now call the *public-check argument*. In general, I cover more ground than Kripke attempts to cover, but in the area of overlap I see nothing important that distinguishes our two interpretations.

For both of us, Wittgenstein hatches a sceptical paradox and then offers a "sceptical solution" to it.

Kripke:

The basic structure of Wittgenstein's approach can be presented briefly as follows: A certain problem, or in Humean terminology, a "sceptical paradox", is presented concerning the notion of a rule. Following this, what Hume would have called a "sceptical solution" to the problem is presented. (pp. 3–4)

Turning to the first edition of my work (and all references in this note are to the first edition), it is not difficult to ferret out a parallel interpretation. The title of Chapter XII is "Sceptical Doubts and a Sceptical Solution to These Doubts." The title of #3 of this section is "A 'paradox' and its solution." The reference is, of course, to Hume's *Enquiry*, a point that is made explicitly for the non-philosophical reader who may have missed it.

What exactly is this paradox? Here is how I put it:

I can introduce what Wittgenstein calls a *paradox* using the following considerations. Suppose we start with the sequence:

$$2 \ 4 \ 6 \ 8 \ 10$$

It is known that however we continue this sequence there will be a function (indeed endlessly many functions) that will yield this continuation. So the sequence of numbers taken this far (or however far) does not, by itself, settle what comes next. (p. 142)

Here is Kripke:

. . . although an intelligence tester may suppose that there is only one possible continuation to the sequence 2, 4, 6, 8, . . . , mathematical and philosophical sophisticates know that an indefinite number of rules (even rules stated in terms of mathematical functions as conventional as ordinary polynomials) are compatible with any such finite initial segment. So if the tester urges me to respond, after 2, 4, 6, 8, . . . , with *the* unique appropriate next number, the proper response is that no such unique number exists, nor is there any unique (rule determined) infinite sequence that continues the given one. (p. 18)

What is this paradox supposed to show? Here I give prominence to a sentence in #201:

What this shews is that there is a way of grasping a rule which is *not* an *interpretation*, . . .

Kripke seems not to appreciate the full significance of this remark for the development of Wittgenstein's argument.

But if interpretations, by themselves, cannot tell us how to follow a rule or, more generally, how to fix meaning, what does? Given this paradox, how does Wittgenstein deal with it? My suggestion, as the very title of the chapter suggests, is that he offers what Hume would call a sceptical solution to this problem. We learn to follow a rule by being *trained* in the *customs* and *practices* of our society. I put it this way:

Here then are two elements in Wittgenstein's account of following a rule: 1 a causal element, which gives Wittgenstein's solution to his paradox more than a passing similarity to Hume's "sceptical solution" to his own "sceptical doubts," and 2 a social element, which explains this causal relationship within the context of institutions, practices and customs. (p. 143)

How do these reflections on the paradox and its sceptical solution bear upon the possibility of a private language? Fogelin:

If we are unaware of this paradox, the possibility of a private language may not seem problematic; if we finally decide that this paradox cannot be solved within a private language, we will then conclude that a private language is, after all, not possible. (p. 154)

Kripke:

The impossibility of private language emerges as a corollary of his sceptical solution of his own paradox, . . . It turns out that the sceptical solution does not allow us to speak of a single individual, considered by himself and in isolation, as ever meaning anything. (pp. 68–9)

At this point our interpretations depart. I considered two themes in the private language argument: one based upon the need for training, the other on the demand for a public check. It is through *training* (not a *public check*) that we are able to halt the regress of interpretations and follow a rule as a matter of course. It is through the appeal to training that Wittgenstein produces his (Humean) sceptical solution to his sceptical paradox. (Kripke seems to miss this: although he correctly identifies Wittgenstein's sceptical paradox, he seems to misidentify his sceptical solution.) It is through a public check that we gain an independent standpoint that allows us to distinguish following a rule from merely thinking that we are following a rule. In Section 3 of Chapter XII, I consider the argument from training and come to the conclusion that it establishes the contingent impossibility of a private language. In Section 4, I consider (what I now call) the public-check argument and conclude that it is not persuasive. (These are now Sections 4 and 5 of Chapter XII in this edition.)

Kripke concentrates almost exclusively on the public-check argument, but here again our interpretations are identical. Fogelin:

> To learn to follow a rule is to become the master of a technique—a technique that is part of a social practice, institution, or custom. *I* know how to do something when I do it the way *it's* done, but the way *it's* done amounts to nothing more than the way in which those people who are members of the institution . . . do it. (p. 144)

Then later:

> . . . the problem with a person following a rule privately is that there is no objective (i.e., independent) standpoint to settle whether he is following a rule or only seems to be. For Wittgenstein, this objective standpoint is supplied by the practice that the person enters into when he is trained to follow the rule. (p. 167)

Kripke:

> . . . if one person is considered in isolation, the notion of a rule as guiding the person who adopts it can have *no* substantive content. . . . There are, as we have seen, no truth conditions or facts in virtue of which it can be the case that he accords with his past intentions or not. As long as we regard him as following a rule "privately", so that we pay attention to *his* justification conditions alone, all we can say is that he is licensed to follow the rule as it strikes him. (p. 89)

In contrast, in the public case, Kripke tells us:

> The solution turns on the idea that each person claims to be following a rule that can be checked by others. (p. 101)

Some loose ends. Wittgenstein's sceptical solution concerning his paradox of rule following (like Hume's sceptical solution to his sceptical doubts) depends upon a broad uniformity in human responses. Fogelin:

> It is a fact of human nature that given a similar training people react in similar ways. For example, those who are trained in mathematics, on the whole, agree on their results. Those who depart from the consensus early in the game are excluded from further training and therefore do not have the opportunity for disagreeing later on at the constructive frontiers of mathematics. (p. 143)

Kripke:

> In fact, our actual community is (roughly) uniform in its practices with respect to addition. Any individual who claims to have mastered the concept of addition will be judged by the community to have done so if his particular responses agree with those of the community in enough cases. . . . Those who deviate are corrected and told (usually as children)

that they have not grasped the concept of addition. One who is an incorrigible deviant in enough respects simply cannot participate in the life of the community, and in communication. (pp. 91–2)

Finally Kripke claims (and he is right) that the series of remarks beginning at #243 do not constitute the private language argument since, as noted, that argument was completed at #202. What, then, is the main point of this later discussion? This is a complicated question, but part of my answer is this:

I think that Wittgenstein recognizes a kind of primitive appeal in the notion of a private language. Part of the reason for this is that our language actually seems to have a component that is essentially private. When I speak about after-images, I seem to be referring to something that only I can know directly. . . . The existence of a private language, we might say, is the best evidence for its possibility. This, then, is one thing that Wittgenstein attempts after #243: he tries to show that reports of sensations are not descriptions of private episodes, but function in an entirely different way. (p. 155)

Kripke:

Now another case [besides mathematics] that seems to be an obvious counter-example to Wittgenstein's conclusion is that of a sensation or mental image. Surely I can identify these after I have felt them, and any participation in a community is irrelevant! Because these two cases, mathematics and inner experience, seem so obviously counterexamples to Wittgenstein's views of rules, Wittgenstein treats each in detail. The later case is treated in the sections following #243. (p. 80)

To conclude this comparison, I offer both an interpretation and an evaluation of the private language argument; Kripke repeatedly claims only to be offering an interpretation. I claim that the training argument provides strong grounds for rejecting the possibility of a private language, whereas the public-check argument does not. My claim is that the public-check argument depends upon the selective use of a sceptical argument which, by a parity of reasoning, could be applied against the possibility of a public language as well. In contrast, as one reads Kripke, it is hard not to get the impression that he thinks quite highly of the public-check argument. At least he never says anything that suggests he rejects it. There is, however, one exception to this: a footnote (#87), which he tells us was added in proof. It is somewhat obscure, but on the surface sounds very much like my criticism of the public-check version of the private language argument:

Does it make any sense to *doubt* whether a response we all agree upon is "correct"? . . . may the individual doubt whether the community may not in fact *always* be wrong, even though it never corrects its error? It *is* hard to formulate such a doubt within Wittgenstein's framework, since it looks like a question, whether, as a matter of "fact", we might always be wrong; and there is no such fact. On the other hand, within Wittgenstein's framework it is still true that, for me, no assertions about community responses for all time need establish the result of an arithmetical problem; that *I* can legitimately calculate the result for myself, even given this information, is part of our "language game."

I feel that some uneasiness may remain regarding these questions. (p. 146)

He should feel uneasiness regarding these questions, for the whole force and significance of the public-check version of the private language argument, as Kripke interprets it, turns upon their answers.

Chapter XIII *Topics in Philosophical Psychology*

1 In this way a philosophical misunderstanding mirrors the concepts it corrupts, for these concepts themselves are often overdetermined in their significance. See PI, #79.

2 The context makes it clear that *normally* the second interpretation is correct. A similar point is made about *longing* in the *Investigations* at #586. He says that the exclamation "I'm longing to see him" may be called "an act of expecting." But he is quick to point out that in some contexts these same words might report the results of self-observation and then might have the force "So after all that has happened, I am still longing to see him." As always, it is the surroundings of the remark that settle the correct *understanding*.

3 The context leaves no doubt that the second alternative is directed.

4 Another pressure drives us in the same direction. People express their anger in *very* different ways: there are people you must know for some time before you can recognize when they are angry. How can we call such diverse behavior expressions of anger without assuming some common principle in back of it? (Here Wittgenstein would support the reasoning given in the text by invoking the doctrine of family resemblance.)

5 Presumably he is alluding to Frege's contrary view as found in "On Sense and Reference," in P. Geach and M. Black (eds), *Translations from the Philosophical Writings of Gottlob Frege*, Oxford, Basil Blackwell, 1952, pp. 56–79.

6 In this way Wittgenstein's general strategy might be worked out within the framework of a Fregean semantics.

7 Wittgenstein takes this for granted in PI #258 when he remarks that "the proposition 'Sensations are private' is comparable to 'One plays patience by oneself.' "

8 For different reasons it would also be odd, in normal contexts, for a person to say that he *knows* that his name is N N. It would not be odd for a person to say that he knows this (or believes this), however, if he is just recovering from amnesia.

9 Either in the "two uses" theory of the *Blue Book* or the "expression" theory of the *Investigations*.

10 Portions of Part II of the *Investigations* often seem less carefully developed than most of the writing of Part I. I do not, however, think that we can use this as an explanation of the lack of a fully developed theory, say, of aspect changes. If anything, Part II comes closer to meeting Wittgenstein's descriptivist ideal than Part I.

11 The *Brown Book* exemplifies this approach better than any of his other writings.

12 Pp. 147 ff.

13 They may, for example, be narrowly aimed at the Gestalt thesis of isomorphism, i.e. the thesis that there is a correspondence between the organization of, say, a visual field and the structure of the nervous system.

14 This is reminiscent of Carlyle's notion of "natural supernaturalism" where all the everyday events of the world are said to be miraculous (*Sartor Resartus*, Book III, Chapter 7).

Chapter XIV *Topics in the Philosophy of Mathematics*

1 Much of this discussion is adapted, some of it verbatim, from my essay "Wittgenstein and Intuitionism," *American Philosophical Quarterly*, 1968, pp. 267–74. I wish to thank the editor of the *American Philosophical Quarterly* for his permission to reuse this material.

2 In a manner of speaking, the formalists, at least in their most militant mood, would also deny that mathematical equations are propositional in character. However, they seem to overshoot the mark by denying not only this, but the very *sense* or *meaningfulness* of mathematical equations.

3 In my essay "Wittgenstein and Intuitionism" (see note 1 above) I suggest Wittgenstein here adopts what Hilary Putnam has called a *modal picture* of mathematics. This in turn accounts for the striking analogy between Wittgenstein's philosophy of mathematics and that of the Intuitionist Movement.

4 This diagram occurs on p. 164 of Schopenhauer's *The Fourfold Root of the Principle of Sufficient Reason*, London, Bell & Sanson, 1897. The same diagram, with a rather fuller discussion, appears in Vol. I, Sect. 15 of Schopenhauer's *The World as Will and Representation*, New York, Dover, 1966. An inspection of these texts leaves little doubt that many of Wittgenstein's central thoughts on mathematics were derived from this source.

5 A. Robinson, "Formalism 64," in *Logic, Methodology, and Philosophy of Science*, edited by Yehoshua Bar-Hillel, Amsterdam, North Holland Publishing Company, 1964, p. 230.

6 Ibid., p. 235.

7 See p. 190.

8 For this argument see especially RFM, II, 18.

Chapter XV *Wittgenstein and the History of Philosophy*

1 G. H. von Wright, "A Biographical Sketch," in *Wittgenstein: A Memoir*, by Norman Malcolm, London, Oxford University Press, 1958, p. 15.

2 See David Sedley's "The Motivations of Greek Skepticism," in *The Skeptical Tradition*, edited by Myles Burnyeat, Berkeley, University of California Press, 1983, pp. 8–29.

3 I have used the notion of general scepticism earlier on pages 00 ff. and 00 ff.

4 See Sextus Empiricus, *Outlines of Pyrrhonism*, Cambridge, Mass., Harvard University Press, 1933, pp. 95 ff.

5 David Hume, *Treatise of Human Nature*, 2nd edn, with text revised and notes by P. H. Nidditch, Oxford, Clarendon Press, 1978, p. 186.
6 Wittgenstein was particularly concerned with two of Moore's essays, "A Defence of Common Sense" and "Proof of an External World." Both are reprinted in his *Philosophical Papers*, London, Allen & Unwin, 1959.
7 Thompson Clark, "The Legacy of Skepticism," *Journal of Philosophy*, LXX, 1972, p. 762.

Selected Bibliography

I *Works by Wittgenstein (in order of composition)*

"Notes on Logic," ed. H. T. Costello, *Journal of Philosophy*, 54, 1957, 230–44. Reprinted in *Notebooks 1914–16*.

"Notes Dictated to Moore in Norway," reprinted in *Notebooks 1914–16*.

Notebooks 1914–16, ed. G. E. M. Anscombe and G. H. von Wright with an English translation by G. E. M. Anscombe, Oxford, Basil Blackwell, 1961.

Prototractatus, ed. B. F. McGuinness, T. Nyberg and G. H. von Wright, trans. D. F. Pears and B. F. McGuinness, Ithaca, New York, Cornell University Press, 1971.

Tractatus Logico-Philosophicus, translated by C. K. Ogden, London, Routledge & Kegan Paul, 1922, and a new translation by D. F. Pears and B. F. McGuinness, London, Routledge & Kegan Paul, 1961.

Letters to Russell, Keynes, and Moore, ed. with an introduction by G. H. von Wright, assisted by B. F. McGuinness, Ithaca, New York, Cornell University Press, 1974.

Letters to C. K. Ogden, ed. G. H. von Wright, Oxford, Blackwell, 1973.

Wörterbuch für Volksschulen, Vienna, Holder-Pichler-Tempsky, 1926.

"Some Remarks on Logical Form," *Proceedings of the Aristotelian Society*, Supp. Vol. 9, 1929, 162–71.

"A Lecture on Ethics," *Philosophical Review*, 74, 1965, 3–12.

Philosophische Bemerkungen, ed. Rush Rhees, Oxford, Basil Blackwell, 1965, English translation by R. Hargreaves and R. White, Oxford, Basil Blackwell, 1975.

Philosophische Grammatik, ed. Rush Rhees, Oxford, Basil Blackwell, 1969. English translation by Anthony Kenny, Berkeley and Los Angeles, University of California Press, 1974.

Bemerkungen über Fraser's The Golden Bough, ed. with a note, Rush Rhees, *Synthese*, 17, 1967, 233–53.

Letter to the Editor, *Mind*, 42, 1933, 415–16.

The Blue and Brown Books, ed. Rush Rhees, Oxford, Basil Blackwell, 1st edn 1958, 2nd edn 1969.

Wittgenstein's Lectures on the Foundations of Mathematics, Cambridge 1939, ed. Cora Diamond, Ithaca, New York, Cornell University Press, 1976.

Remarks on the Foundations of Mathematics, ed. G. H. von Wright, R. Rhees and G. E. M. Anscombe, with a translation by G. E. M. Anscombe, Oxford, Basil Blackwell, 1st edn 1956, 2nd edn 1967.

Lectures and Conversations on Aesthetics, Psychology and Religious Belief, ed. Cyril Barrett, Oxford, Basil Blackwell, 1966.

Philosophical Investigations, ed. G. E. M. Anscombe and R. Rhees with an English translation by G. E. M. Anscombe, Oxford, Basil Blackwell, 1st edn 1953, 2nd edn 1958, 3rd edn 1967.

Zettel, ed. G. E. M. Anscombe and G. H. von Wright with an English translation by G. E. M. Anscombe, Oxford, Basil Blackwell, 1967.

Remarks on the Philosophy of Psychology, Vol. 1, ed. G. E. M. Anscombe and G. H. von Wright, trans. G. E. M. Anscombe, Chicago, University of Chicago Press, 1980.

On Certainty, ed. G. E. M. Anscombe and G. H. von Wright, trans. D. Paul and G. E. M. Anscombe, Oxford, Basil Blackwell, 1969.

Remarks on Colour, ed. G. E. M. Anscombe, trans. Linda L. McAlister and Margarete Schattle, Berkeley, University of California Press, 1977.

Vermischte Bemerkungen, ed. G. H. von Wright, Frankfurt am Main, Suhrkamp, 1977.

II Some books on Wittgenstein

Anscombe, G. E. M., *An Introduction to Wittgenstein's Tractatus*, London, Hutchinson, 1959.

Baker, G. P. and Hacker, P. M. S., *Wittgenstein, Understanding and Meaning*, Vol. 1, Chicago, University of Chicago Press, 1980.

Bartley, William Warren, *Wittgenstein*, Philadelphia, Lippincott, 1973.

Binkley, Timothy, *Wittgenstein's Language*, The Hague, Nijhoff, 1973.

Black, Max, *A Companion to Wittgenstein's "Tractatus"*, Ithaca, New York, Cornell University Press, 1964.

Bogen, James, *Wittgenstein's Philosophy of Language*, London, Routledge & Kegan Paul, 1972.

Bolton, Derek, *An Approach to Wittgenstein's Philosophy*, Atlantic Heights, New Jersey, Humanities Press, 1979.

Cavell, Stanley, *The Claim of Reason*, Oxford, Clarendon Press, 1979.

Dilman, Ilham, *Induction and Deduction, A Study in Wittgenstein*, Oxford, Basil Blackwell, 1973.

Engel, S. Morris, *Wittgenstein's Doctrine of the Tyranny of Language*, The Hague, Nijhoff, 1971.

Engelman, Paul, *Letters from Wittgenstein*, ed. B. F. McGuinness, trans. L. Furtmuller, New York, Horizon Press, 1968.

Fann, Kuang-Ti, *Wittgenstein's Conception of Philosophy*, Berkeley, University of California Press, 1969.

Favrholt, David, *An Interpretation and Critique of Wittgenstein's Tractatus*, Copenhagen, Munskgaard, 1964.

Griffin, James Patrick, *Wittgenstein's Logical Atomism*, Oxford, Clarendon Press, 1964.

Hacker, P., *Insight and Illusion: Wittgenstein on Philosophy and the Metaphysics of Experience*, Oxford, Clarendon Press, 1972.

Hallet, Garth, *Wittgenstein's Definition of Meaning as Use*, New York, Fordham University Press, 1967.

Hallet, Garth, *A Companion to Wittgenstein's "Philosophical Investigations,"* Ithaca, New York, Cornell University Press, 1977.

Hardwick, Charles S., *Language Learning in Wittgenstein's Later Philosophy*, The Hague, Mouton, 1971.

Hartnack, Justus, *Wittgenstein and Modern Philosophy*, trans. Maurice Cranston, New York, New York University Press, 1965.

Janik, Allan and Toulmin, Stephen, *Wittgenstein's Vienna*, New York, Simon & Schuster, 1973.

Kenny, Anthony, *Wittgenstein*, London, Allen Lane, 1973.

Kripke, Saul, *Wittgenstein On Rules and Private Language*, Cambridge, Mass., Harvard University Press, 1982.

Malcolm, Norman, *Ludwig Wittgenstein, A Memoir*, London and New York, Oxford University Press, 1958.

Maslow, Alexander, *A Study in Wittgenstein's Tractatus*, Berkeley, University of California Press, 1961.

Mauro, Tullio de, *Ludwig Wittgenstein: His Place in the Development of Semantics*, Dordrecht, Reidel, 1967.

Morawetz, Thomas, *Wittgenstein and Knowledge*, Amherst, University of Massachusetts Press, 1978.

Pears, David, *Ludwig Wittgenstein*, New York, Viking Press, 1970.

Peursen, Cornelis Anthonio van, *Ludwig Wittgenstein*, trans. Rex Ambler, London, Faber & Faber, 1969.

Pitcher, George Willard, *The Philosophy of Wittgenstein*, Englewood Cliffs, New Jersey, Prentice-Hall, 1964.

Pitkin, Hanna Fenichel, *Wittgenstein and Justice*, Berkeley, University of California Press, 1972.

Pole, David, *The Later Philosophy of Wittgenstein*, London, Athlone Press, 1958.

Rhees, Rush, *Discussions of Wittgenstein*, New York, Schocken Books, 1970.

Specht, Ernest Konrad, *The Foundations of Wittgenstein's Late Philosophy*, trans. D. E. Walford, Manchester University Press, 1969.

Stenius, Erik, *Wittgenstein's Tractatus*, Ithaca, New York, Cornell University Press, 1960.

Waismann, Friedrich, *Wittgenstein and the Vienna Circle*, recorded by F. Waismann, ed. Brian McGuinness, trans. Joachim Shulte and Brian McGuinness, Oxford, Blackwell, 1979.

Wright, Crispin, *Wittgenstein on the Foundations of Mathematics*, Cambridge, Mass., Harvard University Press, 1980.

Index

analysis, attack on, 130–2
Anscombe, Elizabeth, 32, 69
anti-foundationalism, 223
aspect-change, 203–5
atomism: classical, 5, 9; principle of, 4; Wittgenstein's, 9, 14, 42, 126
Axiom of Infinity, 72

behaviourism, 190
belief statements, 75–6
Black, Max, 53, 76
Blue Book, 138, 199–200

Cantor, Georg, 84, 218–21
cardinal numbers, 221–2
causal-historical theory, 139–40
causality, 88–9
causation, 149–50
Church, Alonzo, 82
closure principle, 4
colour, 165, 181; and necessity, 91–2; and ostensive definition, 117–19, 128–30
combinatory theory, 7–8, 10, 12–13
complexes, 14–15, 126
confirmation, theory of, 53
conjunctions, 60–1, 64
constructivism, 78–85
contingency, notion of, 5–6, 11, 33
continuity, law of, 88–9
contradictions, 45–7, 52, 73

demonstratives, 49
depictions, 20
deriving, 147–9
Descartes, René, 166
determinacy, 15–17, 30
determinate relationships, 28
disappearance theory, 42

Donnellan, Keith, 139

elementary propositions, 18–19, 34–6, 39–41, 92, 109; and constructivism, 81–3; demonstratives, 49; functions, 57–61, 65, 83; generality, 54–5, 68–9; primacy of, 36; and probability, 51–3; propositional attitudes, 74–6; *see also* propositions
emotions, 187–92, 197–8
Engelmann, Paul, 99
equations, 85, 97
existence, 127
existential quantifier, 65
experiencing, the because, 149–54
expression, and psychological concepts, 187–9, 191

facts: independence of, 11; logical, 41–2; and pictures, 20–1, 23, 25; and propositional signs, 27; theory of, 3–4, 18
family resemblance, 133–8, 149
Ficker, Ludwig von, 99
finitism, 190, 223
Fogelin, Robert, 82
form, pictorial, 19–24; propositional, 48
formalism, 58–9, 213, 221
Foundations of Mathematics, The, 56
Frege, Gottlob, 31, 55–6, 61, 64–5, 72, 84, 113, 121
functional expressions, theory of, 56
functions, 54–5; expressions, 55–7; theory of, 72; and type theory, 57–60

Geach, Peter, 78–82, 139
generality, 54–77; accidental, 83–4
Gödel, Kurt, 82
grammatical fiction, 190

hedonism, 96
Hume, David, 149, 161, 167, 175, 229, 232, 234

identity, 71–4
identity statements, 214; mathematical, 216
identity-sign, 70–1, 73–4
incongruous counterparts, 90–1
induction, law of, 88
infinite divisibility, 6, 16
infinite totalities, 222
infinity, 218–23
intending, 198–9
internal relations, 204
intuition, 158–9

James, William, 176

Kant, Immanuel, 90–1, 97
Kaplan, David, 139
Kripke, Saul, 139, 241–6

language, motley of, 110–15; workings of, 30
language-games, 112–13, 124–5, 127–8, 131–2, 171, 191, 206, 232–3; and family resemblance, 133–8; and understanding, 153
logical: connectives, 41–4; constants, 32, 39, 44, 49, 66–7, 82, 85–7, 109; form, 22–4, 110; inference, 50–2; necessity, 91; product, 37, 44, 65; space, 4, 6, 8–12, 18, 23–4, 39, 44; truths, 45–7

machine, as symbol, 156–9
mathematical progression, 156
mathematics, 83–5, 163, 182, 214–17; philosophy of, 211–25
meaning, 31–2; and *Tractatus*, 24–5; and use, 121–2, 144
measuring, 162
mental states, inner, 193; and meaning, 120; and understanding, 144–7, 152–3

Mill, John Stuart, 124, 138, 212
Moore, G. E., 131, 137, 229–32
multiply-general propositions, 79

names, 18, 28–30; and propositions, 31–5, 40
naming, 117, 173, 184–5
naturalism, 96
necessary conditions, 121
necessity, 86–92
negation, 39–41, 44, 50
Notebooks, 15–16, 32, 45, 66, 68, 72
number, 133–4, 155–6
numbers, theory of, 84

objects, and generality, 73; naming, 30–4, 40; in ontological atomism, 5–17; and picture theory, 19–20; simple signs, 29–30
Occam's maxim, 59
On Certainty, 226, 229–30
ostensive definitions: private, 184; critique of, 115–18, 121
ostention, 118

pain, 169–72, 190–1, 194–5, 197–8
paradox, 159–65, 167, 175–6; Moore's, 200
Peirce, C. S., 62
peritrope, 228–9; *see also* scepticism
Philosophical Investigations, family resemblance, 136–8; and philosophical psychology, 186–7, 199, 203, 208–9; private language argument, 168, 172–3, 182; proper names, 138–40; and *Tractatus*, 107–11, 115, 120–2, 128–30, 142–3; and understanding, 153, 156
Philosophische Bemerkungen, 92
Philosophische Grammatik, 134
philosophy, 140–3; history of, 226–34
physiological explanation, 207
pictorial form, 19–20, 24, 27, 29, 34–5
picture theory, 3, 18–26, 39–42, 45–6
Platonism, 115, 211–14
pointing, 112, 118
primitive responses, 191–2, 194
Principia Ethica, 131
Principia Mathematica, 72

privacy: and certainty, 169–72; doctrine of, 94
private language argument, 166–85
probability, 51–3
projections, 28
proper names, 138–40
propositional attitudes, 74–7
propositional: form, 48; function, 70; sign, 20, 27–9
propositions: fully general, 66–71; general, 54, 60–5, 76; logic of, 39–53, 62; mathematical, 163–4, 223; meaning of, 24–5; multiply general, 79–81; and names, 31–4; non-elementary, 36–44; sense of, 28–9, 34; see also elementary propositions
Prototractatus, 33
pseudo-propositions, 89, 91, 97
psychological concepts, treatment of, 187–8, 198–200
psychology, philosophical, 186–210
public-check argument, 168–9, 175, 179–84
pure realism, 95
Pythagorean theorem, 217

quantificational theory, 78

radical contingency, doctrine of, 152
Ramsey, F. P., 56, 58, 67, 69, 70
rational numbers, 218–21
realism, naive, 202
reality, 10–11, 13, 37; form of, 23; model of, 18–19; and pictures, 20, 24
Remarks on the Foundations of Mathematics, 176, 190, 218, 225
representation, theory of, 22–4
Robinson, Abraham, 222
rules: following, 175–6, 181; and interpretation, 159–62, 167–8, 185
Russell, Bertrand, 42, 50, 84, 109, 224; critique of Tractatus, 123, 132, 134, 138; and generality, 58–61, 63–5, 70, 72–4, 76

St Augustine, 108–9, 111, 118
sayable, insignificance of, 97–8
scepticism, 166; classical, 233; doubts and solutions, 155–65,

175, 179–83; Pyrrhonian, 226–8, 232–5
Schopenhauer, Arthur, 97, 217
Searle, John, 139
seeing-as, 201–5
Sellars, Wilfrid, 151
sensation: expression of, 198; words, 173–4, 184
sense, and reference, 30–2
Sheffer, 62
showing: critique of, 100; doctrine of, 86
sign: primitive, 120; propositional, 75; simple, 29–35, 56
simples, 14–15, 122–7; doctrine of, 16; and transcendental illusions, 127–30
Sinn and Bedeutung, 31–2
Soames, Scott, 78–82
solipsism, 93–5, 199
spatial relations, 22–3
states of affairs: and elementary propositions, 34–5; in ontological atomism, 5–9, 11–13; picture theory, 18–19, 21, 24
structure, 21
sufficient reason, principle of, 89
symbolism, 18, 22, 42, 59
symbols, 58

tautologies, 26, 85; and generality, 72–3; logical propositions, 45–7, 52; and necessity, 86–90; showing, 101–2; and values, 96–7
Theaetetus, 125
thoughts, 25–6; and propositions, 27–30
Tolstoy, Leo, 99; 'Three Hermits', 99–100
Tractatus: atomistic ontology of, 3–17, 23; critique of, 107–43; error of logic, 78–82; generality and, 67–72; naive constructivism, 78–85; picture theory, 18–26; propositions, 27–38
training, 112, 145, 167
training-argument, 167, 175–9, 185
transcendental: deduction, 6; illusions, 127–30
transfinite cardinals, 218
truth: conditions, 34, 42–3, 46;

mathematical, 163–4, tables, 43;
and *Tractatus*, 24–5
truth-functions, 38, 44, 45–7, 49,
61–2, 75, 79–81, 83
truth-grounds, 50, 52
types, theory of, 72

understanding, 144–54
use, and understanding, 144

values, 96–7, 102–3

Whorf, Benjamin, 214
Whitehead, 72
Wright, G. H. von, 226, 234

"zero-method", 86
Zettel, 187–8, 191, 198, 205, 207–8